A Beginner's Guide to Statistics for Criminology and Criminal Justice Using R

A Beginner's Guide to Statistics for Criminology and Criminal Justice Using R

Alese Wooditch
Department of Criminal Justice, Temple University,
Philadelphia, PA, USA

Nicole J. Johnson
Department of Criminal Justice, Temple University,
Philadelphia, PA, USA

Reka Solymosi
School of Social Sciences, University of Manchester,
Manchester, UK

Juanjo Medina Ariza
Department of Criminal Law and Crime Science, School of Law,
University of Seville, Seville, Spain

Samuel Langton
Netherlands Institute for the Study of Crime and Law Enforcement,
Amsterdam, The Netherlands

 Springer

Alese Wooditch
Department of Criminal Justice
Temple University
Philadelphia, PA, USA

Nicole J. Johnson
Department of Criminal Justice
Temple University
Philadelphia, PA, USA

Reka Solymosi
School of Social Sciences
University of Manchester
Manchester, UK

Juanjo Medina Ariza
Department of Criminal Law and Crime Science,
School of Law
University of Seville
Seville, Spain

Samuel Langton
Netherlands Institute for the Study of Crime
and Law Enforcement
Amsterdam, The Netherlands

ISBN 978-3-030-50627-8   ISBN 978-3-030-50625-4   (eBook)
https://doi.org/10.1007/978-3-030-50625-4

This Springer imprint is published by the registered company Springer Nature Switzerland AG
The registered company address is: Gewerbestrasse 11, 6330 Cham, Switzerland

Contents

Chapter three

Chapter four

Chapter five

Chapter six

Chapter seven

Chapter eleven

Chapter twelve

Preface

This text provides hands-on guidance for researchers and practitioners in criminal justice and criminology to perform statistical analyses and data visualization in the free and open-source software, R. It offers a step-by-step guide for beginners to become familiar with the RStudio platform. It helps users master the fundamentals of the R programming language and functions in addition to program basics, such as understanding R file types (including .Rproj files), performing basic tasks, importing/exporting data, handling different data types and data structures (e.g., variables, matrixes, lists, factors, data frames), data cleaning, different types of loops, and writing functions. It also covers statistical analyses and data manipulation techniques to include measures of central tendency and dispersion, chi-squared, *t*-tests, analysis of variance, hypothesis testing, regression, and data visualizations and graphics. It will also impart best practices in programming and writing R scripts. The text can be used as a stand-alone guide to learning R, or it can be used as an introductory statistics textbook where users learn R along the way. The tutorials include interpretations of R output and explains to the user whether the results suggest that the null hypothesis should be rejected.

Tutorials in each chapter lay out research questions and hypotheses that center around real criminal justice datasets. The survey data used throughout the text include data from the *National Youth Survey, Law Enforcement Management and Administrative Statistics (LEMAS)-Body Worn Camera Survey*, the *Survey of Inmates in State and Federal Correctional Facilities (SISFCF), the National Crime Victimization Survey (NCVS)*, the *British Crime Survey/Crime Survey for England and Wales*, and the *Seattle Neighborhoods and Crime Survey*. The book also relies on real crime data, such as police stop and search data from London, official crime data from Greater Manchester, England, and data used by Professor Patrick Sharkey and his colleagues to study the effect of nonprofit organizations in the levels of crime (dataset contains data from the Uniform Crime Reports, demographic data from the U.S. Census, and data on nonprofits from the National Center for Charitable Statistics).

At the end of each chapter are application activity problems that reinforce the R tutorial examples. As the user goes through the tutorial, they learn the steps necessary to answer these activity questions with the dataset provided. They are designed to help master the software, as well as to provide practice on statistical concepts, data analysis, and interpretation of results/hypothesis testing. Exercises for each chapter may be used for practice in applying skills learned in the chapter, for homework assignments, or as part of a computer lab work session. In completing the exercises, users will get hands-on experience with using actual criminal justice datasets. Instructions are provided to access lab exercises and code online, as well as download the datasets online for free.

Philadelphia, PA, USA   Alese Wooditch
Philadelphia, PA, USA   Nicole J. Johnson
Manchester, UK   Reka Solymosi
Seville, Spain   Juanjo Medina Ariza
Amsterdam, The Netherlands   Samuel Langton

A First Lesson on R and RStudio

Topics Covered

Why learn R?

Technical Skills Covered

Download and install R, RStudio

Creating .R scripts

Customizing RStudio

Using comments

Basic operations in R

A. Wooditch et al., *A Beginner's Guide to Statistics for Criminology and
Criminal Justice Using R*, https://doi.org/10.1007/978-3-030-50625-4_1

R IS A POWERFUL TOOL for statistical analyses and data visualization that is widely used and increasingly popular in criminology and criminal justice. R is open source—and it's free! In early 2020, there were over 15,000 available packages, and the number of things that can be done with R grows exponentially every day as users keep adding new packages. Because it is open source, new statistical methods are quickly implemented, and R offers more analytical solutions, flexibility, and customizability than commonly used statistical software. This book offers a step-by-step guide for beginners to become familiar with the RStudio platform and master the fundamentals of the R programming language quickly and painlessly ☺. The text can be used as a stand-alone guide to learning R, or it can be used as a companion guide to an introductory statistics textbook. Along the way, users will get hands-on experience with using actual criminal justice datasets, and application activity exercises are provided at the end of each chapter to practice covered material.

Why Learn R?

So, why isn't R more widely used in criminal justice and criminology? This is mostly to do with the fact that most criminologists teaching data analysis were trained on SPSS, Stata, and SAS. But this is quickly changing as R becomes the tool of choice for data analysts across a variety of scientific disciplines. Learning R, like learning any other programming language, can be frustrating, and even simple tasks may be a challenge.

But don't worry! This guide offers an easy, step-by-step guide for you to quickly master the R programming language. For the first few chapters, you will be learning the basics of the R programming language, getting familiar with the RStudio interface, and how to visualize your data.

Once you feel comfortable using R, the latter chapters move on to statistical analysis. To be clear, this book is not a statistics book. However, each chapter reviews commonly employed statistical concepts and methods while you learn R, so this text can serve as a great lab companion book to any statistics textbook in criminology and criminal justice.

Along the way, you will be completing walkthroughs using real criminal justice datasets and have the option to complete exercises at the end of each chapter to practice the skills you learned. While this book is intended to be a guide for beginners, it also provides a great reference for intermediate R users. By the end of this book, you will be comfortable using R and confident in your R programming skills.

R and RStudio

R has a command line interface similar to the command prompt in the Windows operating system. R is available for Windows, Mac, and Linux. In the main R console, you encounter a prompt where the user enters programming code that is written in R language to execute tasks. R is different from programs like SPSS because it does not have a graphical user interface (GUI) so there are no drop-down menus to run analyses or execute tasks.

Graphical user interfaces are convenient because you can do analysis by pointing and clicking. You only need to know how to point and click and what the options you are clicking do, but this ease comes with a price. Your analysis becomes less reproducible and it is time-consuming to repeat tasks. Programming for data analysis overcomes these pitfalls, but it too comes at a price. You need to learn the basics of programming. But it also has a massive advantage. Running analysis via programming means you (or others) can always come back to your code and repeat the analysis again in the exact same manner.

RStudio is an integrated development environment (IDE) designed specifically for R. It is at its core a programming code editor. Think of RStudio as the graphical front end to R. Users normally call R via **RStudio** rather than using the command line in R because it offers greater functionality and customization. Since **RStudio** allows you to interact with the R program, you need to download R for it to work. If you just download **RStudio**, you will notice that it will not work since it is just a user-friendly interface to access the R program.

The walkthroughs in this textbook are carried out in **RStudio**, so you will need to download and install both R and **RStudio**. If you are working on a computer at a lab on a university campus, you will want to check whether R and **RStudio** are installed before proceeding with the next steps.

Installing R

Download and install R before installing RStudio. To download R, do the following:

1. Go to https://www.r-project.org/.

2. Click the *download R* link under the *Getting Started* heading.

3. You will be asked to select a Comprehensive R Archive Network (CRAN) mirror. Click the URL closest to your location.

4. Click whichever download link is appropriate for your operating system.

5. Then click the *install R for the first-time* link and proceed to install R.

Install RStudio

After R is installed, download and install RStudio:

1. Go to https://rstudio.com/.

2. Click the *Download* link.

3. Scroll down and then click the *DOWNLOAD* button for the free version of RStudio.

4. You will then be taken to a website to download the free version of RStudio that is appropriate for your computer. Download and then install it.

Open and Explore RStudio

To start, open RStudio. Note that you do not have to open R as well since R runs automatically in the background when you are using RStudio.

When you first open RStudio, you will see (as in Fig. 1.1) that there are three main panes. The bigger one to your left is the console. If you read the text in the console, you will see that RStudio is indeed running R, and you can see what version of R it is using.

Figure 1.1 *RStudio interface*

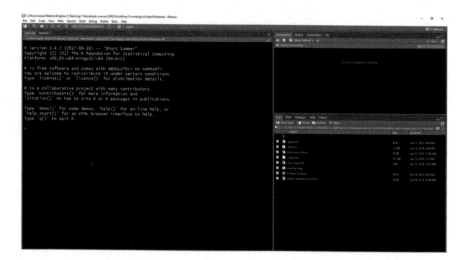

When you work in **RStudio**, you will have four open panes in a regular session. Click on the *File* drop-down Menu, and select *New File* and then *R Script* (see Fig. 1.2). You will now see the four window areas in the display (Fig. 1.3). In each of these areas, you can shift between different views and panels. You can also use your mouse to resize the different windows if that is convenient.

Figure 1.2 *Opening an .R Script*

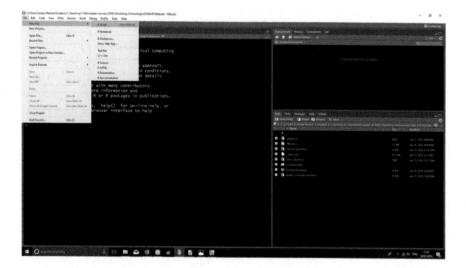

Figure 1.3   *Main Windows in RStudio*

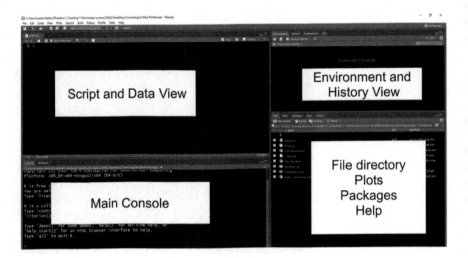

Look, for example, at the bottom right area. Within this area, you can see that there are different tabs, which are associated with different views. You can see in the tabs in this section that there is one for each of the different views available: *Files, Plots, Packages, Help,* and *Viewer.*

Files—The Files tab allows you to see the files in the physical directory that is currently set up as your working environment. You can think of it as a window in Windows Explorer that lets you see the content of a folder.

Plots—Under the Plots tab, you will see any data visualizations or graphical displays of data that you produce. You haven't produced any yet, so it is empty at the moment.

Packages—If you click the Packages tab, you will see the packages that are currently available in your installation. What is a *package* in this context? **Packages** are modules that expand what R can do. There are thousands of them. Few packages come preinstalled when you do a basic R installation. For others, you pick and install them yourself when you have a need to use the functionality of the given package.

Help—The other really useful panel in this part of the screen is the Help viewer. Here you can access the documentation for the various packages that make up R. Learning how to use this documentation will be essential if you want to be able to get the most from R.

In the diagonally opposite corner, the top left, you should now have an open script window. The script window is where you write and keep all of your R programming code. A script is nothing but a text file where you can write. It is associated with the file type .R and is referred to as an R

script. Unlike other programs for data analysis you may have used in the past (Excel, SPSS), you need to interact with R by means of writing down instructions and asking R to evaluate those instructions. R is an *interpreted* programming language; you write code in R programming language, and once executed, it provides instructions for how R should carry out the task. All the instructions we write can and should be saved in a script, so that you can return later to what you did.

As noted above, one of the key advantages of doing data analysis this way is that you are producing a written record of every step you take in the analysis. The challenge though is that you need to learn this language in order to be able to use it. That will be the main focus of this textbook—teaching you how to write R code for the purposes of data analysis.

As with any language, the more you practice it, the easier it will become. Often, you will be typing a lot of code in the script window that is provided to you as you complete the R walkthroughs of each chapter. But we will also expect you to develop a basic understanding of what these bits of code do, so you will be writing your own lines of code to complete the exercises at the end of the chapter.

Another advantage of doing analysis this way is that once you have written your instructions (code) and saved them in a file, you will be able to easily share it with others and run it every time you want in a matter of seconds. This creates a *reproducible* record of your analysis: something that your collaborators or someone else anywhere (including your future self, the one that will have forgotten how to do the stuff) could run and get the same results that you did at some point earlier. This makes science more transparent, and transparency brings with it many advantages. For example, it makes your research more trustworthy. Don't underestimate how critical this is. **Reproducibility** is becoming a key criterion to assess good quality research. And tools like R allow us to enhance it.

Customizing RStudio

RStudio allows you to customize the way the interface looks. For example, working with white backgrounds is not generally a good idea if you care about your eyesight. If you don't want to end up with dry eyes, not only is it good you follow the 20-20-20 rule (every 20 minutes look for 20 seconds to an object located 20 feet away from you), but it may also be a good idea to use more eye-friendly screen displays.

To customize the display, click the *Tools* menu and select *Global options*. This will open up a pop-up window with various options. Select *Appearance*. In this section, you can change the font type and size, as well as background theme that R will use in the various windows. We recommend the *Tomorrow Night Bright* theme because it is easier on your eyes over long periods of time, but you may prefer a different one. You can preview them and then click *apply* to select the one you like. This will not change your results or analysis so changing the appearance is up to you. Under *Global options*, you can navigate to *Pane layout* if you want to change the location of the four panes in your RStudio interface.

Commenting Your Code

As you follow along with the sections of code in this chapter, you will notice part of the code is grayed out. Here is one example:

```
# This is a comment
```

You can see that after the hashtag, all the text is being grayed out. What is this? What's going on? These are **comments**. Comments are simply annotations that R will know is not code (and therefore doesn't attempt to understand and execute). We use the hashtag symbol to specify to R that what comes after is not programming code, but simply bits of notes that we write to remind ourselves what the code is actually doing. Including these comments will help you to understand your code when you come back to it. You can use this sign to include *annotations* when you are coding. These annotations are a helpful reminder to yourself (and others reading your code) of *what* the code is doing and (even more important) *why* you are doing it.

It is good practice to often use annotations. You can use these annotations in your code to explain your reasoning and to create *scannable* headings in your code.

Just keep in mind:

- You need one # per line, and anything after that is a comment that is not executed by R.

- You can use spaces after it (it is not like a hashtag on Twitter).

Basic Operations

The best way to get comfortable with R is to practice carrying out simple operations. You are able to compute simple calculations in R using common arithmetic operations. The result is printed in your console. For example, try the following:

```
# Addition
5 + 5

## [1] 10

# Subtraction
10 - 3

## [1] 7

# Multiplication
2 * 5

## [1] 10

# Division
6 / 2

## [1] 3
```

There are more than just these operators. Table 1.1 presents some of the operations you can use:

Table 1.1   Basic operations in R

OPERATION	R OPERATOR
Absolute value	abs()
Addition	+
Ceiling	ceiling()
Division	/
Exponentiation	^ or **
Floor	floor()
Logarithm	log()
Modulus	%%
Round	round()
Subtraction	-
Square root	sqrt()

For the round() function, you are able to specify the number of decimal places to round to such as round(x, digits=2). The operators that are expressions (e.g., log, sqrt) rather than symbols (e.g., +, -) are carried out a little differently. Try the following:

```
# Calculating the Logarithm
log(100)
```

```
## [1] 4.60517
```

```
# You can also combine operators
log(100 + 5)
```

```
## [1] 4.65396
```

Take note that R is case sensitive; capitalizing the *L* in `log()` will throw an error:

```
# Error... since R is case sensitive :-/
Log(100)
```

```
## Error in Log(100): could not find function "Log"
```

Objects

What do we mean by object? Everything that exists in R is an **object**. You can think of objects as boxes where you put stuff. This is done using the **assignment operator**. The assignment operators in R are presented in Table 1.2.

Table 1.2   R assignment operators

OPERATION	R OPERATOR
=, <-, <<-	Left assignment
->, ->>	Right assignment

The assignment operators `<-` and `=` can be used almost interchangeably, while operators `<<-` and `->>` are used as assignment operators within functions.

By far, the most common is the standard left assignment operator using the `<-` or `=` symbols. See the example below:

```
a <- 10
A = 15
```

You can assign anything to objects. It could be a dataset, a string of text, or a matrix, to name a few. Here, you will see that we assigned text to an object. Also, note that the name of your object does not have to be only one letter, and it can contain numbers.

```
abc123 <- "Hello!"  # Assign object
abc123   # Print object

## [1] "Hello!"
```

After you have completed those examples, look at the **environment** window in the right top corner. We can see that this object is now listed there. You can think of the environment as a warehouse where you store your different objects. Is there a limit to this environment? Yes, your RAM. R works on your RAM, so you need to be aware that if you use very large objects, you will need loads of RAM.

Data Structures

To practice more interesting tasks in R, you generally need to work with more complex data structures. There are several types of data structures, which define the ways in which R stores data, so data can be accessed in an efficient way according to its purpose. All data structures in R are objects. Five of the most common data structures in R are as follows: *atomic vector, array, matrix, list,* and *data frame.* As presented in Table 1.3, the data structures can be distinguished by the type(s) of elements they store and number of dimensions.

| Table 1.3 | Characteristics of common data structures in R |

# OF DIMENSIONS	HOMOGENOUS	HETEROGENOUS
One	Atomic vector	List
Two	Matrix	Data frame
More than two	Array	

Atomic vectors, arrays, and **matrixes** are categorized as homogenous (meaning that the elements they store need to be the same type at any given point in time). You can also visualize differences in the number of dimensions between these homogenous data structures in Fig. 1.4.

Figure 1.4   *Homogenous data structures: Vectors, arrays, and matrixes*

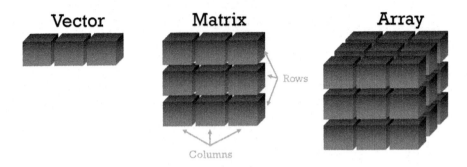

Lists and **data frames** are heterogenous data structures (meaning that different types of elements can be stored at the same time). For example, even though matrixes and data frames are both two-dimensional, matrixes can only have one type of data at any given point in time (e.g., integers OR character text), whereas data frames can combine multiple types at once (e.g., a column for integers AND a column of character text). This is depicted in Fig. 1.5.

Figure 1.5   *Comparison of matrixes and data frames in R*

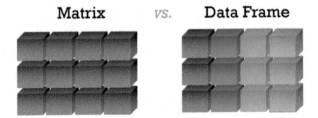

As described in Table 1.3, both atomic vectors and lists have only one dimension. Technically speaking, they are both vectors. Atomic vectors are homogenous vectors, while lists are heterogenous vectors (as depicted in Fig. 1.6). You can even create a list of lists!

Figure 1.6   *Data structures stored in lists*

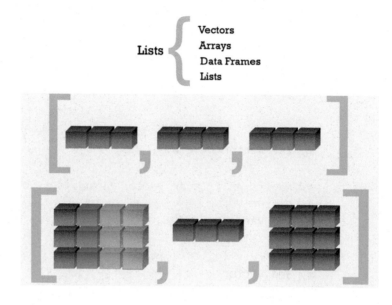

Atomic Vectors

Let's get a bit more specific. An atomic vector is an ordered set of objects that are *of the same class*. Typically, these classes are as follows: *character, complex, integer, logical,* and *numeric.* Table 1.4 includes examples for each object class.

Table 1.4   Classes stored in an atomic vector

CLASS TYPE	EXAMPLE
Character	a, b, c
Complex	1 + 1a, 2 + 2b, 3 + 3c
Integer	1, 2, 3
Logical	TRUE, FALSE
Numeric	1.01, 2.01, 3.01

The types of classes stored in vectors are discussed further below. To populate an atomic vector, you will use the `c()` function (c stands for concatenate) to create vectors. The code below exemplifies how to create vectors of different classes (numeric, logical, etc.). Notice how the listed elements are separated by commas, and you will see how all these vectors are added to your *global environment* and stored there. In vector 6 below, we are going to use the colon (:) operator, which generates a regular sequence.

```
# Creates a numeric vector with 3 elements
my_1st_vector <- c(0.5, 8.9, 0.6)

# Creates an integer vector by adding L at the end
## of the value
my_2nd_vector <- c(1L, 2L, 3L)

# Creates a logical vector
my_3rd_vector <- c(TRUE, FALSE, FALSE)

# Creates a logical vector using abbreviations of True
## and False, but you should avoid this formulation and
## instead use the full word.
my_4th_vector <- c(T, F)

# Creates a character vector
my_5th_vector <- c("a", "b", "c")


my_6th_vector <- c(1:6)  # Vector with sequence of values
my_6th_vector  # Print this vector in your console
## [1] 1 2 3 4 5 6

# Vectors can also be more complex
my_7th_vector <- c(1+0i, 2+4i)
```

The beauty of an object-oriented statistical language like R is that once you have these objects, you can use them as *inputs* in functions, use them in operations, or use them to create other objects. This makes R very flexible. See some examples on the next page.

```
my_1st_vector + 2 # Add a constant to each element
## of the vector

## [1]  2.5 10.9  2.6

# Creates a vector that contains my_1st_vector
## elements plus a constant of 1
my_8th_vector <- my_1st_vector + 1

# Adds the two vectors and auto-prints the results
## (note how the sum was done)
my_1st_vector + my_6th_vector
## [1]  1.5 10.9  3.6  4.5 13.9  6.6
```

Notice how the following code throws an error because you are asking R to use addition with a vector of characters:

```
# Error :-(
my_1st_vector + my_5th_vector

## Error in my_1st_vector + my_5th_vector: non-numeric
argument to binary operator
```

Matrix

A matrix is a specific type of array, which has at least two columns and two rows. In the example below, we are assigning a 2 x 2 matrix to the object *m* and then using the `print()` function to print the objects in the matrix in our *console*. You can specify whether you would like the matrix to be populated row-wise or just populated by row.

```
m = matrix(1:4, nrow=2, ncol=2, byrow=FALSE) # 2x2

print(m)

##      [,1] [,2]
## [1,]    1    3
## [2,]    2    4
```

The difference between `byrow = TRUE` and `byrow = FALSE` in row population is presented in Fig. 1.7.

Figure 1.7   *Illustration of differences in row population options*

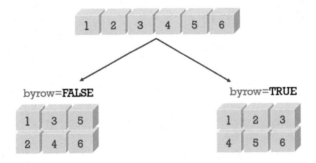

Array

As we discussed, an array is similar to a vector and matrix. It has an ordered set of objects that are the same type (see the `c()` function that creates the vector), but it also has dimension attributes (see the `dim()` function) that make it three-dimensional.

```
MyArray = array(c(1:6), dim = c(3, 2))
```

Lists and Data Frames

Lists and data frames are both used to store elements, but they differ in important ways. Lists are not restricted on the length, structure, or class of the included elements. In contrast, data frames are defined by their number of columns and rows. Data frames permit elements of multiple classes; however, data frames do not permit multiple data classes in the same column/variable. Unlike lists, the vectors included in a data frame (columns) must be of the same length.

Lists are created using the `list()` function. You can use the `class()` function to verify that the elements have been defined as a list. For both lists and data frames, we can also use the dollar sign ($) to identify attributes/variables.

```
TopVioCrimeCities2019 <- list("St. Louis", "Detroit",
                              "Baltimore")

class(TopVioCrimeCities2019)

## [1] "list"

# You can also name the components
names(TopVioCrimeCities2019) <- c("Highest1", "Highest2",
                                  "Highest3")

TopVioCrimeCities2019$Highest2

## [1] "Detroit"
```

Data frames can be created in R using the `data.frame()` function. In certain situations, you have the option to coerce a data frame (see `as.data.frame()` in Appendix 6).

```r
TopVioCities <- c("St. Louis", "Detroit", "Baltimore")
VioRatePer1k <- c(20.8, 20.6, 20.3)
State <- c("Missouri", "Michigan", "Maryland")
# Join to make a data frame
df <- data.frame(TopVioCities, VioRatePer1k, State)
# View the data frame with the View() function
View(df)
```

Logical Operators

Now that you know the basic data types, let's review **logical operators**, which are Boolean operators that return **TRUE** or **FALSE** (see Table 1.5).

Table 1.5   Boolean operations in R

OPERATION	R OPERATOR
And	&, &&
Or	| or ||
Not equal to	!=
Equal to	==
Less than	<
Less than or equal to	<=
Greater than	>
Greater than or equal to	>=

How about we start with some simple examples of the operators in the table above?

```r
1 == 1
## [1] TRUE

0 == 1
## [1] FALSE

0 == 0 || 0 == 1
## [1] TRUE

0 == 0 && 0 == 1
## [1] FALSE
```

You should be mindful when applying these operations to Boolean vectors because sometimes they will only be conducted on the first element in the vector. Also, you will see how the *or* operator works differently by | or ||.

```
c(TRUE, FALSE, FALSE) || c(TRUE, TRUE, FALSE)

## [1] TRUE

c(TRUE, FALSE, FALSE) | c(TRUE, TRUE, FALSE)

## [1]   TRUE   TRUE FALSE

c(TRUE, FALSE, FALSE) && c(TRUE, TRUE, FALSE)

## [1] TRUE

c(TRUE, FALSE, FALSE) & c(TRUE, TRUE, FALSE)

## [1]   TRUE FALSE FALSE
```

Application Activities

For the problems below, you will want to be writing your syntax in a script file; you do not want to be typing directly into your console window. To open a new script, go to *File > New File > R Script*. Then, save your script file, making sure that at the end of the name, you type .R (e.g., *Chapter1_Problems.R*). Remember to save your script file again one you have completed the problems below.

Problem 1:

Suppose that we have a document containing (among others) the following crimes and crime counts:

Robbery: 5
Arson: 2
Burglary: 7
Assault: 6
Vandalism: 3
Prostitution: 5

(a) Using the c() function, create a character atomic vector called **types** that contains these crime types, and then create another numeric atomic vector called **counts** that contains the crime counts (in their respective positions).

(b) Combine the two vectors into a data frame called **crime.counts** using the **data.frame()** function.

Problem 2:

(a) Using `matrix()` and `byrow=`, create a 5 × 5 matrix named `PoliceBeats` comprised of the integers 1 through 25 (populated row-wise from top left to bottom right).

(b) Convert the matrix you named `PoliceBeats` into a data frame using `data.frame()`, and assign this to a new object `BeatsDF`.

(c) Test the equality of the objects `PoliceBeats` and `BeatsDF` using the `==` logical operator. What is R actually comparing? What type of object is created by this operation?

Key Terms

Array A three-dimensional data structure that can contain homogenous elements (of the same class).

Assignment operators Symbols used to make assignations to objects.

Atomic vector A one-dimensional data structure that can contain homogenous elements (of the same class).

Comments Code annotations that are not interpreted by R.

Data frame A data structure that is defined by the number of rows and columns.

Environment Where objects are stored.

List A one-dimensional data structure that can contain heterogenous elements (of different classes).

Logical operators Boolean operators that return TRUE or FALSE.

Matrix A specific type of array that has at least two columns and two rows and can contain homogenous elements (of the same class).

Object A specialized data structure; everything in R is an object.

Packages Modules that expand what R can do.

R A language and free software environment used for statistical computing.

R Script Where R programming code is written and stored.

Reproducibility When there is a record of one's research such that these steps can be repeated by others and the findings reproduced.

RStudio An integrated development environment (IDE) designed specifically for R.

Functions Introduced in this Chapter

FUNCTION	DESCRIPTION (PACKAGE)
abs()	Calculates the absolute value (base **R**)
as.data.frame()	Checks if data frame and tries to coerce if not (base **R**)
array()	Stores data in 1 dimension (vector) or 1+ dimension (matrix) (base **R**)
c()	Concatenates elements to create vectors (base **R**)
ceiling()	Always round up (base **R**)
class()	Checks the class of an object (base **R**)
dim()	Checks the dimensions of an R object (base **R**)
data.frame()	Creates a new data frame object (base **R**)
floor()	Always round down (base **R**)
list()	Creates a list (base **R**)
log()	Computes the natural logarithm (base **R**)
matrix()	Creates a vector with two dimensions (base **R**)
names()	Provides the element names (base **R**)
print()	Prints arguments and returns it invisibly (base **R**)
round()	Rounds to the nearest whole number/specified number decimals (base **R**)
sqrt()	Finds the square root (base **R**)
View()	View data in new window (base **R**)

Getting to Know Your Data

Topics Practiced

Levels of measurement

Technical Skills Covered

Viewing data types and variable labels

Formatting classes, value labels, and variable labels

Recoding and creating new variables

Sorting and subsetting data

R Packages Required

here, haven, labelled, sjlabelled, tidyverse (includes dplyr and tibble)

Now that you are familiar with creating data in different formats in R, we can start to discuss one of the most important steps of the data analysis process—transforming your data into what Hadley Wickham (Wickham, 2014) calls *tidy data*. Fittingly, many useful functions for data tidying are in a set of packages called the `tidyverse`. Data tidying is a very important step that will ensure your data are in the format you need to conduct your analyses. It includes steps such as viewing data types; viewing, editing, and adding both variable labels and value labels; formatting classes; and recoding and creating new variables. Learning basic techniques to determine, for example, how different variables in your dataset are stored or whether a variable has too many missing cases can be extremely useful when you are planning what you can feasibly analyze and how to do it. In pretty much any research project involving data analysis, you can expect that your data will require some level of manipulation. We rarely receive data that are perfectly clean and set up for our purpose! Fortunately, R offers a great deal of flexibility in how to accomplish these tasks. In this section, we will walk through some examples of common data transformations you may need to perform in your own analysis while at the same time practicing the concept of levels of measurement using data from the National Crime Victimization Survey.

Data

Dataset Source: National Crime Victimization Survey

File Name: NCVS lone offender assaults 1992 to 2013.sav

Dataset Description: The National Crime Victimization Survey (NCVS) is administered annually to a nationally representative sample of households in the United States. The survey asks respondents a variety of questions related to their criminal victimization experience in the previous 6 months, including details about the crime and its severity, injuries sustained, and characteristics of the offender. This dataset includes information on respondents who reported being victims of assault collected from the 1992 through 2013 surveys.

R Projects

Managing your workflow in **R** is much easier if you work inside a **project**. Rather than loading in data and using scripts from multiple different locations on your computer, which can get rather confusing and cluttered, projects help you keep your work self-contained and organized in a single working directory. When you are throwing yourself into a new assignment or research project, it's best to set up an associated project in **RStudio**.

There is a tab in the top right of your **RStudio** interface to set up a new project called *Project: (None)*. Click on this and then click *New Project*. This will bring up a new window with a few different options, but we want to create our project in a *New Directory*. The project type in the next list will be *New Project*. You will have to choose a name for your project (e.g., r_crim_course) and a location (working directory) where your project will be created. This is the folder in which your project, and associated folders such as data and scripts, will be stored. Once done, you can click *Create Project*, and your new project will be launched in **RStudio**.

You'll notice that anything you do within a project begins from this folder location. The **getwd()** function (Appendix 1.5) will output your current working directory (i.e., the location of your project). It is up to you how this folder is organized, but a common approach is to have separate folders containing things like scripts, data, outputs, and visuals. You can create these now in the same working directory as your project. If you'd prefer, these can be created within **R** using the function **dir.create()**. For instance, to create a new folder called *Datasets*, you'd run **dir.create("Datasets")** in your console. To ensure your code is completely reproducible when loading in data from a folder, it is good practice to refer to each part of the working directory containing the data using the **here()** function, as demonstrated below. You can read more about this in the Appendix too (see Appendix 1.3).

Installing Packages

Packages can be installed using the **install.packages()** or **library()** functions (Appendix 1.1). Remember that while you only need to install packages once, they need to be loaded with **library()** each time you open **RStudio**. Let us install the package **dplyr** and load it.

```
install.packages("dplyr")
library(dplyr)
```

Notice you may get a series of warnings when you run this code. You will want to make a habit of reading these warnings. Most of the time, the warnings explain to you what is being loaded and confirm that the package is successfully loaded. However, sometimes, you may get an error when loading packages. If that happens, or if simply you want to check whether a package has been successfully installed, please see the troubleshooting steps in Appendix 1.1. If you receive no error, congrats!

When we install **dplyr**, you will see that it is telling us that some functions from certain packages are being masked. One of the things with a language like **R** is that sometimes packages introduce functions that have the same name as those that are already loaded into your session. When that happens, the newly loaded ones will override the previous ones. You can still use them but you will have to refer to them explicitly (Appendix 1.2).

Once you have installed **dplyr** correctly, go back and edit your code to install the other packages listed at the beginning of this chapter. You especially want to make sure that the **haven** package is installed since it is needed to open your dataset in the next section.

Import the NCVS Dataset with the read_spss() Function

Now, let's load our dataset. The NCVS dataset used in this chapter is in the SPSS data format (.sav). You can load this into your project using **read_spss()** from the **haven** package (see Appendix 1.6.8.). In doing this, you must also specify where the file is located. Wherever your **R** project is saved will be the default working directory. This is very helpful when it comes to loading or saving data because you don't have to specify the whole working directory each time and only need to use the **here()** function from the **here** package. While it is recommended to work with projects, please see the function **setwd()** in Appendix 1.4 if you are not using a project/loading the dataset with the **here()** function.

Within the **read_spss()** function of the example below, we are telling **R** to load the *NCVS lone offender assaults 1992 to 2013.sav* dataset. We are specifying that this file is located in a folder named *Datasets*. This folder is saved in the same place as our current project. Additionally, we tell **R** that we want the object containing the dataset to be named **ncvs**. One thing you will not want to forget when opening files in **R** is that you must specify the file extension after the file name (will be *.sav* for this dataset).

```
# Importing our SPSS dataset and naming it, "ncvs"
ncvs <- read_spss(here("Datasets", "NCVS lone offender
    offender assaults 1992 to 2013.sav"))
```

Once you have completed this process, make sure you have loaded your dataset correctly by viewing the data frame via `View(ncvs)` (Appendix 1.7).

Viewing Data Types

Recall from Chapter 1 that base **R** has three main classes of vectors: numeric, character (or string), and factors. When we say base **R**, we mean basic **R** programming rather than code/functions introduced by packages. The way you capture a variable within a vector should relate to its level of measurement:

Nominal—While **nominal** variables (also called categorical unordered) can be of string or character class, it is preferable to use the factor class and assign value labels to each category. Use the character or string class if you want to store text that will not be used in descriptives or analysis, such as a notes field.

Ordinal—Mathematical operations (addition, multiplication, etc.) should not normally be conducted on **ordinal** variables (also called categorical ordered), so it is good practice that ordinal variables be of the factor class since it allows ordering. In instances when researchers treat an ordinal variable as a ratio scale (such as computing the mean of a variable that is a Likert scale), the variable should be classified as numeric in **R**.

Interval/Ratio—**Interval-/ratio**-level variables can be continuous or discrete variables and should be stored as numeric class.

While vector classes should pertain to the variable level of measurement, sometimes you need to change the class of a vector for a given variable into a different one if the vector class is not appropriate for its level of measurement. For example, you may find that gender is stored in **R** as numeric (which is often coded using the values of 0 and 1), and you need to change the variable to the factor class.

Using class()

First, let's take a look at the class of vectors (i.e., columns) in our data frame. The following loops the function **class()** through every variable in the data frame object:

```
sapply(ncvs, class)
```

You can see here that there are many **haven_labelled** variables. What are these? This is a particular type of vector introduced by the *haven* package, which we used for importing SPSS data into R. A labelled vector is a common data structure in other statistical environments, allowing you to assign text labels to specific values. In survey research, it was common to use numbers to denote categories and then to assign a separate text label to these numbers. Historically, this made data input and storage easier to manage.

When we use the `haven()` function to import data, R kept the metadata associated with that file type, that is, the SPSS variable information and value labels that were in the dataset. So what this means in practice is that you can find categorical data in R embedded in very different type of vectors (character, factor, or haven labelled) depending on decisions taken by whoever created the data frame.

Whether you need to change your object class depends ultimately on what makes sense conceptually and what analytic tasks you need to perform. For example, some functions in R may expect that you use a factor when working with categorical data, whereas others won't make this requirement.

Note that you can also print the class of a single variable at a time. The `$` symbol allows us to access specific variables in a data frame object. If objects are *boxes* in your environment, this symbol allows you to open and access compartments within those boxes.

```
class(ncvs$injured)

## [1] "numeric"
```

Using attributes()

Let's take another look at the injured variable.

```
attributes(ncvs$injured)

## $label
## [1] "Victim Sustained Injuries During Victimization"
##
## $format.spss
## [1] "F8.2"
##
## $display_width
## [1] 10
##
## $labels
## uninjured    injured
##         0          1
```

We said that objects are like boxes in your environment and that the injured variable is like a compartment in this box. The `attributes()` function allows us to look even closer at what we have inside this haven labelled vector.

Viewing Labels

Unlike in a normal character vector that you can use for encoding a categorical variable, with a haven labelled vector, you can also record a variable label that helps you to understand better what this variable measures (*victim sustained injuries during victimization*). It tells you the original format in which it came recorded, but also the text labels and how they match the values in the variable. If you just run a frequency distribution of the injured variable using the `table()` function, what you will see displayed is not the text labels but the values (which may be harder to interpret).

```
table(ncvs$injured)

##
##     0     1
## 16160  7809
```

We can get more information on haven labelled vectors using the `var_label()` and `get_labels()` functions. What all these two functions are doing is accessing the information we obtained when using `attributes()`.

View Variable Labels Using `var_label()`
You can use the `var_label()` function to view a variable's label:

```
var_label(ncvs$injured) # Print variable label

## [1] "Victim Sustained Injuries During Victimization"
```

View Value Labels Using `get_labels()`
You can use the `get_labels()` function to view value labels of a variable:

```
get_labels(ncvs$injured) # Print value labels

## [1] "uninjured" "injured"
```

Removing Labels

You can use the `remove_var_label()` function to remove variable labels (`labelled` package) and the `remove_labels()` function to remove the values (`sjlabelled` package). We are first going to create a new variable so we don't lose the labels on one of our key variables of interest.

```
# Create a new variable
ncvs$injured_no_labels <- ncvs$injured

# Print variable label
var_label(ncvs$injured_no_labels)

## [1] "Victim Sustained Injuries During Victimization"

# Print value labels
get_labels(ncvs$injured_no_labels)

## [1] "uninjured" "injured"
```

The new variable, injured no labels, has the same variable and value labels as the injured variable. In the next sections, we will remove them.

Remove Variable Labels Using `remove_var_label()`

You can remove a variable's labels with the `remove_var_label()` function:

```
# Remove variable labels
ncvs$injured_no_labels <- remove_var_label
        (ncvs$injured_no_labels)

# Check that they were removed
var_label(ncvs$injured_no_labels)

## NULL
```

Remove Value Labels Using `remove_labels()`

You can remove a variable's value labels with the `remove_labels()` function. Here, even though our variable is coded 0/1, we are specifying to remove 1 through 2 because we want the first and second value labels removed on the variable.

```
# Remove value labels
ncvs$injured_no_labels <- remove_labels(
    ncvs$injured_no_labels, labels = c(1:2))

# Check that they were removed
get_labels(ncvs$injured_no_labels)
## NULL
```

Adding Labels

Adding Variable Labels Using `var_label()`

We have the option to remove or change the variable label. Note that you may also want to change the class of a variable to the numeric class (e.g., if you treat an ordinal variable as a ratio to compute the mean), which can be done with the **as.numeric()** function (see Appendix 3.1.1.).

```
# Add variable label
var_label(ncvs$injured_no_labels) <- "Whether Victim
            Sustained Injured"

# Check that they were added
var_label(ncvs$injured_no_labels)

## [1] "Whether Victim Sustained Injured"
```

Adding Values Labels Using `add_labels()`

```
# Add variable label
ncvs$injured_no_labels <- add_labels
        (ncvs$injured_no_labels, labels =
        c(`uninjured` = 0, `injured` = 1))

# Check that they were added
get_labels(ncvs$injured_no_labels)
## [1] "uninjured" "injured"
```

Formatting Classes and Value Labels Using factor()

Now that you have determined the class of your variables and viewed variable labels, you can decide if you want to make changes to how the variables are formatted or labelled. Value labels are very useful when we have a nominal- or ordinal-level variable in our dataset *that has been assigned numeric values*. Most of the time, these numeric values do not mean anything in and of themselves, so we need a little help to make sure we interpret them correctly. For nominal variables, the order of the values does not matter. Although, for ordinal variables, the order of the values does matter, so we need to tell R how they should be ordered and that ordering is important for these variables.

Since the level of measurement of the injured variable is nominal, let's change the class of this variable so it is a factor using the `factor()` function. In doing so, we are going to create a new variable, retaining the value labels, rather than overwrite the existing variable. Remember, you can use the `class()` and `get_labels()` functions to make sure the class and value labels on the injured variable are correct.

```
# Name the newly created factor *injured_r*
ncvs$injured_r <- factor(ncvs$injured, labels =
    c("Uninjured", "Injured"))
table(ncvs$injured_r)

##
## Uninjured    Injured
##     16160       7809
```

It is important to note that with ordinal variables, you must specify that the variable is ordered when creating a factor.

Recoding and Creating New Variables

Sometimes you may need to recode some of your variables before you can work with them. Recoding could mean anything from collapsing multiple values of your variable into a single category or setting some values of your variable to be missing.

You might even want to create a brand-new variable, for instance, a composite of two variables in your dataset. Fortunately, R makes this simple to accomplish with vectorized operations. For example, let's say we want to create a new variable in our NCVS data that tells us about the severity of the victimization experienced by the respondent. Let's assume, in this case, that severity will be measured as whether the offender had a weapon and whether the victim sustained an injury during their victimization. These are not necessarily the best variables to use in measuring victimization severity; however, this example should illustrate how you might combine variables to create a new variable.

Creating a New Variable from 1 Existing Variable

Before getting into how to combine variables, sometimes you may want to add a totally new column to your data frame (which may or may not use an existing variable). In the first example, we are creating a new variable named InjuredNew, and we are making a duplicate of the existing variable named injured. The code from the second example is one that you learned above. However, it is important to take note that this is another example of how to create a new variable since the code is telling R to create a new variable named injured_r, by using the existing variable, injured. It also allows you to specify the class of the new variable and the labels. In this third example, we are using the `add_column()` function from the `tibble` package (also from `tidyverse`) to create a new ID variable that is simply equal to the row number (see Chap. 4 for discussion about tibbles).

```
# Create the new variable
ncvs$InjuredNew <- ncvs$injured

## New variable but specify that order is important
ncvs$injured_r <- factor(ncvs$injured, labels =
    c("Uninjured", "Injured"), ordered = TRUE)

## Create a new column that has a row ID
add_column(ncvs, newid = 1:nrow(ncvs))
```

Creating a New Variable from >1 Existing Variables

Producing a quick tibble using the `count()` function for the injured variable tells us again that this nominal-level variable is stored as an integer, where the 0 value means the victim was uninjured and the 1 value means they were injured. You will often see this way of coding in data, in which 0 represents the absence of the feature being measured and 1 means the presence of such feature.

```
count(ncvs, injured)
```

And looking at the weaponpresent variable with the `count()` function, we see this is also a nominal variable stored as an integer. In this case, there are more victims reporting that the offender did not use a weapon during the offense as opposed to using one. We also note that there are a number of missing values for this question.

```
## # A tibble: 3 x 2
##   weaponpresent     n
##           <dbl> <int>
## 1             0 15814
## 2             1  6652
## 3            NA  1503
```

Creating a New Variable Using mutate()

We can use the mutate() function in the dplyr package to create a new column that is comprised of the sum of both of these variables. An important thing to note is that while mutate() keeps the old variables that comprise the new variable, the similar function transmute() drops old variables once the new variable is calculated.

```
# Create the new variable with mutate
ncvs <- mutate(ncvs, severity = injured + weaponpresent)
```

Check it by comparing it with the old variables. Note the use of the *pipe* operator (%>%), which means that we only need to specify the data frame object once at the beginning. In all subsequent functions, the object is *piped* through saving us some repetition.

```
ncvs %>%
select(injured, weaponpresent, severity) %>%
sample_n(10)

##    injured weaponpresent severity
## 1        0             0        0
## 2        1             0        1
## 3        1             1        2
## 4        0             1        1
## 5        1             1        2
## 6        0             0        0
## 7        0             1        1
## 8        0             0        0
## 9        1             1        2
## 10       1             0        1
```

Notice that now our variable is considered ordinal, where 0 is the least severe (neither a weapon was used nor the victim was injured), 1 is more severe (either the offender wielded a weapon or the victim reported being injured), and 2 is the most severe (the respondent and the offender both reported being injured and having a weapon, respectively). You can go ahead and add value labels to indicate this if you like.

The previous example was pretty straightforward in that it was only necessary to add two existing variables together to get our new variable. We can also tackle more complex recoding. Often, we need to collapse multiple categories of a variable into one. For example, let's assume we wanted to turn the variable in the NCVS dataset that includes the relationship between the victim and the offender into a dichotomous variable that indicates whether the offender was a stranger (0) or was known to the victim (1) that we will name notstranger. Before doing this, take a look at how the variable is coded using the **count()** function. We see that there are four categories:

```
## # A tibble: 5 x 2
##   relationship       n
##           <dbl> <int>
## 1             0  6547
## 2             1  2950
## 3             2  4576
## 4             3  9227
## 5            NA   669
```

Conditional Change of a Variable Using case_when()

Using the **dplyr** package from **tidyverse**, the functions **mutate()** and **case_when()** allow us to make changes to a variable that are conditional on some requirement. Think of **case_when()** like an *if* logical statement. Note below that this turns our new categories into character values. In this example, we are creating a new variable named notstranger using the existing variable relationship. In doing so, we tell R that if the case is coded as a *0* on the relationship variable, code the new notstranger variable as *Stranger*. Also, if the case is coded as a *1, 2,* or *3* on the relationship variable, code the new notstranger variable as *Not a stranger*.

```
ncvs <- ncvs %>%
  mutate(notstranger = case_when
         (relationship %in% 0 ~ "Stranger",
          relationship %in% 1:3 ~ "Not a stranger"))
```

Alternatively, we could run the following code to make the character values numeric rather than string (e.g., stranger vs. not a stranger) instead:

```
ncvs <- ncvs %>%
  mutate(notstranger = case_when(relationship == 0 ~ 0,
                                 relationship <= 3 ~ 1))
```

Sorting Using arrange()

You might have noticed when viewing your data frame using `View()` that you can sort rows according to a variable by clicking on the variable name. This is useful, but it is only temporary, and does not actually alter your data frame object. To sort our data frame by the age of the respondent in our NCVS data frame, for instance, we can use the `arrange()` function.

```
# View age of the top 5 respondents before sorting
head(ncvs$age_r, n=5)

## [1] 34 51 20 38 71

# Sort ascending, changing existing object.
ncvs <- arrange(ncvs, age_r)
```

Now it's been sorted, check the data by viewing the top five youngest respondents.

```
head(ncvs$age_r, n=5)

## [1] 12 12 12 12 12
```

You can sort descending by adding the `desc()` argument.

```
ncvs <- arrange(ncvs, desc(age_r))  # Sort descending
```

Subsetting

Subsetting (Non-tidyverse Way)

It is common to want to subset your data based on some criteria. The syntax for subsetting using the built-in functionality of R is to use the name of the data frame (or vector, if you're filtering from that) followed by the square brackets. Inside the square brackets, you enter the criteria you want to filter for rows and columns, separated by a comma. Row criteria are always on the left of the comma, and column criteria are always on the right. If you leave either side of the comma blank, that indicates that you want all of those.

To select all rows of the first two columns of our dataset, you would type ncvs[, 1:2]. If you want to use this subset data frame later, don't forget to assign it to an object! So, to create a new data frame, which we are calling ncvs_Df (the first two columns of ncvs dataset), you type:

```
ncvs_Df <- ncvs[ ,1:2]
```

You can have a look at the new data frame you have created using View(). Similarly, if you wanted the first two rows of the dataset, then you would put your criteria on the left (row) side of the comma within the square brackets:

```
firstTwoRowsOfncvs <- ncvs[1:2, ]
```

To test whether an observation (row) meets the criteria, we can test for each row whether the == returns true or false. In the subsetting, we get back all the rows where == returned TRUE. As you recall, we want to filter rows, and row criteria goes in the left half of the brackets. We want all of the columns, so we leave the right-hand side (column criteria) blank:

```
OnlyInjured <- ncvs[ncvs$injured == 1, ]
```

You can add multiple criteria to your selection. To do this, you use the *and* (&) and *or* (|) operator.

```
# Select respondents who knew their offender and were
## injured
KnewOffandInjured <- ncvs[(ncvs$relationship > 0 &
    ncvs$injured == 1), ]
```

Subsetting Using select()
Another way of subsetting data frames (or vectors) is to use functions within the tidyverse package. It is increasingly common to use such functions instead of the indexing above, although it is useful to know both. Using select(), we can subset variables by number or name:

```
# This:
ncvs_Df <- ncvs %>%
  select(1:2)

# Does the same as this, with the variable names:
ncvs_Df <- ncvs %>%
  select(varname1:varname2)
```

Subsetting Using `slice()`

Using `slice()`, we can subset rows by number, and combine it with `select()`.

```
# Get the first two rows
firstTwoRowsOfncvs <- ncvs %>%
  slice(1:2)

# Combine with select to get the first two variables,
## and first two rows
firstTwoRowsCols <- ncvs %>%
  select(1:2) %>%
  slice(1:2)
```

Subsetting Using `filter()`

We can use the `filter()` function to subset observations (i.e., rows) based on conditions. For instance, to replicate the condition example from earlier, for which we only wanted those who have a value of 1 on the <u>injured</u> variable, we could run:

```
OnlyInjured <- ncvs %>%
  filter(injured == 1)
```

These filters can be combined using conditions like **&** and **|** just as we did earlier.

```
KnewOffandInjured <- ncvs %>%
  filter(relationship > 0 & injured == 1)
```

Application Activities

Problem 1:

Using `mutate()` and `case_when()`, create a new variable named ReportedandNotStranger, where *YES* indicates that the victim both reported the offense to the police (victimreported variable) and knew their offender in some capacity (relationship variable), and use *NO* to indicate otherwise.

Problem 2:

Use the `View()` function to scan the data frame to identify the gender and age variables. Then, using those variables and the `filter()` function, subset the NCVS data frame such that it contains only male respondents between the ages of 16 and 34. Save the subset as a data frame named `ncvsAgeSubset`. Using `arrange()`, sort the dataset so the oldest respondents are at the top and younger respondents are at the bottom.

Problem 3:

Using `mutate()` and `case_when()`, create a new variable called age_cat using the age_r variable, whereby the respondent's age is placed into one of four categories: 12–24, 25–40, 41–60, and 60+. Make sure all aspects of the new variable's class is appropriate for its level of measurement by running the `class()` function. Last, add a variable label and appropriate value labels using the `var_label()` and `add_labels()` functions, respectively.

Key Terms

Project A self-contained working directory.

Nominal variables Categorical, unordered variables.

Ordinal variables Categorical, ordered variables.

Interval/ratio variables Numeric variables with equal intervals between values; they are functionally the same, yet ratio-level variables have a true zero.

Functions Introduced in this Chapter

FUNCTION	DESCRIPTION (PACKAGE)
add_column()	Adds columns to a data frame (tibble)
add_labels()	Adds value labels to a variable (sjlabelled)
arrange()	Sorts rows by a given variable(s) (dplyr)
case_when()	Allows users to vectorize multiple if / if else statements (dplyr)
count()	Counts the number of occurrences (dplyr)
factor()	Creates a factor (base R)
filter()	Subsets a data frame to rows when a condition is true (dplyr)
get_labels()	Returns value labels of labelled data (sjlabelled)
head()	Returns first parts of a vector, matrix, table, or data frame (base R)
here()	Finds a project's files based on the current working directory (here)
install.packages()	Installs non-base R packages (base R)
library()	Loads the installed non-base R package (base R)
mutate()	Creates new vectors or transforms existing ones (dplyr)
nrow()	Counts the number of rows (base R)
read_spss()	Imports SPSS .sav files (haven)
remove_labels()	Removes value labels from a variable (sjlabelled)
remove_var_label()	Removes a variable's label (labelled)
sapply()	Applies a function over a vector or list (base R)
select()	Select columns to retain or drop (dplyr)
slice()	Select rows based on their position in the data frame (dplyr)
table()	Generates a frequency table (base R)
var_label()	Returns or sets a variable label (labelled)

Reference

Wickham, H. (2014). Tidy data. *Journal of Statistical Software, 59*(10), 1–23.

Chapter three

Data Visualization

Topics Practiced

Data visualization by level of measurement

Technical Skills Covered

Using bar charts to represent nominal and ordinal data

Using graphs/plots to represent ratio/interval data

Scatterplot, histogram, line graph, and box-and-whiskers plot

Color palettes and themes

R Packages Required

dplyr, ggplot2, here, readr

© The Editor(s) (if applicable) and The Author(s), under exclusive license to
Springer Nature Switzerland AG 2021
A. Wooditch et al., *A Beginner's Guide to Statistics for Criminology and
Criminal Justice Using R*, https://doi.org/10.1007/978-3-030-50625-4_3

ARE YOU SICK of those drab-looking graphs and plots in Stata and SPSS? We are too! So, this chapter covers data visualization in R. Specifically, you will be working with `ggplot2`, a package within the `tidyverse` set of packages, for making high-quality, reproducible graphics. Data visualization is an accessible, aesthetically pleasing, and powerful way to explore, analyze, and convey complex information. It is an integral part of investigating data and disseminating findings to wider audiences. Learning the basics of data visualization in R can improve your workflow and make your findings easier to interpret and more impactful. This chapter reviews how to visually represent nominal and ordinal data using bar charts and how to visualize ratio and interval data using histograms, scatterplots, line graphs, and box plots in R. Crime data from Greater Manchester, England, will be used to demonstrate these visualization techniques.

Data

Dataset Source: Official crime data from England and Wales

File Name: gmp_2017.csv; gmp_monthly_2017.csv

Dataset Description: Police forces in England and Wales release crime records on a monthly basis for public usage. These data can be aggregated to neighborhood-sized census units, known as Lower Super Output Areas (LSOA), to visualize associations between demographic characteristics and crime concentrations. The first dataset contains LSOA-level data for Greater Manchester, England, including burglary counts for 2017 and deprivation measures. The second data set contains crime counts for Greater Manchester that have been aggregated by crime type and month. The raw crime data are available from open records at data.police.uk/data, and the deprivation and resident population data are made available by the Office for National Statistics and the Ministry of Housing, Communities and Local Government, under Open Government License v3.0.

Getting Started

1. Open up your existing R project as outlined in Chap. 2 (see also Appendix 1.3).

2. Install and load the required packages using the `install.packages()` and `library()` functions (see Appendix 1.1).

3. Open the datasets containing crime data from Greater Manchester, England, (*gmp_2017.csv* and *gmp_monthly_2017.csv*) using the `read_csv()` function to import the datasets (see Appendix 1.6.3), specifying the working directory with `here()` (see Appendix 1.3). When doing so, respectively name the data frames `burglary_df` and `monthly_df` by using the `<-` assignment operator.

Grammar of Graphics

You will be working with **ggplot2**, a package within the **tidyverse** set of packages, for making high-quality, reproducible graphics. This is one of the most popular packages in R, and for good reason. The package builds on Leland Wilkinson's (1999) work, *The Grammar of Graphics*, and revolves around the idea that graphics are made up of *layers*. The three primary layers in visualizations are (1) the data, (2) the aesthetics, and (3) the geometries.

- **Data** The first layer is the data itself, which would typically be a data frame with *tidy* rows and columns.

- **Aesthetics** These describe the visual characteristics that represent the data (i.e., variables) you are interested in. At a minimum, these might be an x- and y-axis, but these can be extended to aesthetics, such as color, size, and shape, which are *mapped* to variables.

- **Geometries** These describe the objects that represent the data, such as points or lines.

When you are creating graphs using **ggplot2**, you can build the graph up using these layers. As we will see in the following examples, the way of conceptualizing these layers is reflected in how we write **ggplot2** code. It is a different way of thinking about graphs compared to, say, using a template for a plot in Excel, but don't worry! Over time, it will be intuitive and allow you to make high-quality visuals quite quickly. Importantly, you will find that you can simply reuse chunks of code to create numerous different types of graphics or reproduce identical graphics, using different datasets.

It is important to be familiar with your data and its structure before attempting anything in **ggplot2**. So, take a look at your first dataset using **View(burglary_df)**, and consider exploring how **R** is treating each variable using **class()**, e.g., **class(burglary_df$IMDscore)**. Remember, you can also examine the attributes of the dataset under the *Environment* tab in **RStudio**.

We can see that in our dataset, **burglary_df**, there are number of variables:

- LSOAcode Official code to identify the LSOA

- burglary count Discrete measure that is a count of the burglaries recorded by police in 2017

- LAname Name of the local authority in which the LSOA is nested

- IMDscore Index of multiple deprivation (IMD) score for 2019

- IMDrank Rank of the LSOA in terms of deprivation for England

- IMDdeci Deprivation decile for England (1, most deprived; 10, least deprived)

- incscore Income score of residents, a component of the IMD

- pop Resident population count for 2011

The IMDscore variable is an official measure that combines seven domains of deprivation into one index: income, employment, education, health, crime, barriers to housing/services, and living environment. While IMDrank is a variable that ranks all 32,844 LSOAs from highest to lowest, you will see by using **range()** function, **range(burglary_df$IMDrank)**, that not all LSOAs are included, since this dataset only contains cases from Greater Manchester.

If you now examine the second dataset with the **View()** function, **monthly_df**, you will note that it only contains three variables, but quite a lot of information. We have the crime count for various different crime types, spread across 12 months of the year. Note that the data are in *long* format. This is a useful (and common) format for longitudinal data, because our time variable (i.e., months) is contained in one variable. As we'll see later, this makes it easier to create graphics demonstrating change over time.

- Month Month of the year (1, January; 12, December)

- crime type Crime type (e.g., burglary, vehicle crime)

- n Crime count

Now, let's learn to make some fancy plots. Yeah buddy!

Scatterplot

There are a number of research questions that can be answered using these data. We might be interested in the relationship between deprivation and burglary victimization. Since the <u>IMDscore</u> measure makes use of police recorded crime data, it is probably best to use the <u>incscore</u> variable instead. So, we are asking: *What is the relationship between burglary counts and income?* We can explore this question using a scatterplot, which is a graph that depicts the relationship between two ratio/interval variables.

First, let's generate the data layer.

```
ggplot(data = burglary_df)
```

As you can see, not a lot actually happens, but your *Plots* window will pop up and will be blank. This is the first layer of the graphic, defining the data, but it still needs aesthetics and a geometry. Working step-by-step, we now want to define the aesthetics, i.e., the variables we want to map to visual properties. Since we are interested in the relationship between <u>burglary count</u> and <u>inscore</u>, it seems intuitive to map these variables to the x- and y-axis aesthetics.

We can specify this within the **ggplot()** function using the **mapping** argument:

```
ggplot(data = burglary_df, mapping = aes
       (x = incscore, y = burglary_count))
```

With the data and aesthetic layers complete, our graphic is beginning to emerge. Notice that the function has automatically specified the extent of axis and the break labels. Users can alter these manually later.

The final layer is geometry, which is defined by numerous functions, each of which begin with **geom_**. Here, we want a scatterplot, which has the corresponding geometry, **geom_point()**. All we need to do is add this geometry to our current code using **+**, which works similarly to the **%>%** operator. The information stated in our initial **ggplot()** function is passed through to **geom_point()**. It is important to mention that the **+** symbol needs to be placed at the end of the line of code and cannot be placed at the beginning of the row before your code because **R** will throw an error.

```
ggplot(data = burglary_df, mapping = aes
       (x = incscore, y = burglary_count)) + geom_point()
```

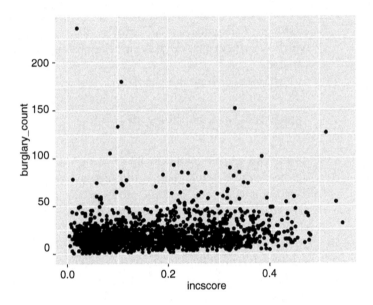

What are your conclusions from this? Is there a meaningful relationship? Are there any outliers to be concerned about?

We might also be interested in incorporating other variables into our scatterplot. *How do local authorities factor into this relationship?* We can color each dot by the LAname variable using the **color** aesthetic.

```
ggplot(data = burglary_df, mapping = aes(x = incscore,
       y = burglary_count, color = LAname)) + geom_point()
```

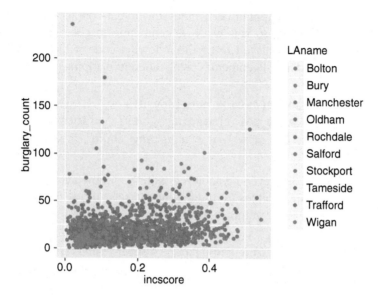

There are a number of different aesthetic options beyond those used above, such as **shape**, **linetype**, **size**, **fill**, and **alpha** (transparency), and the usage of which will depend on the geometry being used and the class of variable being mapped to an aesthetic.

Try the **shape** aesthetic for <u>LAname</u>, which would vary the shape of each point according to the local authority. What is the warning message telling you? How does the graphic reflect this issue? It's problematic. This relates back the grammar of graphics and how people interpret visual information: **ggplot2** is good at guiding your decisions, and it will warn you when appropriate. You can override such behavior, but then you might run the risk of creating a graphic that is difficult to interpret or, perhaps even worse, misleading.

Code Structure

It is worth being aware that **ggplot2** code can be constructed in different ways depending on what you are trying to achieve or what you think makes your code clearer. We can write **geom_point()** with no information inside the brackets because we have already specified the aesthetics within **ggplot()**. If you do this (i.e., specify the aesthetics first within the **ggplot** function), then any subsequent **geoms** (short for geometries) will have that same mapping. Sometimes, this might conflict with what you are trying to achieve, so it is worth remembering that the above plot could also have been achieved using the following code, which would allow you to use additional geometries using different mappings, but the same data, later on:

```
ggplot(data = burglary_df) +
  geom_point(mapping = aes(x = incscore,
             y = burglary_count, color = LAname))
```

It could even be achieved with the following, which would permit you to map variables from different datasets, and with different geometries, onto the same graphic:

```
ggplot() + geom_point(data = burglary_df, mapping = aes
  (x = incscore, y = burglary_count, color = LAname))
```

Color Palettes

Let's extend this example to learn some new skills within **ggplot2**. The first thing you might be wondering is: Where did the color scheme come from? The one used above is the default palette for discrete scales, but it is one of a number available automatically. We can apply different palettes using an additional layer, **scale_color_brewer()**, which specifically dictates to the color aesthetic. Later, you might be using the **fill** aesthetic, and in which case, you'd define the color palette using **scale_fill_brewer()**, for instance. In this example, we'll use **Spectral**. It is worth exploring online to find out about the other color palettes available.

```
ggplot(data = burglary_df, mapping = aes(x = incscore,
  y = burglary_count, color = LAname)) +
  geom_point() +
  scale_color_brewer(palette = "Spectral")
```

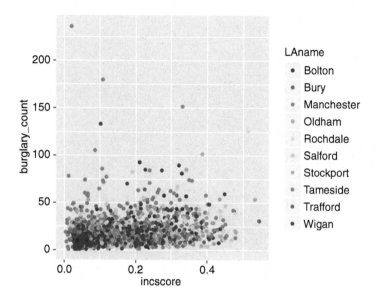

A note that is relevant to anyone creating data visualizations is color blindness. It might leave many readers unable to differentiate between different colors on your graphic. Fortunately, there are packages in **R** which address this. The **viridis** package contains a number of palettes that are easier to interpret for people with such a deficiency. This package is integrated into **ggplot2**. Instead of the standard color (or fill) brewer used above, one can use a viridis-specific scale. For instance, to replicate the graph above using the default **viridis** palette for a discrete variable (LAname), you could run the below code chunk:

```
ggplot(data = burglary_df, mapping = aes(x = incscore,
    y = burglary_count, color = LAname)) + geom_point() +
# or scale_color_viridis_c() for a continuous variable
    scale_color_viridis_d()
```

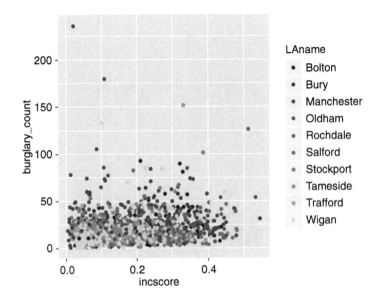

Just like with the default brewer, `viridis` has a number of different palettes. You can explore them using the `option` argument, e.g., `scale_color_viridis_d(option = "magma")`.

Sizes and Transparency

Alterations can be made to the visual appearance of geometries within the geometry layer, in this case, `geom_point()`. These include things like size, transparency, and thickness, depending on what geometry we are using. To increase the size of points and make them transparent, we can use the `size` and `alpha` arguments. The default for `size` is 1, so anything lower (e.g., 0.5) will make points smaller, and anything larger (e.g., 10) will make points bigger. The default for `alpha` is also 1, which specifies absolute opaqueness, so you can only go lower to make things less opaque (more transparent).

```
ggplot(data = burglary_df, mapping = aes(x = incscore,
    y = burglary_count, color = LAname)) +
    geom_point(size = 3, alpha = 0.5) +
    scale_color_brewer(palette = "Spectral")
```

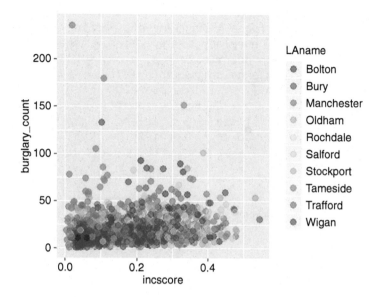

Note that in making these tweaks to the visual appearance of geometries, *we have not specified them as aesthetics*, even though `size` and `alpha` could be used as aesthetics (i.e., changing the size of points according to a variable or changing the transparency according to a variable). In other words, the `size` and `alpha` arguments have been made outside of `aes()`. This is because we are making changes to the general visual appearance of the point geometry, rather than changing the size or alpha according to a variable in our data frame. Remember, anything specified within `aes()` should be a variable in your data! One of the most common mistakes in `ggplot2` code is to accidentally try and map variables outside of the `aes()` argument.

What would you expect to happen if you placed `size` within `aes()` in relation to a variable, such as `size = LAname`? What happens if you tried to map it to a variable *outside* of the aesthetic argument?

Labels

Our graphic is shaping up well, but you'll notice that all our labels have been defined automatically based on variable names. We can alter them using the `labs()` layer. There are a few standard label types, such as x, y, title, and caption (and whichever aesthetics are being used, e.g., color).

```
ggplot(data = burglary_df, mapping = aes(x = incscore,
    y = burglary_count, color = LAname)) +
  geom_point(size = 3, alpha = 0.5) +
  scale_color_brewer(palette = "Spectral") +
  labs(x = "Income score",
       y = "Burglary count",
       title = "Income and burglary and victimization",
       color = "Local Authority")
```

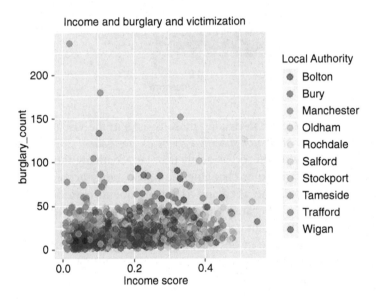

Built-In Themes

A final touch you might want to incorporate is **themes**. These will alter the general appearance of your plot with only a small amount of code. The default we are seeing now is `theme_gray()`, for instance. For a simple, minimalist look, we might want to try `theme_minimal()`, as demonstrated below. You can read more about customized themes using the `theme()` function in Appendix 4.3.

```
ggplot(data = burglary_df, mapping = aes(x = incscore,
    y = burglary_count, color = LAname)) +
  geom_point(size = 3, alpha = 0.5) +
  scale_color_brewer(palette = "Spectral") +
  labs(x = "Income score",
       y = "Burglary count",
       title = "Income and burglary and victimization",
       caption = "Income score from 2019 IMD.
                   Burglary counts from 2017.",
       color = "Local Authority") +
  theme_minimal()
```

Income and burglary and victimization

Income score from 2019 IMD. Burglary counts from 2017.

The above example dealt only with scatterplots using the geometry **geom_point()**, but there are numerous other geometries available. We cover a few additional examples below, but this list is by no means exhaustive. However, it will cover the fundamentals of different visuals using **ggplot2** and equip you with the skills needed to get you creating your own graphics.

Geometry Examples

Histograms

While creating a scatterplot needs two existing variables, mapped to the x- and y-axis, some geometries perform calculations in the background. Histograms, for instance, visualize the distribution of a ratio or interval variable by creating bins and counting the number of values in each one. The **geom_histogram()** geometry will do this automatically, and thus you only need to specify the x aesthetic. The y-axis (a count) is being generated for us. Let's take a look at IMDscore, the overall score indicating the level of deprivation in each neighborhood:

```
ggplot(data = burglary_df) +
  geom_histogram(mapping = aes(x = IMDscore))
```

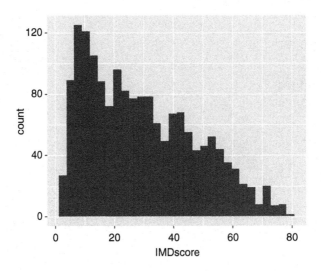

The appearance of histograms, and thus the conclusions drawn from the visual, is sensitive to the number of bins, so it is worth investigating several options before settling on a number. You'll notice that **ggplot** gives you a warning if you don't specify it yourself. You can mess around with the **bins** argument within **geom_histogram()** if you'd like to explore this, remembering that such an argument should go *outside* of **aes()**.

Recall from what you learned in the prior chapter that you can assign your histogram to an object. Executing the name of the object in your script (or console) will simply output the graphic to the plot window.

```
my_plot <- ggplot(data = burglary_df) +
            geom_histogram(mapping = aes(x = IMDscore))


my_plot
```

Bar Graphs

A common descriptive visual to explore the count distribution of nominal and ordinal variables is a bar graph. In our data, we might want to know the number of neighborhoods falling into each IMD (deprivation) decile, a key indicator of criminality. As noted earlier, the structure of your data is integral to using **ggplot2** effectively. You can take a look at the counts per decile manually using **table(burglary_df$IMDdeci)**, but these figures don't actually exist within the **burglary_df** object. Rather than creating a new data frame object to make a bar graph from scratch, you can let **ggplot** calculate these frequencies for you in the background just by specifying the x-axis.

```
ggplot(data = burglary_df) +
# convert IMDdeci to a factor on-the-fly
  geom_bar(mapping = aes(x = as.factor(IMDdeci))) +
  labs(x = "Deprivation Score",
       y = "Number of Lower Super Output Areas")
```

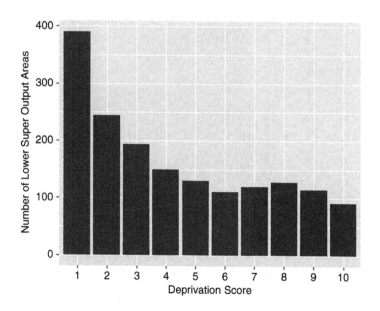

Note that we treat the decile variable as a factor for this plot. This is not strictly necessary, but you will notice that **ggplot2** treats it as a continuous variable otherwise because its class is numeric. This makes the default x-axis values somewhat misleading because it includes non-integer values (e.g., 7.5), which are not possible. Alternatively, you could convert the IMDdeci variable to a factor beforehand or create a new variable that is a factor using the **as.factor()** function.

Grouped Bar Graph

How might you explore the distribution of these deprivation deciles by local authority? There's a number of ways you could do this. One might be to fill the color of each bar by local authority and then arrange the bars side-by-side. You can do this using **fill** and an option called **position** whereby bars dodge one another.

```
ggplot(data = burglary_df) +
  geom_bar(mapping = aes(x = as.factor(IMDdeci),
           fill = LAname), position = "dodge") +
  labs(x = "Deprivation Score",
       y = "Number of Lower Super Output Areas",
       fill = "Local Authority")
```

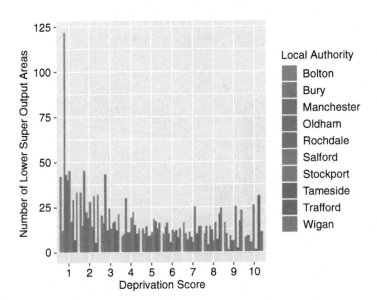

Another way you can explore such things is through a facet, which is covered later in this chapter.

Multiple Graphs Using *facet_wrap()*

Sometimes, it is useful to generate different plots for each level of a factor rather than trying to portray lots of information in one graphic. This is where the `facet_wrap()` layer is especially useful. Returning to our scatterplot from earlier, we colored each point by local authority, which generated lots of information, and led to many points overlapping one another. An alternative would be to facet the scatterplot by using ~ and local authority (~LAname). Note that by default, `facet_wrap()` fixes the y-axis of each graph to facilitate comparisons.

```
ggplot(data = burglary_df) +
  geom_point(mapping = aes(x = incscore,
                           y = burglary_count)) +
             facet_wrap(~LAname)
```

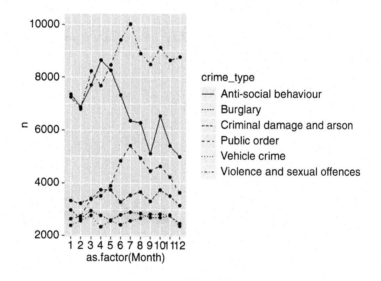

Line Graphs

There has been an increasing movement toward longitudinal studies in criminology and criminal justice research. With that comes a demand for effective ways of visualizing change over time. A staple graphic for showcasing developmental trends are line graphs. First, ensure that you have the `monthy_df` data object loaded into your environment, as demonstrated at the beginning of the chapter.

Take a few moments to explore the structure of these data. Remember that it is in long format. Even though we have 12 months' worth of data, we only have a single month variable (rather than each being spread across 12 columns). This allows us to specify the aesthetics (e.g., x- and y-axis) easily.

Here, we're going to plot these counts over time to show the longitudinal trends of different crime types over the course of the year using **geom_line()**. Intuitively, we want the time variable, <u>month</u>, running along the x-axis, and the count variable, <u>n</u>, on the y-axis. To show each crime type separately, we're going to use the **group** aesthetic and introduce a new aesthetic, **linetype**, which uses different patterns for each group.

To clearly show our time measurement points, we also add **geom_point()**. This demonstrates how everything within the **ggplot()** function gets passed into subsequent layers.

```
ggplot(data = monthly_df, aes(x = as.factor(Month), y = n,
    group = crime_type, linetype = crime_type)) +
    geom_line() +
    geom_point()
```

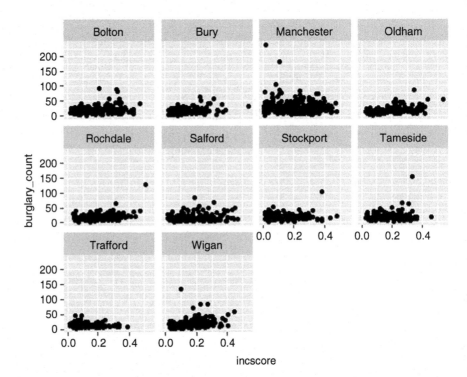

You can also change the color, size of the lines, alpha (transparency), and line type. There are several line types to choose from in R, such as dashed, dotted, solid, and dotdash. These get automatically mapped to a variable when specified as an aesthetic, as demonstrated above for crime types. However, line types can be changed uniformly for all lines by specifying options *outside* of the aesthetics, just as we did earlier with geom_point().

You will have noticed that, for the purposes of this demonstration, our time variable Month is treated as a factor. However, there are specific ways of treating dates in R which are especially useful with more complex date-time variables. These are covered in the Appendix (see 3.2 and 3.3).

Box Plots

Another common way to explore and visualize distributions is a box-and-whiskers plot (box plot). It shows a bit more information than a histogram, because it includes the interquartile range and helps us identify specific outliers. We could quickly take a look at the distribution of burglary count using the geom_boxplot() layer, specifying the variable as a y aesthetic. Here, we go one step further and generate a box plot for each deprivation decile. This demonstrates how LSOAs in the most deprived deciles tend to have a higher median burglary count.

```
MyWhiskerPlot <- ggplot(data = burglary_df) +
  geom_boxplot(mapping = aes(x = as.factor(IMDdeci),
                             y = burglary_count,
   group = as.factor(IMDdeci), fill = as.factor(IMDdeci)))


MyWhiskerPlot +
    labs(x = "Deprivation Scale",
         y = "Number of Burglaries")
```

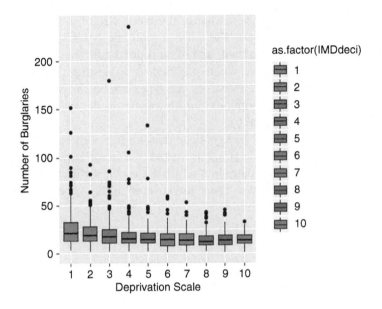

Application Activities

Problem 1:

Using the `burglary_df` data frame, visualize the distribution of IMDscore with a histogram (using the geometry `geom_histogram()`). To explore how the distribution varies between local authorities, use a facet wrap (`~facet_wrap()`) to plot a visual for each local authority in LAname. If you want, use an additional fill aesthetic within `geom_histogram()` to fill in the color of each histogram according to LAname.

Problem 2:

Using the `burglary_df` data frame, visualize the deprivation decile counts using IMDdeci, but fill the color of each bar by decile. This will involve adding `fill = as.factor(IMDdeci)` within your aesthetics. Remember that we want IMDdeci to be treated as a factor to ensure an appropriate (discrete, not continuous) color palette is used. Try changing the color palette to something which you think best aligns with the ordinal nature of IMDdeci (1, most deprived; 10, least deprived). You can use the `scale_fill_brewer()` layer to specify a suitable color palette.

Problem 3:

Using the `monthly_df` data frame, create a new variable that transforms the raw crime counts to a rate per 100,000 people. The population of

Greater Manchester is around 2.6 million. To create this new variable, you will need to use the `mutate()` function introduced in Chap. 2. It is part of the `dplyr` package, so first load this package using `library(dplyr)` as we learned previously. Once you've created the variable, construct a line graph that displays the crime rates across months by crime type. The code for this will be very similar to the earlier demonstration of line graphs, but you will use your new rates variable instead of n. Make the lines semi-transparent red and thinner than the default. Still make each crime type have a different line type. The x-axis title should be labelled *Month*, and the y-axis should be labelled *Crimes per 100,000 people*.

Problem 4:

Using the `burglary_df` data frame, add a line of best fit to the scatterplot that visualizes the relationship between the burglary counts and income (without including local authorities) which we generated earlier. For that, you will make use of a geometry layer called `geom_smooth()` which adds smoothed lines to your plots, helping you determine patterns from the points. If your code mimics the example from the walk-through, the aesthetics will be specified within `ggplot()`, and thus the `geom_point()` and `geom_smooth()` layers can be added without any aesthetics. Within `geom_smooth()`, you should include `method = "lm"` to draw a *linear* trend line.

Problem 5:

Create a graph or chart in R to visualize one or multiple variables from either the `burglary_df` or `monthly_df` datasets that were not used in the examples above. Be mindful to select a means of visualizing the variable(s) that is appropriate for their level of measurement.

Problem 6:

Recreate the scatterplot that visualizes the relationship between income score and burglary victimization using `burglary_df` but use a new measure that is the burglary rate, i.e., counts standardized by population. You can create this new variable using the pop variable, which tells us the resident population of each neighborhood and of course the raw count `burglary_count`.

Key Terms

Aesthetics Describe visual characteristics that represent the data.

Data Information used to answer a research question; typically will be stored in a data frame. Data (plural) are made up of numerous datum (singular).

Geom Abbreviation for geometries from the `ggplot2` package.

Geometries Describe the objects that represent the data.

Themes Customizations that can alter the general appearance of a plot.

Functions Introduced in this Chapter

FUNCTION	DESCRIPTION (PACKAGE)
aes()	Mapping aesthetics to variables (ggplot2)
as.factor()	Convert to factor, including specifying levels (base R)
facet_wrap()	Facet graphics by one or more variables (ggplot2)
geom_bar()	Geometry layer for bar plot (ggplot2)
geom_boxplot()	Geometry layer for box plot (ggplot2)
geom_histogram()	Geometry layer for histograms (ggplot2)
geom_line()	Geometry layer for line charts (ggplot2)
geom_point()	Geometry layer for scatterplots (ggplot2)
geom_smooth()	Geometry layer for smoothed lines (ggplot2)
ggplot()	Initialize a ggplot graphic, i.e., specify data, aesthetics (ggplot2)
labs()	Specify labels for ggplot object, e.g., title, caption (ggplot2)
range()	Provides the minimum and maximum values (base R)
read_csv()	Read in comma separated values file (readr)
scale_color_brewer()	Default color scheme options (ggplot2)
scale_color_viridis_d()	Color-blind-friendly palettes from viridis package (ggplot2)
theme()	Customize ggplot graphics (ggplot2)
theme_minimal()	Default minimalist theme for ggplot graphics (ggplot2)

Reference

Wilkinson, L. (1999). *The Grammar of Graphics*. Springer. ISBN 978-0-387-98774-3.

Descriptive Statistics: Measures of Central Tendency

Topics Practiced

Measures of central tendency

Technical Skills Covered

Calculating the mean (ratio, interval)

Calculating the median (ratio, interval, ordinal)

Calculating the mode (ratio, interval, ordinal, nominal)

Detecting outliers and skewness

R Packages Required

dplyr, ggplot2, here, modeest, moments, skimr

A. Wooditch et al., *A Beginner's Guide to Statistics for Criminology and
Criminal Justice Using R*, https://doi.org/10.1007/978-3-030-50625-4_4

THIS CHAPTER COVERS some basic and commonly used methods of describing your data, including calculating measures of central tendency. When we talk about measures of central tendency, we are referring to cases that fall in the middle of a distribution. In other words, we can think of these as being the typical or average case. Measures of central tendency are very efficient ways of describing how some variable is distributed in the population. It is very important in the early stages of data analysis to examine your dataset descriptively, particularly looking at the various measures of central tendency (the focus of this chapter), and dispersion (the focus of Chap. 5). Performing descriptive analyses on your data is an important part of the analysis process. Chances are, whether you are working with a dataset you have compiled or commonly available criminal justice datasets, your data will likely be a sample of some population. R makes it simple to describe your sample using the various measures of central tendency. The three common measures of central tendency reviewed in this chapter are the mean, the median, and the mode. We will demonstrate how to compute these statistics using the 2016 Body-Worn Camera Survey from the Law Enforcement Management and Administrative Statistics Survey.

Data

Dataset Source: Law Enforcement Management and Administrative Statistics (LEMAS)-Body-Worn Camera Supplement (BWCS) Survey

File Name: 37302-0001-Data.Rda

Dataset Description: The core LEMAS Survey has been administered by the Bureau of Justice Statistics (BJS) every 3 to 4 years since 1987 to a representative sample of law enforcement agencies in the United States. The survey collects key administrative data on agencies, including information on staffing, budget, and operational capacity. The BWCS is a supplemental survey administered in 2016 focusing on the adoption, planned adoption, and use of body-worn cameras. Data on approximately 4,000 law enforcement agencies are included in the dataset.

Getting Started

1. Open up your existing **R** project as outlined in Chap. 2 (see also Appendix 1.3).

2. Install and load the required packages using the `install.packages()` and `library()` functions (see Appendix 1.1).

3. Open the 2016 LEMAS-BWCS dataset (*37302-0001-Data.Rda*). We obtained these data from the Inter-university Consortium for Political and Social Research (ICPSR) website so the dataset name refers to the ICPSR study number. Our data are stored in an **R** data file format (.rda). We just need to use the `load()` function to import the data frame into our environment (see Appendix 1.6.1.), specifying the working directory using `here()` as we have previously (see Appendix 1.3). When you do this, name the data frame **bwcs** by using the `<-` assignment operator.

4. Use the function `View(bwcs)` to make sure the file is loaded successfully and to get a feel for the data structure. You can also use the function `dim(bwcs)` to see the number of observations and variables.

Calculating Mean, Median, and Mode

Measures of central tendency describe what is average or typical in a distribution of data (the center/middle of data values). Mean, median, and mode are all measures of central tendency. The **mean** is commonly referred to as the average. Mean values are incredibly useful when we want to quickly summarize some variable in the population. However, one thing to keep in mind is that the mean is sensitive to **outliers**. This means that extreme values above and below the average can actually inflate the average or pull the average down, giving us a biased measure of central tendency.

Because of potential outliers, we might also want to look at the **median** value of our variable. The median is the middlemost value in the distribution and is unaffected by extreme values. Therefore, it can provide a less biased estimate of central tendency.

We often want to examine both the mean and the median values that we will use in our analysis. Finally, we need a way of determining the typical case of a nominal- or ordinal-level variable. This is called the **mode** and simply tells us the most frequently occurring case of a variable.

We are interested in exploring the adoption of body-worn cameras (BWCs) and their usage in this sample of agencies. Now, to start, it may be helpful to know how many agencies reported adopting BWCs as of 2016:

```
# Check the class of the variable asking
## whether the agency has adopted BWCs
class(bwcs$Q_10A)  # we see this is a factor variable

## [1] "factor"

# Print a tibble to your console that gives
## the frequency of each response
bwcs %>%
  group_by(Q_10A) %>%
  summarize(n())

## # A tibble: 2 x 2
##    `bwcs$Q_10A`                                      `n()`
##    <fct>                                             <int>
## 1 (1) Agency has acquired in any form acquired
          in any form (including testing)             1915
## 2 (2) Agency has not acquired                      2013
```

(Note that a **tibble** is a more modern version of base R's data frame).

According to our frequency table, most agencies had *not* acquired BWCs at the time of the survey. We can get the same information by asking for the **mode** of variable Q_10A.

```
# Save the mode of Q10_A into the object "mode_adopted"
mode_adopted <- mlv(bwcs$Q_10A)
mode_adopted
## [1] (2) Agency has not acquired
## 2 Levels: (1) Agency has acquired in any
   form (including testing) ...
```

We used the `mlv()` function (referring to the most likely values) from the **modeest** package to obtain the mode of variable Q10_A. Unsurprisingly, the modal response of all agencies was *No*, indicating that they had not adopted BWCs as of the 2016 survey.

Now, we want to know more about the camera adoption among agencies who *did* report having acquired BWCs in 2016. We will examine the variable Q_12 to determine the average number of cameras agencies reported having in service. We can use the `summarize()` function in the **dplyr** package to accomplish this, in addition to using the `mean()` function provided in base R. First, let's examine this variable using the `min()`, `max()`, and `table()` functions.

```
# Reports the minimum value
min(bwcs$Q_12, na.rm=TRUE)

## [1] 0

# Reports the maximum value
max(bwcs$Q_12, na.rm=TRUE)

## [1] 1200

# table() provides a count for each unique value of a
## variable.
# Since we see all values with the table() function,
## we do not need the na.rm=TRUE code
table(bwcs$Q_12)

##
##    0    1    2    3    4    5    6    7    8    9   10   11   12   13   14   15
##   97  191  137  112  127  107  102   46   89   49   72   19   62   27   21   62
##   16   17   18   19   20   21   22   23   24   25   26   27   28   29   30   31
##   16   22   26    7   48    8   18    6   12   20    9    6    9    4   18    3
##   32   33   34   35   36   37   38   39   40   42   43   44   45   46   47   48
##    8    1    1    9    8    5    2    3   14    4    4    1    3    1    3    7
##   49   50   52   53   54   55   56   57   58   59   60   61   65   66   68   70
##    2   25    4    2    4    3    3    3    4    1   15    1    7    2    1    5
##   71   72   75   76   78   80   82   85   86   87   88   89   90   91   92   93
##    1    2    3    1    1   11    1    7    2    1    2    2    8    1    1    1
##   95   99  100  101  105  106  107  110  111  112  114  115  116  117  119  120
##    1    1   19    1    1    1    1    4    1    2    2    3    1    1    1    4
##  122  123  125  127  130  133  134  135  137  140  145  150  160  163  165  168
##    1    1    2    1    3    1    1    2    1    3    1    7    3    1    1    1
##  175  188  190  200  210  220  224  225  230  236  239  240  245  250  260  270
##    3    1    2    6    1    2    1    2    2    1    1    1    1    4    1    2
##  274  292  298  300  312  325  330  347  350  351  355  360  400  402  429  430
##    1    1    1    5    1    1    1    1    1    1    1    2    2    1    1    1
##  450  500  544  600  630  661  815  825  900 1079 1100 1200
##    2    2    1    1    1    1    1    2    1    1    1    3
```

You will need to tell R that you have missing (NA) cases when calculating measures of central tendency. When we use certain functions to calculate measures of central tendency, we can use the option na.rm=TRUE so R excludes cases that have already been defined as missing. If, for instance, we don't include this code when using the mean() function, it will return *NaN* for those agencies who have acquired BWCs because the Q_12 variable has missing data. And don't think you did something wrong if you see *NaN* for the row defining agencies that have not acquired BWCs. They will be *NaN* because there are no cases.

```
# We only want to include agencies who reponded
## "Yes" to Q_10A

# dplyr method
bwcs %>%
  group_by(Q_10A) %>%
  summarize(mean_deployed = mean(Q_12, na.rm = TRUE))

## # A tibble: 2 x 2
##   Q_10A                                    mean_deployed
##   <fct>                                    <dbl>
## 1 (1) Agency has acquired in any
##         form (including testing)           31.8
## 2 (2) Agency has not acquired              NaN

# Base R method
mean(bwcs$Q_12, na.rm = TRUE)

## [1] 31.82024
```

You should get the same answer using both methods. And we do!

Since this survey contains state, local, and county agencies of varying sizes, there may be a lot of variation in how many BWCs are being deployed. Because the mean is not robust to outliers, it will be useful to examine the median of the same variable.

```
# Use the same format as above, this time using
## the median() function

# dplyr method
bwcs %>%
  group_by(Q_10A) %>%
  summarize(med_deployed = median(Q_12, na.rm = TRUE))

## # A tibble: 2 x 2
##   Q_10A                                    med_deployed
##   <fct>                                    <dbl>
## 1 (1) Agency has acquired in any
##       form (including testing)             8
## 2 (2) Agency has not acquired              NA

# Base R method
median(bwcs$Q_12, na.rm = TRUE)

## [1] 8
```

The mean and median differ quite a bit! Now that we know how to calculate measures of central tendency for a given variable, we can condense our code to obtain all of our measures of central tendency in one code chunk:

```
# tibble containing the mean, median, mode, total number of
## BWCs deployed
bwcs %>%
  group_by(Q_10A) %>%
  summarize(mean_deployed = mean(Q_12, na.rm = TRUE),
            med_deployed = median(Q_12, na.rm = TRUE),
            mode_deployed = mlv(Q_12, method='mfv',
                                         na.rm = TRUE),
            total = sum(Q_12, na.rm = TRUE))
## # A tibble: 2 x 5
##    Q_10A               mean_deployed med_deployed mode_deployed total
##    <fct>                       <dbl>        <dbl>         <dbl> <dbl>
## 1 (1) Agency has
       acquired in any~          31.8            8             1 60363
## 2 (2) Agency has
       not acquired               NaN           NA           NaN     0
```

You may need to adjust the size of your console window to view tibble tables correctly. Another handy function that provides summary statistics according to the class of your variables is the **skim()** function from the **skimr** package. It also works with the pipe operator. For numeric classes, **skim()** produces measures of central tendency that we are covering here (like the mean and median), as well as measures of dispersion (see Chap. 5) and other useful information like the number of missing values. A really cool feature is that the output includes a miniature histogram of the numeric variables you specify. If you do not want to specify a particular variable, **skim()** will simply summarize your entire data frame, which may be helpful depending on the size of your dataset!

```
# Produce a summary of your Q_12 variable, grouped by Q_10
## using skim()
bwcs %>%
  group_by(Q_10A) %>%
  skim(Q_12)
```

Data summary

NAME	PIPED DATA
Number of rows	3928
Number of columns	260

Column type frequency: numeric	1

Group variables	Q_10A

Variable type: numeric

SKIM_ VARIABLE	Q_10A	N_ MISSING	COMPLETE_ RATE	MEAN	SD	P0	P25	P50	P75	P100	HIST
Q_12	(1) Agency has acquired in any form (including testing)	18	0.99	31.82	92.27	0	3	8	20	1200	█ _ _ _
Q_12	(2) Agency has not acquired	2013	0.00	NaN	NaN	NA	NA	NA	NA	NA	

Identifying Outliers

As you might guess from the last table we produced, there are perhaps some agencies who are skewing the average number of BWCs deployed. We can check for outliers in our data using R; however, you must decide how you are going to define outliers in your analysis.

We might assume that outliers are observations that lie above or below `1.5 * the Interquartile Range (IQR)` or, for more extreme outliers, beyond `3 * IQR`. The IQR is simply the 75th percentile observation minus the 25th percentile observation in your distribution. These thresholds are known as Tukey fences. Let's find and save the outliers for the Q_12 variable using this method.

```r
# First, let's get the IQR of the Q_12 variable using
## the IQR function
bwc_deployed_iqr <- IQR(bwcs$Q_12, na.rm = TRUE)
bwc_deployed_iqr
```

```
## [1] 17
```

```r
# Then, get the 1st and 3rd quartiles of the Q_12
## variable using quantile()
bwc_deployed_1st <- quantile(bwcs$Q_12, 0.25, na.rm = TRUE)
bwc_deployed_1st
```

```
## 25%
##   3
```

```r
bwc_deployed_3rd <- quantile(bwcs$Q_12, 0.75, na.rm = TRUE)
bwc_deployed_3rd
```

```
## 75%
##  20
```

```r
# Next, calculate the fences
# Lower Fence
lower_inner_fence <- bwc_deployed_1st - 1.5 * bwc_deployed_iqr
lower_inner_fence
```

```
##    25%
## -22.5
```

```r
# Upper Fence
upper_inner_fence <- bwc_deployed_3rd + 1.5 * bwc_deployed_iqr
upper_inner_fence
```

```
##  75%
## 45.5
```

```r
# You can also calculate the "outer fences"
lower_outer_fence <- bwc_deployed_1st - 3 * bwc_deployed_iqr
lower_outer_fence
```

```
## 25%
## -48
```

```r
upper_outer_fence <- bwc_deployed_3rd + 3 * bwc_deployed_iqr
upper_outer_fence
```

```
## 75%
##  71
```

```r
# And save them in a separate object
outliers <- bwcs %>%
  filter(Q_12 > upper_inner_fence| Q_12 < lower_inner_fence)
summary(outliers$Q_12)
```

```
##    Min. 1st Qu.  Median    Mean 3rd Qu.    Max.
##    46.0    60.0   100.0   162.1   167.2  1200.0
```

```r
outliers_extreme <- bwcs %>%
  filter(Q_12 > upper_outer_fence| Q_12 < lower_outer_fence)
summary(outliers_extreme$Q_12)
```

```
##    Min. 1st Qu.  Median    Mean 3rd Qu.    Max.
##    72.0   100.0   130.0   215.4   241.2  1200.0
```

Outliers can also be identified and visualized in R for the <u>Q 12</u> variable using the `boxplot()` function or using the `geom_boxplot()` layer of `ggplot` as we covered in Chap. 3. Note that we introduce the `theme()` function here simply to adjust the position of the plot title. This is discussed in more details in Sect. 4.2 in the Appendix.

```
# Prints the outliers
OutlierVals <- boxplot(bwcs$Q_12)$out
```

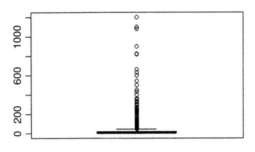

```
bwcs$Q_12[ (bwcs$Q_12 %in% OutlierVals )]
##   [1] 101  544   85  100 312   50   47   90   50   91   50  160 360 100 150
##  [16]  82  300   60  150  60   86   90  450   71   50  112   55 270 116  70
##  [31]  80  402   58   60 225  355   65  200  188 230 120   65 351  50  60
##  [46] 210   48   65  100 175  190 260   52   80   57   55  175  65 300 225
##  [61] 160  115  239   75 200  111 165   54  500 250   68   54 150  85  89
##  [76]  88   70   61  600  80  300   66  125  107 168   46  112 123 400 135
##  [91]  65  110   48 1200  52  190   60  661  220  50   60   89 105 100 350
## [106] 110 1079  140  117 250  300 140   90  114 325 127  430 100  80 230
## [121]  60  140   80   80  66   48   50  100  130  57   90  100 145  85 150
## [136] 130  245  330   50 450   70 120   60  220  48 100  133  50 150 100
## [151] 160   56   85   50  90  292 360   50   59 134  92   50 100  99 200
## [166]  85   76   80  236 250   90  50   60  200 150  50   56  80 119  50
## [181]  48   50   47  150  80   90 429   80  900  60  47   52  86 100  50
## [196]  60  100  825   88 815  110  95  100  137 106  75   50  49 240  50
## [211]  85   80  120   57 825  110  72  135   48 115  65  630  93  50  58
## [226]  60   54   60  100  58   75  90 1100   50  53  78  100  50 298 130
## [241]  48   60  120 1200  56   58 300 500   60 200 115   65 224  55 100
## [256] 347   49  100   70  70   85 400 163   72 125  87   54 100 122 274
## [271] 200   50   53  250  50  100 270 114   50  52 175 1200
```

```
# Visualize outliers
ggplot(data = bwcs, mapping = aes(x = " ", y = Q_12)) +
  geom_boxplot(outlier.color = "red", outlier.shape = 2,
               coef = 3) +

  labs(x = " ", y = "Number of BWCs",
       title = "Boxplot of # BWCs Deployed
                (Outliers in Red)") +
       theme(plot.title = element_text(hjust = 0.5))

## Warning: Removed 2031 rows containing
##          non-finite values (stat_boxplot).
```

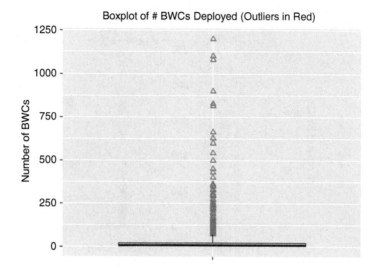

Boxplot of # BWCs Deployed (Outliers in Red)

You may get few warnings from the above functions. If you get the error, `Error in plot.new() : figure margins too large`, then execute this function, `par(mar=c(1,1,1,1))`, to adjust the margins, and rerun the code in the above step.

There may also be a warning that **ggplot** removed 2031 rows when creating the box plot. This is because the agencies who did not adopt BWCs are missing (NA) on the Q 12 variable. The outliers in the box plot are denoted in red. We specified that we wanted outliers to be determined by `3 * IQR` in the **coef** option.

It may also be informative to evaluate the outliers for different types of agencies (i.e., Sheriff's Offices, State Police, Local Police), as well as agencies of different sizes. To view it easier, we are going to use the **facet_wrap()** function to create multiple box plots (see Chap. 3). We can accomplish this through the use of grouped box plots.

```
# By Agency Type
ggplot(data = bwcs, mapping = aes(x = SAMPTYPE, y = Q_12)) +
  geom_boxplot(outlier.color = "red", outlier.shape = 2,
               coef = 3) +
  labs(x = "Agency Type", y = "Number of BWCs" ) +
  ggtitle(expression(atop("Boxplot of # BWCs Deployed
                     (Outliers in Red)"))) +
  theme(plot.title = element_text(hjust = 0.5)) +
  facet_wrap( ~ SAMPTYPE, scales="free")
## Warning: Removed 2031 rows containing
         non-finite values (stat_boxplot).
```

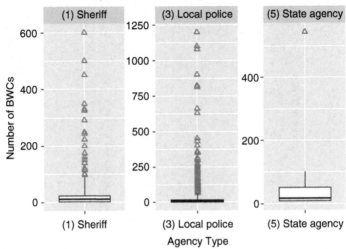

```
# By Agency Size
# First, collapse number of Full-time sworn officers
## into categories
bwcs <- bwcs %>%
  mutate(agcysize=case_when(
    Q_8 %in% 0:10 ~ "0-10 FTS",
    Q_8 %in% 11:50 ~ "11-50 FTS",
    Q_8 %in% 51:100 ~ "51-100 FTS",
    Q_8 %in% 101:500 ~ "101-500 FTS",
    Q_8 %in% 501:1000 ~ "501-1000 FTS",
    Q_8 >= 1001 ~ ">1000 FTS"))

# Boxplot
ggplot(data = bwcs, mapping = aes(x = agcysize, y = Q_12)) +
  geom_boxplot(outlier.color = "red", outlier.shape = 2,
               coef = 3) +
  labs(x = "Agency Size", y = "Number of BWCs" ) +
  ggtitle(expression(atop("Boxplot of # BWCs Deployed
                          (Outliers in Red)"))) +
  theme(plot.title = element_text(hjust = 0.5))
## Warning: Removed 2031 rows containing
            non-finite values (stat_boxplot).
```

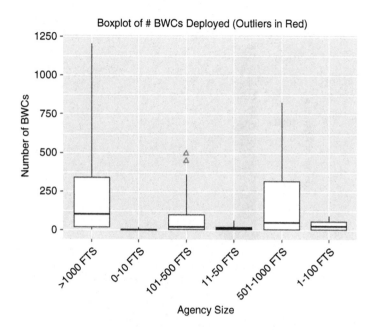

Boxplot of # BWCs Deployed (Outliers in Red)

Skewness

In addition to potential extreme values that may be influencing your estimates, understanding the general shape of your distribution is also important. We can produce a histogram of number of BWCs an agency reported deploying.

```
# Histogram of # BWCs deployed
ggplot(data = bwcs, mapping = aes(x = Q_12)) +
  geom_histogram(bins = 15, fill = "red") +
  labs(x = "Number of BWCs Deployed",
       y = "Number of Agencies") +
  ggtitle("Histogram of Number of BWCs Deployed") +
  theme(plot.title = element_text(hjust = 0.5))

## Warning: Removed 2031 rows containing
##          non-finite values (stat_bin).
```

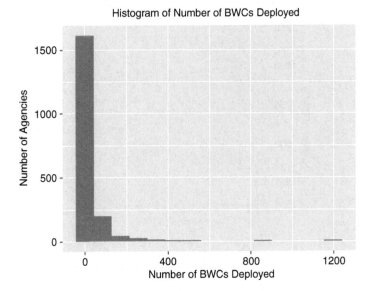

We can tell right away from this graph that most agencies deployed fewer than approximately 250 BWCs and only a handful deployed more than 800. This asymmetric distribution is referred to as a *positively skewed* distribution. That is, one tail of the distribution is longer than the other due to **outliers**. There are many cases in criminal justice in which we might expect some variable to be non-normally distributed like this.

There are several ways of detecting skewness in your sample using R. For this example, we are going to use the **skewness()** function from the **moments** package to examine the distribution of the Q_12 variable in our sample. Skewness of 0 refers to a symmetrical distribution. If the skewness is a positive value, this means our data are positively skewed or skewed right. Alternatively, if the skewness is a negative value, this indicates a negative skew in our data or left skew. From the histogram above, do you think the skewness coefficient will indicate there is negative skewness, positive skewness, or no skewness?

```
bwc_skew <- skewness(bwcs$Q_12, na.rm = TRUE)
bwc_skew

## [1] 7.640767
```

When we print the object **bwc_skew**, we see that our skewness coefficient is indeed positive!

Application Activities

Problem 1:

In the LEMAS-BWCS dataset, examine the variable Q 15 NUMBER (variable indicating the anticipated number of body-worn cameras that will be deployed) using the functions `min()`, `max()`, and `table()`. Find the measures of central tendency using the `mean()` and `median()`. Next, group your data by agency type (SAMPTYPE variable) using the `group_by()` function/**dplyr** method, and find those two measures of central tendency again.

Problem 2:

Examine the agency size variable (Q 8) measured as the number of full-time sworn officers (FTS) using the functions `min()`, `max()`, and `table()`. Then, use the `mean()` function to determine the average size of law enforcement agencies in the United States reporting in this LEMAS Survey. Are there any outliers? Show this visually with a graph, and then print the outliers by relying on the **boxplot()** and **ggplot()** functions, as well as **$out** and **%in%**.

Problem 3:

Choose any variable measured at the ratio level from the data frame. Test for skewness using **skewness()** function. Make sure to specify **na. rm=TRUE**. Then add a comment in your code that specifies whether the distribution is positively skewed or negatively skewed.

Key Terms

Mean A measure of central tendency calculated by dividing the sum of the scores by the number of cases.

Measures of central tendency Descriptive statistics that allow us to identify the typical case in a sample or population. Measures of central tendency are measures of typicality.

Median A measure of central tendency calculated by identifying the value or category of the score that occupies the middle position in the distribution of scores.

Mode A measure of central tendency calculated by identifying the score or category that occurs most frequently.

Outliers A single or small number of exceptional cases that substantially deviate from the general pattern of scores.

Tibble Modern version of base R's data frame (simpler and more user-friendly) that is from the **tidyverse** package.

Functions Introduced in this Chapter

FUNCTION	DESCRIPTION (PACKAGE)
`boxplot()`	Produce a box-and-whiskers plot (base **R**)
`element_text()`	Refer to a text element in thematic options (see Appendix 4.2) (**ggplot2**)
`group_by()`	Group observations by variable(s) for performing operations (**dplyr**)
`IQR()`	Compute interquartile range (base **R**)
`max()`	Returns the maximum value (base **R**)
`mean()`	Compute arithmetic mean (base **R**)
`median()`	Compute the median (base **R**)
`min()`	Returns the minimum value (base **R**)
`mlv()`	Compute the mode (**modeest**)
`par()`	Set graphics parameters such as margins (base **R**)
`quantile()`	Compute quantiles as per specified probabilities (base **R**)
`skewness()`	Calculate degree of skewness in a numeric vector (**modeest**)
`skim()`	Provide summary statistics specific to object class (**skimr**)
`sum()`	Sum values in a vector (base **R**)
`summarize()`	Create new summary variable(s), e.g., counts, mean (**dplyr**)
`summary()`	Produce summary of model results (base **R**)
`table()`	Generates a frequency table (base **R**)

Reference

United States Department of Justice. Office of Justice Programs. Bureau of Justice Statistics. (2016). Law enforcement management and administrative statistics body-worn camera supplement (LEMAS-BWCS) [Data file]. Ann Arbor, MI: Inter-university Consortium for Political and Social Research [distributor], 2019-06-20. Retrieved from https://doi.org/10.3886/ICPSR37302.v1.

Chapter five

Measures of Dispersion

Topics Practiced

Measures of dispersion

Technical Skills Covered

Calculating range, variance, standard deviation

Calculating variation ratio, index of qualitative variation

Calculating coefficient of relative variation

R Packages Required

dplyr, here, modeest, qualvar, skimr

In the last chapter, we covered how to use **R** functions to calculate various measures of central tendency. But while it is certainly useful to know the mean of a given variable you are examining, it is even more helpful if you also know the spread, or *dispersion*, of cases around this mean. For this chapter, we will focus on measures of dispersion for both nominal-/ordinal-level variables (*variation ratio* and *index of qualitative variation*) and ratio-/interval-level variables (*range, variance, standard deviation*, and *coefficient of relative variation*). We will use data from the 2004 Survey of Inmates in State and Federal Correctional Facilities, a nationally representative sample of US prison inmates to demonstrate some of these concepts.

Data

Dataset Source: 2004 Survey of Inmates in State and Federal Correctional Facilities (SISFCF)

File Name: 04572-0001-Data.Rda

Dataset Description: The SISFCF survey has been conducted periodically since 1976. It is a nationally representative survey of inmates held in state and federal correctional facilities in the United States. From the ICPSR website, the survey contains information on their current offense and sentence, criminal history, family background and personal characteristics, prior drug and alcohol treatment programs, gun possession and use, and prison activities, programs, and services. We will be working with the data file that contains information garnered from federal institutions. Similar to the body-worn camera survey in Chap. 4, the current survey can be accessed at the ICPSR website and downloaded as an .Rda file.

Getting Started

1. Open up your existing R project as outlined in Chap. 2 (see also Appendix 1.3).

2. Install and load the required packages using the `install.packages()` and `library()` functions (see Appendix 1.1).

3. Open the SISFCF survey dataset (*04572-0001-Data.Rda*) using the `load()` function to import the dataset (see Appendix 1.6.1), specifying the working directory with `here()` (see Appendix 1.3). Note that the dataset will load into R with the name `da04572.0001`.

4. Change the name of the dataset from `da04572.0001` to `inmatesurvey04` by using the `<-` assignment operator. This will create an identical object under the new name.

5. Since we only are dealing with one dataset for this exercise, use the function `attach(inmatesurvey04)` (see Appendix 1.8). Just remember to use `detach("inmatesurvey04")` once you are done with the exercises in this chapter.

Dispersion Measures for Nominal- and Ordinal-Level Variables

Variation Ratio

Understanding variation is at the heart of all data analysis questions. Even if you are working with nominal data, it can be useful to describe the variation of your categorical variables. One way of assessing this is to calculate the **variation ratio (VR)**, which tells us the proportion of cases that are *not* in the modal category. It can be computed on nominal- or ordinal-level variables. The `qualvar` package, which is a package for indices of qualitative variation, does not contain a function for the variation ratio, so let's calculate this ourselves.

First, take note of the formula for the VR in Eq. 5.1:

Variation Ratio Formula

$$VR = 1 - \frac{N_{\text{modalcat}}}{N_{\text{total}}} \qquad \textbf{Equation 5.1}$$

Here, N_{modalcat} refers to the frequency of cases in the modal category, and N_{total} refers to the total number of cases. This formula tells us that the VR is equal to 1 minus the proportion of cases that are in the modal category $\frac{N_{\text{modalcat}}}{N_{\text{total}}}$, which is the same as saying the proportion of cases that are *not* in the modal category.

To illustrate how to calculate the variation ratio, let's suppose that we want to know about federal inmates' work histories prior to their arrests. Specifically, we would like to know if inmates mostly reported working full-time, part-time, or occasionally in the month prior to their arrest. Then, we want to know how dispersed these data are, that is, if the modal category describes the sample very well or if there is a lot of differentiation in responses from inmates. We show how to calculate the variation ratio for this variable, V1748, below. We draw on the `mlv()` function (most likely value) to identify the mode. Before we do this, we are going to first examine the V1748 variable with the `table()` and `skim()` functions. Then, we are going to use the `is.na()` function within the `table()` function to get a summary of any missing cases. Since we have missing (NA) cases, we are going to use the `na.rm=TRUE` option within the `mlv()` function.

```
# Let us first take a look at our variable of
## interest: V1748
table(V1748)

## V1748
##  (1) Full-time (2) Part-time (3) Occasional (7) Don't know (8) Refused
##          2180           284            65            0             1

# Or use skim()
skim(inmatesurvey04$V1748)
```

Data summary

NAME	INMATESURVEY04$V1748
Number of rows	3686
Number of columns	1
Column type frequency:	
factor	1
Group variables	None

Variable type: factor

SKIM_VARIABLE	N_MISSING	COMPLETE_RATE	ORDERED	N_UNIQUE	TOP_COUNTS
data	1156	0.69	FALSE	4	(1): 2180, (2): 284, (3): 65, (8): 1

```
# Check if we have cases defined as missing
table(is.na(inmatesurvey04$V1748))

##
## FALSE   TRUE
##  2530   1156

# While we can tell from the tables above that
## "Full-time" is the mode
# We can also get R to provide the mode and save
## it in an object
mode_employment <- mlv(V1748, na.rm = TRUE)
mode_employment

## [1] (1) Full-time
## 5 Levels: (1) Full-time (2) Part-time (3) Occasional ... (8) Refused
```

We can see here that most federal inmates responding to this question reported working full-time hours prior to their arrest. Now, we will calculate the variation ratio using the formula described above. But first, you'll want to recode the responses of *Don't Know* and *Refused* as missing because if you don't, R will think that they are valid cases. To do this, we are going to create a new variable so we don't write over the original one and then tell R that the given variables should be considered missing (**NA**).

Note that even though the **attach()** function is on, we need to first specify our new variable's name along with the name of the dataset. Otherwise, R will turn it into an object rather than a new variable in our dataset.

Now, we can get the number of cases in the modal category, as well as the total number of cases.

```
# Store this value in the object n_mode
n_mode <- inmatesurvey04 %>%
  filter(employment == "(1) Full-time" ) %>%
  summarize(n = n())

# Get the number of cases  who reported being
## employed prior to arrest
# Store this value in the object n_employed
n_employed <- inmatesurvey04 %>%
  filter(!is.na(employment)) %>%
  summarize(n = n())

# Calculate the proportion
# Store this value in the object proportion_mode
proportion_mode <- n_mode/n_employed


# Get the V ratio
# Subtract proportion of cases in the modal category from 1

vratio <- 1 - proportion_mode

vratio

##              n
## 1 0.1383399
```

The smaller the variation ratio, the larger the number of cases falling in the modal category. So, it appears that with a variation ratio of 0.1383399, the employment status among federal inmates prior to their arrest is relatively concentrated in the modal category.

Index of Qualitative Variation

In addition to the variation ratio, you may also gauge dispersion by calculating the **index of qualitative variation (IQV)** for variables that are nominally or ordinally distributed. This is a measure that lies between *0* and *1*, and it gives an indication of the variability of the distribution. It is similar to the variation ratio, but it also incorporates variation across all categories (not just modal versus non-modal). To do this, we are going to use the DM( ) function in the `qualvar` package (which requires us to store the frequencies of the categorical variable in a vector).

```
# Get the index of qualitative variation for
## the same variable: V1748

IQV <- as.vector(table(inmatesurvey04$V1748))
DM(IQV, na.rm = TRUE)

## [1] 0.1729249
```

Dispersion Measures for Ratio- and Interval-Level Variables

Calculating measures of dispersion with ratio- or interval-level data may be more familiar to most readers. These measures give us an indication of the *spread* of cases around a mean. Common measures of dispersion that you may want to calculate when analyzing your variables include the range, variance, standard deviation, and coefficient of relative variation.

Range

R provides numerous functions that allow one to calculate the **range** of a given variable. The range is simply the difference between the maximum and the minimum value in a given distribution. Let us explore a variable from our SISFCS data that is measured at the ratio level. We can see that there is a variable that represents the age at which the inmates reported that they first started smoking cigarettes regularly, V2254.

```
# Examine the variable
str(V2254)

##  num [1:3686] NA NA 19 NA 16 15 18 NA NA NA ...
##  - attr(*, "value.labels")= Named num [1:3] 98 97 0
##  ..- attr(*, "names")= chr [1:3] "Refused" "Don't know"
"Never smoked regularly"

attributes(V2254)

## $value.labels
##                Refused  Don't know Never smoked regularly
##                     98          97                      0

# This variable has codes that do not indicate the number
## of times smoked.

# These are 0 - never smoked; 97 - Don't know; and
## 98 - Refused

table(V2254)
## V2254
##  0  1  2  5  6  7  8  9 10 11  12  13  14  15  16  17  18  19 20 21
## 17  1  1  1  7 18 19 35 55 69 177 203 184 246 250 143 182 102 77 60
## 22 23 24 25 26 27 28 29 30 31  32  33  34  35  36  37  38  39 40 42
## 53 31 26 41 22 19 18  6 13  5  13   8   5  11   6   3   5   2  6  1
## 44 45 47 50 53 55 57 97 98
##  1  1  1  1  2  1  1 21  4
```

We want to ask R for the minimum and maximum (i.e., the range) values, but we know from how it is coded that it will not produce an accurate summary of the age range. That is, the values for *0, 97,* and *98* are not ages, but rather codes that represent inmates who reported *never* smoking regularly (coded as *0*), who responded *Don't know* (coded as *97*), or who refused to answer the question (coded as *98*). See what happens when we run the base **R** summary() function on this variable or the skim() function from the skimr package.

```
summary(V2254) # Note the minimum and maximum values

##    Min. 1st Qu.  Median    Mean 3rd Qu.    Max.   NA's
##    0.00   13.00   16.00   17.57   19.00   98.00   1512

skim(V2254)
```

Data summary

NAME	V2254
Number of rows	3686
Number of columns	1
Column type frequency:	
numeric	1
Group variables	None

Variable type: numeric

SKIM_VARIABLE	N_MISSING	COMPLETE_RATE	MEAN	SD	P0	P25	P50	P75	P100	HIST
data	1512	0.59	17.57	10.41	0	13	16	19	98	---

One way to solve this problem is to tell **R** that the values *0*, *97*, and *98* indicate missing data:

```
# Create a new variable so we don't write over the old one
AgeSmokerRange <- V2254

# Code 0, 97, and 98 values as missing
AgeSmokerRange[AgeSmokerRange==0] <- NA
AgeSmokerRange[AgeSmokerRange==97] <- NA
AgeSmokerRange[AgeSmokerRange==98] <- NA
```

You can now use the range() function in base **R** to calculate the range. However, you will notice that the function actually provides the minimum and maximum values of the variable. We are then going to use the diff() function to calculate the actual range.

```
# range() function prints the minimum and maximum values
# Doesn't provide the actual range :-(
range(AgeSmokerRange, na.rm = TRUE)
## [1]  1 57
# Compute the range by assigning the min and max
## values to an object
# Then, calculate the difference of that object
SmokerRange <- range(AgeSmokerRange, na.rm = TRUE)
diff(SmokerRange)
## [1] 56
```

Now, you have computed the range. We see that the range of federal inmates' age they first started smoking is 56, meaning that the difference between the lowest age an inmate reported they first started smoking and the highest age an inmate reported they first started smoking is 56 years. You can see how calculating the range of your distribution can be helpful in the data cleaning process as well, as in practice we might want to exclude responses of 1-year-old in our analyses!

Variance

Variance (s^2) is another measure of dispersion that gives us a sense of how spread out cases are around their mean. To compute the variance of some variable, you can use the **var()** function from the **stats** package that comes preinstalled in **R**. We will demonstrate using the continuous variable, V2529, which records the number of times inmates reported being written up for verbally assaulting a prison staff member.

```
# First, let's take a look at the variable
summary(V2529)

##    Min. 1st Qu. Median  Mean 3rd Qu.    Max.  NA's
##    1.00    1.00   1.00 31.45    3.00  998.00  3545

attributes(V2529)

## $value.labels
##     Refused Don't know
##         998        997

# Create a new variable so we don't write over the old one
# Then, code 997 and 998 values as missing
VerbAssaultVar <- V2529
VerbAssaultVar[VerbAssaultVar>=997] <- NA

# Now let's calculate the variance
var1 <- var(VerbAssaultVar, na.rm = TRUE)
var1

## [1] 82.64384
```

We see that even though most inmates reported only one instance of being written up, the variance for this distribution is fairly sizable. This is because we have one inmate reporting being written up 99 times for verbal assault on a staff member. This is no doubt influencing the mean of the distribution, as well as the measures of dispersion.

Standard Deviation

The **standard deviation (SD)** is a related measure of how cases are dispersed around the mean. It is specifically the square root of the variance. The smaller the standard deviation, the closer cases are to the mean, while larger standard deviations indicate a wider distance. We can calculate the standard deviation of our VerbAssaultVar variable using the sd() function.

```
# Calculate SD of the VerbAssaultVar variable and
## save it to an object
sd <- sd(VerbAssaultVar, na.rm = TRUE)
```

Since the standard deviation of a distribution is simply the square root of the variance, we can actually check this against our measure of variance above by squaring it.

```
# We will call this var2.
var2 <- sd^2

# Now print both objects to see if they match
var1

## [1] 82.64384

var2

## [1] 82.64384
```

And indeed, they are the same!

Coefficient of Variation

While the standard deviation is a good measure of variability and dispersion for one set of values, the **coefficient of variation (CV)**, or the relative standard deviation, is good for comparing multiple sets of values. Much like the name suggests, this coefficient represents the standard deviation of a distribution relative to its mean. It is easily calculated by dividing the standard deviation by the mean. The CV is often presented as a percentage. Let's use the same VerbAssaultVar variable to calculate the CV.

```
# First, let's get the mean
mean <- mean(VerbAssaultVar, na.rm = TRUE)

# Then, divide the SD we have already calculated by the mean
CV <- sd/mean * 100
CV

## [1] 279.8761
```

Application Activities

Problem 1:

Find both the variation ratio and index of qualitative variation for the variable V2549 (recent violations). Use the equation presented in the example to compute the variation ratio and then use the DM() function to compute the IQV, but first you will want to check whether any values need to be coded as missing by examining this variable with table().

Problem 2:

Calculate the range (range() and diff() functions), standard deviation (sd() function), and variance (var() function) for the variable V0663. This question asked inmates who were under pretrial detention how many days they spent in jail prior to being sentenced to prison. Before obtaining these measures of dispersion, check to make sure that there are no values that need to be coded as missing.

Problem 3:

Calculate the coefficient of variation for the variable CH_SERVEDMTH for federal inmates using the **mean()** function, **sd()** function, and equation presented in text. This question asked inmates how many months they had served as of the interview date. Again, make sure to code missing values appropriately if needed.

Problem 4:

Calculate the coefficient of variation for the variable CH_SERVEDMTH for each offense type at the same time (CO_CURRENTOFFENSE_COL). Hint: refer to *Summarize a Data Frame by Groups* in Appendix 2.10, which relies on the **summarize()** and **group_by()** functions.

Problem 5:

And just one last reminder, once you are finished with this chapter, remember to use **detach("inmatesurvey04")** to tell **R** you are no longer only using the SISFCF dataset.

Key Terms

Coefficient of variation (CV) A measure of dispersion calculated by dividing the standard deviation by the mean.

Index of qualitative variation (IQV) A measure of dispersion calculated by dividing the sum of the possible pairs of observed scores by the sum of the possible pairs of expected scores (when cases are equally distributed across categories).

Range A measure of dispersion calculated by subtracting the smallest score from the largest score. The range may also be calcu-

lated from specific points in a distribution, such as the 5th and 95th percentile scores.

Standard deviation (SD) A measure of dispersion calculated by taking the square root of the variance.

Variance (s^2) A measure of dispersion calculated by adding together the squared deviation of each score from the mean and then dividing the sum by the number of cases.

Variation ratio (VR) A measure of dispersion calculated by subtracting the proportion of cases in the modal category from 1.

Functions Introduced in this Chapter

FUNCTION	DESCRIPTION (PACKAGE)
as.vector()	Coerce an object into a vector (base **R**)
attach()	Commonly used to attach a data frame object for easier access (base **R**)
attributes()	Access object attributes, such as value labels (base **R**)
diff()	Computes differences between values in a numeric vector (base **R**)
DM()	Computes deviation from the mode (**qualvar**)
is.na()	Returns **TRUE** when values are missing, **FALSE** if not (base **R**)
sd()	Computes standard deviation of a numeric vector (base **R**)
str()	Returns internal structure of an **R** object (base **R**)
var()	Computes variance (base **R**)

Chapter six

Inferential Statistics

Topics Practiced

Populations and sampling

Central limit theorem

Confidence intervals and standard error

Technical Skills Covered

Creating synthetic data

Random sampling

Computing confidence intervals

R Packages Required

dplyr, ggplot2, mosaic

$I_{\text{N MANY TOPICS}}$ within criminology and criminal justice research, we want to draw conclusions from our data that are generalizable to wider populations. These make our findings relevant to the real world, and not specific to any one study or any one dataset. This is where inferential statistics are particularly useful. There are a number of key concepts underlying inferential statistics that we can demonstrate visually within R. This chapter will review sampling from a population, standard error/confidence intervals, and how to generate data based on a distribution in R. In doing so, you will generate a synthetic dataset of intelligence quotient (IQ) scores for each of the approximately 3.6 million probationers in the United States.

Data

Dataset Source: Synthetic data created in R

File Name: Not applicable

Dataset Description: Synthetic data containing information about probationer IQ scores in the United States

Getting Started

1. Open up your existing R project as outlined in Chap. 2.

2. Install and load the required packages using the `install.packages()` and `library()` functions (see Appendix 1.1).

Populations Versus Samples

Let's say we want to know how pervasive robbery has been in the United States during the last 12 months. Given that we know that many people do not report crimes to the police, it would be unwise to rely solely on police-recorded crime data to tell us this information. One alternative might be to survey the entire **population** of the United States, asking them whether they were a victim of robbery in the past year or perhaps how many times they were robbed. While it is likely more accurate than police-recorded crime data, it is logistically and financially unfeasible to conduct such a survey. Instead, we can take a **sample** of the population and produce estimates of the extent to which robbery victimization is common in the population as a whole. This is what surveys like the National Crime Victimization Survey (NCVS) are designed to do. They allow researchers to make estimates about a population based on a sample.

This approach is deployed in countless fields in criminology. The population of interest does not have to be the citizens of a country. It might be prison inmates, as was the case when we used the SISFCF survey in the last chapter. In that case, we were using a sample of inmates in the United States to draw conclusions about the entire prison population. We could do the same for a particular county or city; the population is simply the collection of observations (e.g., victims, offenders, inmates, neighborhoods) for which we want to create generalizable estimates using a sample.

The problem then becomes: How can we ensure that our sample is generalizable to the wider population? To what extent are our sample estimates, like the mean of a variable, representative of the population? This is where we can use **inferential statistics**, an approach which is often more broadly termed *frequentist statistics*.

Synthetic Data

To demonstrate how one can use inferential statistics to create estimates about a population, this chapter will make use of **synthetic data** which represent a fake population. This way, we can clearly demonstrate the concept of using samples to make inferences about a wider population, since data on entire populations (whatever that may be) is rarely available in the real world. So let's start by creating some synthetic data. Doing this requires some reliance on creating "randomly" generated numbers. We have put randomly in inverted commas simply because it is actually impossible to create truly random numbers on a computer. That said, for our purposes, R can do a pretty good job of creating synthetic random data which represent some characteristics of our population. Let's suppose that this population is every probationer in the United States, of which there are approximately 3.6 million across the entire country and that we have the intelligence quotient (IQ) score of each probationer. For the purposes of creating this synthetic data, let's assume that the IQ scores of probationers reflect that of IQ scores more generally, for which the mean is a score of 100 and the standard deviation is around 15 (see Chap. 5). We can create this **population distribution** using the `rnorm()` function, specifying the mean and standard deviation, respectively, assigning these numbers to a vector object.

```
prob_iq <- rnorm(n = 3600000, mean = 100, sd = 15)
```

We can plot this distribution using the visualization skills we learned from the **ggplot2** package in Chap. 3. Here, we don't even need to specify the data object, because all our numbers are stored in a single vector, unlike a data frame which contains multiple vectors (columns) of information. Thus, we can leave the **ggplot()** function empty. Notice that we add a line manually which represents the mean of the population IQ.

```
ggplot() +
    geom_histogram(mapping = aes(x = prob_iq), bins = 60) +
    geom_vline(mapping = aes(xintercept = mean(prob_iq)),
        col = "red", linetype = "dashed")
```

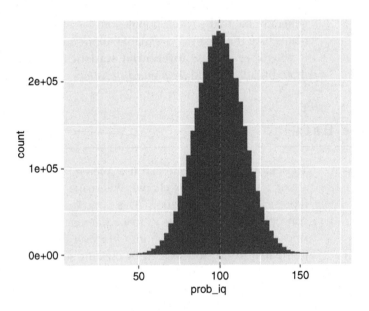

We can see that IQ scores are normally distributed (sometimes called a **Gaussian distribution** or **bell curve**). The vast majority of probationers have an IQ around the mean of 100, with no skewness on either side (see Chap. 4). We can check descriptive statistics more specifically using skills we learned in Chap. 4 too.

```
mean(prob_iq)      # 100.01
## [1] 100.0147

median(prob_iq)    # 100.01
## [1] 100.0115

sd(prob_iq)        # 14.9
## [1] 14.999
```

You will notice that your figures are different from those in the comments above. This goes back to how computers create random numbers. To ensure that we all get the same results, we can set a seed from which the numbers are generated. Once we do this, subsequent random numbers, and thus things like the mean and median, will match those in these examples and, in any subsequent reruns, on the assumption we have used the same seed number. Let's do this now, and then create a data frame with an ID column for each probationer, and rerun the creation of the normal distribution representing the IQ scores. Note that we wrap the `rnorm()` function with `round()`, which we've specified to round each IQ score to a whole number (zero decimal places), since IQ scores are integers. We use `set.seed()` so R *should* generate the exact same distribution for your R session. It also allows you to replicate the distribution again. Don't worry if your results slightly differ from those presented in this chapter because the `set.seed()` will not generate consistent results across R versions.

```
set.seed(1612) # Use this number!

prob_off <- data.frame(
  probationer_id = 1:3600000,
  IQ = round(rnorm(3600000, mean = 100, sd = 15), 0)
  )

mean(prob_off$IQ)    # 100.0028
median(prob_off$IQ)  # 100
sd(prob_off$IQ)      # 14.99976
```

With the seed set, the descriptive statistics above should match what you get in your own R session. The data frame object **prob_off** is now our synthetic population data, containing an identification number for each probationer in the country, and their associated IQ score. For that reason, the *true* mean probationer IQ is 100.0028, *true* median is exactly 100, and the *true* standard deviation is 14.99976. That said, in the real world, we'd rarely ever have access to the IQ score of a population containing millions of people, so the true score would be unknown. Instead, we can sample from that population to calculate an estimate of this unknown value. But how accurate would an estimate of these statistics be from samples of the population? We can demonstrate this now using the synthetic data.

Sampling and Sampling Variability

First off, let's take a single random sample from our synthetic probationer population data using the **sample()** function from the **mosaic** package. All we need to do is specify the data frame (our population) and the number of observations (i.e., probationers) we want to randomly draw from the population. We can assign this to a new data frame object.

```
sample1 <- sample(x = prob_off, size = 100)
```

You can examine this new object using functions like **head()** and **View()**. You'll notice that we have successfully drawn a random sample of 100 probationers from the population of 3.6 million. How do our descriptive statistics look?

```
mean(sample1$IQ)    # 101.59
median(sample1$IQ)  # 101.5
sd(sample1$IQ)      # 16.27485
```

These figures look pretty close to our *true* population, but if we didn't set the same seed, you will likely be getting different results. This is a realistic problem: each time we draw a random sample from a population, whether it be probationers, prison inmates, or US citizens, things like the mean of a variable (e.g., IQ) are probably going to be different each time. You can see this for yourself by rerunning the **sample()** function above and recalculating the mean, median, and standard deviation figures each time. What you are witnessing is sampling variability, an inevitable outcome when randomly sampling observations from population data.

Sampling Distribution

Sampling variability can be demonstrated on a larger scale by automating the process of resampling. Fortunately, the **mosaic** package makes this quite straightforward using the **do()** function, which loops the sampling of our population data frame **prob_off** as many times as we specify. In this case, a thousand times. The outcome is a data frame containing a thousand samples from our population, each containing 100 probationers.

```
sample100 <- do(1000) * sample(x = prob_off, size = 100)
```

Notice that a number of additional variables are added to the outputted data frame **sample100** to help us keep track of each sample. This helps us calculate the mean IQ of each sample, of which there are now 1000. The .index variable is a sample identification number. We can use **group_by()** to group observations based on the .index and then calculate the mean IQ. This will calculate the mean IQ for each unique value of .index (i.e., each sample).

```
sample_means100 <- sample100 %>%    # Select the sample100
                                    ## data frame
  group_by(.index) %>%              # Group by .index (the
                                    ## sample id)
  summarize(meanIQ = mean(IQ))      # Creating new variable
                                    ## of mean IQ
```

You'll notice that the mean in **sample_means100** is very close to the *true* population IQ mean of 100. The mean of the sample means can be considered to be the same as the true population mean, because if we'd taken more samples, they would eventually be identical. This is pretty useful to demonstrate using synthetic data, because in the real world, we rarely know the true mean of a population.

```
mean(sample_means100$meanIQ)

## [1] 100.1112
```

We can plot the frequency of these sample means to showcase what is called the **sampling distribution**. The sampling distribution is the frequency distribution of sample means drawn from the same population. In this case, it is the frequency distribution of the mean IQ found in each of our 1000 samples of 100 probationers. We have overlaid a red dotted line, which is the mean of the sample means.

```
ggplot(data = sample_means100) +
  geom_histogram(mapping = aes(x = meanIQ)) +
  geom_vline(mapping = aes(xintercept = mean(meanIQ)),
             col = "red", linetype = "dashed")

## `stat_bin()` using `bins = 30`. Pick better value
   with `binwidth`.
```

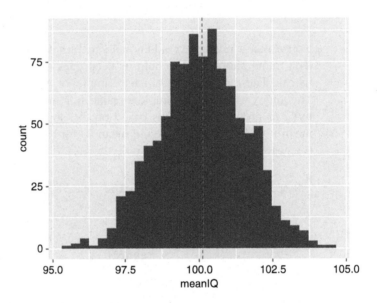

The above visualization of our sampling distribution demonstrates a key concept in inferential statistics. That is, if you randomly draw many samples from a population (such as probationers), for a given variable (in this case, IQ scores), calculate a **sample statistic** (in this case, the mean of each sample), and plot a frequency distribution of these means, you will get a normal distribution. This sampling distribution is sometimes called the probability distribution of a statistic. Why is this important? Well, it means that most samples we take from our population of probationers will have a mean that is close to the true population mean. Based on the above sampling distribution, we'd be highly unlikely to draw a sample with a mean IQ score that was very different from the true population mean IQ score. Most samples will be a fairly good representation of the population, providing a reasonably accurate estimation of the mean. The same could be said of other point estimates, such as the median or standard deviation; we just happen to have chosen the mean.

Sample Sizes

That said, in the above example, we used samples containing 100 probationers. What if we'd gone big and each sample contained a thousand
probationers? Or been lazy and only taken 30 in each sample? We can try
this out to see what happens. First, we'll rerun the sampling from the
population using one larger ($N = 1000$) and one smaller ($N = 30$) sample,
combine them into one data frame with the original sample ($N = 100$), and
then replot the sampling distributions in the same graphic for comparison.
The function **bind_rows()** is useful for combining data frames that contain the same columns, because we essentially stick them to the bottom of
one another. Remember that the number of actual samples remains the
same; at 1000, we are just changing the number of observations (probationers) in each sample.

```
# 1000 probationers in each sample
sample1000 <- do(1000) * sample(x = prob_off, size = 1000)

# 30 probationers in each sample
sample30   <- do(1000) * sample(x = prob_off, size = 30)

# Calculate the mean IQ scores for each sample
sample_means1000 <- sample1000 %>%
  group_by(.index) %>%
  summarize(meanIQ = mean(IQ))
sample_means30 < - sample30 %>%
  group_by(.index) %>%
  summarize(meanIQ = mean(IQ))

# Bind them with our first example, which had 100
## probationers in each sample
sample.means.total <- bind_rows(sample_means30,
    sample_means100, sample_means 1000, .id = "sample.size")

# Density plot for comparison
ggplot(data = sample.means.total) +
    geom_density(mapping = aes(x = meanIQ,
                fill = sample.size), alpha = 0.5) +
    scale_fill_discrete(labels = c("30","100","1000"))
```

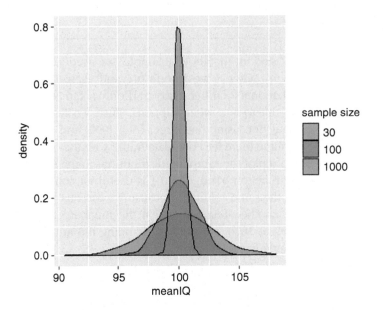

What can you conclude from the above visualization? All three **sample distributions** are fairly normally distributed, and all three have means that are similar to the true population mean. You can check this using `mean(sample_means1000$meanIQ)` for each one. That said, the larger the sample size, the more likely the sample means are to be closer to the population mean. This is evidenced by the *pointy* distribution when $N = 1000$ and the *flatter* distribution when $N = 30$. The likelihood of drawing a sample from our probationer population with an extreme, nonrepresentative mean IQ score is much higher when the sample size is smaller. In other words, our estimate of mean probationer IQ scores is likely to be more accurate (i.e., closer to the population mean) and reliable when using larger samples, which have much less variability.

Standard Error

You can quantify this variability using the standard deviation of the sampling distribution. We covered standard deviations more generally in Chap. 5. Remember, the standard deviation is a useful way of finding out how well the mean represents your data. A large standard deviation suggests that the mean is a poor representation of your population, because there is so much variability. By contrast, a small standard deviation indicates that most values are fairly close to the mean and, as such, the mean is a fairly accurate way of summarizing your data. The standard deviation of sample means is known as the **standard error** *of the mean*, and the principle is the same. We can calculate it using skills we've already picked up to demonstrate how the standard error of sample means decreases as the sample size gets bigger. Remember that your figures might differ slightly, but the relationship between sample size and standard error should be the same (the larger the sample size, the smaller the standard error).

```
sd(sample_means30$meanIQ)

## [1] 2.695511

sd(sample_means100$meanIQ)

## [1] 1.485388

sd(sample_means1000$meanIQ)

## [1] 0.4774102
```

What we have covered so far illustrates a key part of the **central limit theorem**, which is useful because it allows us to estimate error when using samples in the real world. We've been following these exercises using a synthetic population. As we noted earlier, in reality, population data often do not exist; we do not know the true population mean, and we cannot take thousands of samples from a population, produce a sampling distribution, and calculate the standard deviation of these sample means (i.e., the standard error). That said, using the central limit theorem and the concepts demonstrated earlier in R, we can rely on approximations of the standard error. We do this by dividing the standard deviation of our variable (e.g., IQ) by the square root of our sample size. You'll notice that this figure is very close to the standard deviation of the sample means computed above.

```
sample1000 %>% # Select our data frame with all 1000 samples
  filter(.index == 1) %>% # Filter the first one (choose any)
  summarize(SE = sd(IQ)/sqrt(1000))  # Calculate the error

##             SE
## 1 0.4783743
```

With this information, we can gauge the extent to which the mean of a sample, drawn from a population with an unknown mean, is likely to be a precise estimation of the true mean contained in the population. One way of illustrating this accuracy more usefully is by using confidence intervals.

Confidence Intervals

As noted above, statistics like the standard error are a useful way of assessing how imprecise estimates from samples, such as the mean of a variable, are likely to be relative to the true (unknown) mean in the population. Interpreting this number in isolation might not be that intuitive. Fortunately, we can augment the standard error with something called a **confidence interval**. Confidence intervals are especially useful because they convey the extent of uncertainty we have in our mean estimates. So, instead of simply reporting the mean IQ score from a sample of probationers, we can report a bandwidth on both sides of the mean value, which gives some margin for error. This margin of error was broadly demonstrated earlier when we looked at sampling variability; while many of the samples we looked at had mean IQ scores fairly close to the population mean, evidenced by the peaks in the middle of the distributions, there were a handful of extreme values that went wide of the mark, represented by the *tails* either side of our density distributions.

The question then becomes: *How can we calculate these intervals to convey the margin of error in our mean estimates?* To do this, we need to return to our normal distribution. One of the characteristics of a normal distribution is that 95% of values will fall within 1.96 standard deviations of the mean. Using the sampling distribution of the mean, which we know from earlier had a normal distribution, we can calculate an upper and lower boundary that captures this 95%. Remember that if you have not set a seed or you are using a different version of R than we are, your results might differ slightly to those below, but it should be fairly similar.

```
# Select our data frame with 1000 samples,
## get the sample mean for each

many_samples <- sample100 %>%
  group_by(.index) %>%
  summarize(samples_means = mean(IQ))

mean(many_samples$samples_means) # Mean
## [1] 100.0354

# Upper and Lower boundary
mean(many_samples$samples_means) + 1.96*sd
(many_samples$samples_means)
## [1] 102.9959

mean(many_samples$samples_means) - 1.96*sd
(many_samples$samples_means)
## [1] 97.07488
```

We know from this that 95% of our sample means fall between 97.07488 (lower boundary) and 102.9959 (upper boundary), with the mean of 100.0354 directly in the middle. Adding these bandwidths to our original sampling distribution visual will help make this clearer.

```
ggplot(data = many_samples) +
  geom_density(mapping = aes(x = samples_means)) +
  geom_vline(mapping = aes(xintercept =
           mean(samples_means)), col = "red",
                               linetype = "dashed") +
  geom_vline(mapping = aes(xintercept =
           mean(samples_means) + 1.96*sd(samples_means)),
           col = "blue", linetype = "dashed") +
  geom_vline(mapping = aes(xintercept =
           mean(samples_means) - 1.96*sd(samples_means)),
           col = "blue", linetype = "dashed")
```

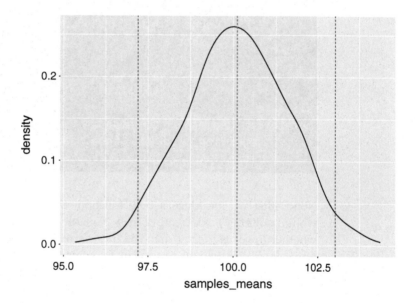

But why is this useful? Well, we know from the sampling distribution earlier that there is some degree of variability in the means of different samples taken from the same population, even if most of them tend to cluster around the true population mean. For that reason, there will also be variability in the confidence intervals, since the bandwidths sit on both sides of the mean for any given sample. What's interesting, and useful to demonstrate, is that if we resample our probation population 1000 times and calculate the mean for each sample, the true population mean will fall within the corresponding confidence intervals 95% of the time. That is, 5% of the confidence intervals calculated from these samples will fail to capture the true population mean.

Let's demonstrate this now and continue working with the object called `sample_means100` in your R session, which contains 1000 samples of 100 probationers. We can just take the mean and standard deviation of these, take the first 100 of these means, compute the confidence intervals for each one, and then create a new variable that specifies whether the true population mean was captured by the intervals. There is quite a lot going on in this code, so take care to read the comments.

```r
# Create a vector containing the true population mean
true.mean <- mean(prob_off$IQ)

# select the df with sample sizes of 100
new.sample.ci100 <-sample100 %>%
  group_by(.index) %>% # group by the .index
  summarize (meanIQ = mean(IQ),  # compute sample mean
             sample_sd = sd(IQ), # compute sample sd
             lower = meanIQ-1.96*sample_sd/
               sqrt(100), # compute lower boundary
             upper = meanIQ+1.96*sample_sd/
               sqrt(100)) %>% # compute upper boundary
# If lower > true mean or upper < true mean then
## capture.mean will be "yes"
# If not, capture.mean will be "no"
slice(1:100) %>% # Take the first 100 means
mutate(capture.mean = if_else
       (condition = lower > true.mean | upper < true.mean,
           true = "no"  false = "yes"))
```

Notice that we introduce a new function: `if_else()`. Here, we use it within `mutate()` to create a new variable <u>capture.mean</u>, which tests whether <u>lower</u> is greater than the true mean *or* (denoted by |) whether <u>upper</u> is smaller than the true mean. In either circumstance, the confidence interval will have failed to capture the true population mean, and <u>capture. mean</u> would be *no*, but otherwise, the confidence interval will have captured it, and thus it would be *yes*.

Producing a frequency table of this new variable tells us how many of our confidence intervals managed to capture the true population mean. We'd expect that around 95% will have.

```r
table(new.sample.ci100$capture.mean)

##
## no yes
##  3  97
```

Your result might differ slightly depending on the set seed, but in this example, 97% of the confidence intervals captured the mean, and 3% did not, so this is pretty close to what we expected. We can plot this finding visually to make more sense of the result. Note that we are specifying the point estimate mean IQ for each sample of probationers, with error bars around both sides representing the confidence intervals, and then coloring each based on whether the confidence intervals captured the true population mean, which is shown as a black dotted line.

```
ggplot(data = new.sample.ci100) +
  geom_vline(mapping = aes(xintercept = true.mean),
             linetype = "dashed") +
  geom_errorbarh(mapping = aes(xmin = lower, xmax = upper,
                 y = .index, colour = capture.mean)) +
  geom_point(mapping = aes(y = .index, x = meanIQ,
             colour = capture.mean))
```

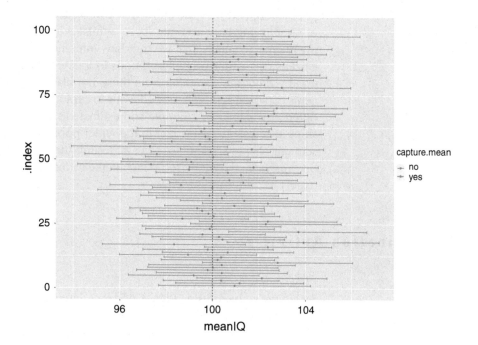

This visual illustrates that if we were to continuously resample from our population of probationers and calculate the mean IQ and corresponding confidence intervals for each sample, 97% of the time the true population mean would fall within these boundaries. Of course, this also means that 3% of the time, the confidence intervals around the sample mean will fail to capture the true population mean. Importantly, we can extrapolate this finding to single samples taken from a population, since most of the time we only have one sample. So, in practice, if we were to take a single sample of 100 probationers from our population, we could calculate a mean IQ score for that sample, with 95% confidence intervals on both sides. As far as we know, this mean point estimate and surrounding confidence intervals are our best guess of the mean IQ score of probationers nationwide, which in the real world is unknown. But we also know that there is a reasonable chance that our confidence intervals have captured the true population mean, because if we'd taken a hundred samples, 95% of them would have done so correctly. In reality, there is no way of knowing whether we have actually captured the true mean, but this degree of confidence is considered good enough in most fields of research, and it is useful to state these intervals when reporting your findings.

So, we now know that we can use samples to make estimates about a population, and we now know that confidence intervals are a useful way of establishing how accurate these estimates are. This opens up an exciting prospect, namely, that we can draw inferences about populations (e.g., citizens of a country, neighborhoods in a city, total number of probationers) by randomly sampling from these populations. Even better, the concepts explored in this chapter allow us to explore the relationships between different variables in a sample and estimate to what extent these relationships are likely to be evident in the wider population. As we'll see in subsequent chapters, there are ways of testing these relationships in R based on prespecified hypotheses, which make formal proposals about what we expect to find from our data.

Application Activities

Problem 1:

So far, we've been using 95% confidence intervals as our cutoff. Although this is the popular choice in criminology, it is not definitive. We could have used an interval of 2.58 standard deviations from the mean, which captures 99% of values in a normal distribution. What do you think the impact of using this interval will be? Try the final exercise again (under the *Confidence Interval* heading using the `summarize()`, `mean()`, and `sd()` functions), but replace `1.96` with `2.58`, and assess the result in your visualization using `ggplot()`.

Problem 2:

Let's assess it the other way—90% of values in a normal distribution fall within around 1.65 standard deviations from the mean. Now, what will happen if we rerun our visualization using these 90% confidence intervals? Again, assess the impact of making this change. Change the color and the line attributes in your plot.

Problem 3:

Recreate the density plot that shows the density of scores for 30, 100, and 1000 as a scatterplot. Make sure that the three sampling distributions have different colors and different symbols (see Appendix 4 for customization options).

Key Terms

Bell Curve See Gaussian distribution.

Central limit theorem A theorem that states: "If repeated independent random samples of size N are drawn from a population, as N grows large, the sampling distribution of sample means will be approximately normal." The central limit theorem enables the researcher to make inferences about an unknown population using a normal sampling distribution.

Confidence interval An interval of values around a statistic (usually a point estimate). If we were to draw repeated samples and calculate a 95% confidence interval for each, then in only 5 in 100 of these samples would the interval fail to include the true population parameter. In the case of a 99% confidence interval, only 1 in 100 samples would fail to include the true population parameter.

Gaussian distribution Normal distribution or bell curve.

Inferential statistics A broad area of statistics that provides the researcher with tools for making statements about populations on the basis of knowledge about samples. Inferential statistics allow the researcher to make inferences regarding populations from information gained in samples.

Population The universe of cases that the researcher seeks to study. The population of cases is fixed at a particular time (e.g., the population of the United States). However, populations usually change across time.

Population distribution The frequency distribution of a particular variable within a population.

Sample A set of actual observations or cases drawn from a population.

Sample distribution The frequency distribution of a particular variable within a sample drawn from a population.

Sample statistic A characteristic of a sample—for example, the mean number of previous convictions in a random sample of 1,000 prisoners.

Sampling distribution A distribution of all the results of a very large number of samples, each one of the same size and drawn from the same population under the same conditions. Ordinarily, sampling distributions are derived using probability theory and are based on probability distributions.

Standard error The standard deviation of a sampling distribution.

Synthetic data Computer-generated data.

Functions Introduced in this Chapter

FUNCTION	DESCRIPTION (PACKAGE)
bind_rows()	Combine data frame(s) together row-wise (dplyr)
do()	Loop for resampling (mosaic)
geom_density()	Geometry layer for density plots (ggplot2)
geom_errorbar()	Draw error bars by specifying maximum and minimum value (ggplot2)
geom_vline()	Geometry layer for adding vertical lines (ggplot2)
if_else()	Tests conditions for true or false, taking on values for each (dplyr)
rnorm()	Create synthetic normally distributed data (base R)
sample()	Randomly sample from a vector or data frame (mosaic)
scale_fill_discrete()	Specify fill of discrete aesthetics, e.g., color palette (ggplot2)
set.seed()	Random number generator start point (base R)

## Chapter seven

Defining the Observed Significance Level of a Test

Topics Practiced

Probability theory (multiplication rule, arrangements)

Applying the binomial formula

Technical Skills Covered

Calculating probabilities

Writing *for loops* and *while loops*

R Packages Required

stats

A. Wooditch et al., *A Beginner's Guide to Statistics for Criminology and Criminal Justice Using R*, https://doi.org/10.1007/978-3-030-50625-4_7

IT IS PROBABLY CLEAR to you now that research in criminal justice is often concerned with making inferences to a population based on a sample statistic. During the course of our research, we may often use tests of statistical significance to determine whether we can safely reject a null hypothesis as being true for our population of interest. But, when we conduct these tests, we will always have some risk of what is called a *type I error* (mistakenly concluding that an intervention or strategy is effective or efficacious). This chapter will illustrate some of the basics of probability theory in **R** that demonstrates how we identify the risk of type I error. In doing so, you will be posed with scenarios where you will compute binomial probabilities of a criminal court judge delivering a guilty verdict in bench trials using *for loops* and *while loops*. This chapter will be using binomial probabilities as an example (covering the *multiplication rule* and *arrangements*, specifically).

Calculating Probabilities Using the Multiplication Rule

Before walking through the application of the binomial test, it may be useful to illustrate some of the rationale underlying the functions used to calculate binomial probabilities and the risk of type I error in **R**. But before we get into it, recall that type I errors refer to the risk of a false positive. Figure 7.1 illustrates type I error as well as type II errors, which is the risk of a false negative.

Figure 7.1   *Type I and type II errors*

One way in which it is possible to calculate your risk of type I error is to use the **multiplication rule**, which is a simple rule derived from probability theory about the likelihood of obtaining a certain number of outcomes in a row, given that we are drawing an infinite number of samples from a population. The multiplication rule rests on the assumption that each event (e.g., a coin toss) in a sample is **independent** of other events in the sample. Put differently, the outcome of each event should not be affected by the outcome of any other events in the sample. Just because I got heads on my first coin toss, that does not affect whether I flip heads again on my second coin toss. This rule is called the multiplication rule because the likelihood of a given series of events happening is equal to the probability associated with each event happening multiplied together.

We can illustrate the multiplication rule using a simple example. For instance, let's say there is a criminal court judge holding a series of bench trials, where he hears evidence provided in each case and makes a judgment of guilt. Let's also say that this judge did not pay attention as much as he should have in law school and must now flip a coin to determine the outcome of each trial (i.e., if the coin lands on heads, he rules that the defendant is guilty, and vice versa).

Let's write out our hypothesis...

Hypotheses

H_0: There is an equal probability that the coin will land on heads or tails every time it is tossed by the judge (coin is fair).

H_A: There is not an equal probability that the coin will land on heads or tails every time it is tossed by the judge (coin is not fair).

You hear one day that the judge has recently delivered eight guilty verdicts in a row! You start to suspect that the coin used by the judge may not be fair. Before you confront him, however, you want to know, what is the likelihood of finding eight defendants guilty in a row? Assuming that each trial is independent, we can use the multiplication rule to find the probability of this scenario.

The multiplication rule applied—the likelihood of getting eight guilty verdicts in a row.

```
# Probability of judge finding defendant guilty = 0.5
prob <- 0.5

# Number of trials
num_trials <- 8

# Prob of getting 8 guilty verdicts in a row =
# prob(trial1) * prob(trial2) *....prob(trial8)
prob_8 <- prob^num_trials
prob_8
## [1] 0.00390625
```

We can see the probability of delivering eight guilty verdicts in a row (getting eight heads) is close to 0.004. What this also means is that the observed risk of making a type I error in rejecting the null hypothesis that the coin the judge uses is *fair* is about 0.004. To put this differently, the chance of us saying that the judge did not have a fair coin when, in fact, we were wrong, and the coin was fair, is about 4 in 1,000. This number is quite small and much smaller than conventional benchmark used in criminal justice of 0.05, or 5 in 100. Therefore, we observed eight guilty verdicts in a row; we would conclude that the coin is not fair (reject the null hypothesis).

Hypotheses Conclusion

H_0: ~~There is an equal probability that the coin will land on heads or tails every time it is tossed by the judge (coin is fair).~~

H_A: There is not an equal probability that the coin will land on heads or tails every time it is tossed by the judge (coin is not fair). [REJECT NULL]

Calculating Multiple Probabilities Using a *For Loop*

If we were interested in seeing the probability of delivering a certain number of guilty verdicts in a row over a range of verdicts decided, we can write a *for loop*. This saves us time because we don't have to manually compute each probability by hand. A *for loop* tells R to repeat specified operations until a certain condition is met. Before we apply a *for loop* to our problem, let's start out with some easy loops so you get the hang of it. Try the *for loop* below. This loop tells R to print the value of x starting at the value 1 and continuing sequentially until x is equal to 10.

```
for (x in 1:10) {

print(x)

}
## [1] 1
## [1] 2
## [1] 3
## [1] 4
## [1] 5
## [1] 6
## [1] 7
## [1] 8
## [1] 9
## [1] 10
```

Let's add some additional arguments… Have the loop multiply the value of x by 5 and then report the result. As with our loop above, x takes on a value of 1, 2, 3, …, 10.

```
for (x in 1:10) {
z<- x * 5
print(z)

}
## [1] 5
## [1] 10
## [1] 15
## [1] 20
## [1] 25
## [1] 30
## [1] 35
## [1] 40
## [1] 45
## [1] 50
```

Now that you have the hang of it, let's use a *for loop* with our example of a judge flipping a coin to determine guilty verdicts. See the *for loop* below. On the first loop, R is going to give the object `num_verdicts` a value of *1* to indicate that the judge decided a total of one verdict and then going to exponentiate the number of verdicts decided (`num_verdicts`) by the probability of delivering a guilty verdict from a flip of a coin (*0.05*) and then have R print the probability of deciding a given number of guilty verdicts in a row. We have told our *for loop* to run `1:10`, which will examine the probability of one guilty verdict, then loop to examine two guilty verdicts in a row, then loop to examine three guilty verdicts in a row, and so forth all the way up to ten. The `print()` function is needed for our loop to return a result to us, but we also need the `paste()` function since we are having our loop print not only the value of an object but also some string text.

```
for (num_verdicts in 1:10) {

  prob <- 0.5 ^ num_verdicts

  print(paste("The probability of ", num_verdicts,
              " guilty verdicts in a row is ", prob))

}

## [1] "The probability of 1 guilty verdicts in a row is 0.5"
## [1] "The probability of 2 guilty verdicts in a row is 0.25"
## [1] "The probability of 3 guilty verdicts in a row is 0.125"
## [1] "The probability of 4 guilty verdicts in a row is 0.0625"
## [1] "The probability of 5 guilty verdicts in a row is 0.03125"
## [1] "The probability of 6 guilty verdicts in a row is 0.015625"
## [1] "The probability of 7 guilty verdicts in a row is 0.0078125"
## [1] "The probability of 8 guilty verdicts in a row is 0.00390625"
## [1] "The probability of 9 guilty verdicts in a row is 0.001953125"
## [1] "The probability of 10 guilty verdicts in a row is 0.0009765625"
```

Calculating Multiple Probabilities Using a *While Loop*

But what if we were only interested in the number of guilty verdicts in a row for us to get really suspicious that the judge was not using a fair coin? We can use a *while loop* to do this. Let's start with an easy example so you get used to writing *while loops*. In the example below, we are telling R to print the value of x but to stop once the value of x is greater than 10. Notice that we need to define the object x before the *while loop* initiates, and once the value of x is printed, we will add x plus 1, so the value of x increases by 1 with each loop.

```
x<-0

while( x <= 10) {

print(x)

x<- x + 1  }

## [1] 0
## [1] 1
## [1] 2
## [1] 3
## [1] 4
## [1] 5
## [1] 6
## [1] 7
## [1] 8
## [1] 9
## [1] 10
```

I think you have the hang of it! Let's get back to our judge example. We would like to know the number of guilty verdicts in a row we would need to observe for us to get really suspicious that the judge was not using a fair coin. For this while loop, we are telling R to continue to calculate the probability of a given number of guilty verdicts in a row but to stop calculating once the probability of what is being observed is less than or equal to 0.05.

For a *while loop*, we need to first specify the objects that are going to be used in the loop. As such, we specify **num_verdicts** equal to the value 1 (the number of verdicts delivered to start with in the loop) and **prob** as 0.5 (the probability of getting a guilty verdict based on a fair coin toss). To initialize our *while loop*, we are telling R to continue calculating the number of sequential guilty verdicts in a row until the observed probability is equal to or less than 0.05. Notice that with each loop, we are writing over our **prob** and **num_verdicts** objects, and we are also having our loop print the results. Now when you run this *while loop*, you should find that the loop stops looping once five guilty verdicts in a row were decided because the probability falls below 0.05.

```
prob<-0.5    # Probability 1 guilty verdict
num_verdicts<-1  #Start Loop by examining 1 guilty verdict

# Compute Likelihood until the observed probability is
## greater than 0.05.
while (prob > 0.05) {

prob <- 0.5^num_verdicts

print(paste("The probability of ", num_verdicts,
            " guilty verdicts in a row is ", prob))

# Examine the likelihood of one additional guilty verdict
## on the next loop
num_verdicts <- num_verdicts + 1
}

## [1] "The probability of 1 guilty verdicts in a row is 0.5"
## [1] "The probability of 2 guilty verdicts in a row is 0.25"
## [1] "The probability of 3 guilty verdicts in a row is 0.125"
## [1] "The probability of 4 guilty verdicts in a row is 0.0625"
## [1] "The probability of 5 guilty verdicts in a row is 0.03125"
```

Arrangements

You might also be curious as to the likelihood of the judge delivering eight guilty verdicts out of a certain number of trials. If the judge adjudicated ten trials, there are a number of ways that he could have delivered the eight guilty verdicts. For instance, he could have tossed four heads, two tails, and four heads, in that order. The different combinations of delivering eight guilty verdicts in ten trials can also be referred to as **arrangements**. To determine the probability of the judge delivering eight guilty verdicts out of ten trials, we would first need to determine the number of arrangements of getting this number of guilty verdicts in ten trials.

We will use Eq. 7.1 to calculate the number of arrangements, where N refers to the number of trials in our sample and r is the number of guilty verdicts passed down in the number of trials. The exclamation point (!) denotes the factorial of a value and can be obtained by using the **factorial()** function from base R.

Formula to Calculate Arrangements

$$\binom{N}{r} = \frac{N!}{r!(N-r)!}$$

Equation 7.1

Let's calculate this in R.

```
# Calculate N (number of trials in sample)
N <- 10

# Calculate N! (N factorial)
N_fact <- factorial(N)
N_fact
## [1] 3628800

# Calculate r (number of guilty verdicts, or number of heads)
r <- 8

# Calculate r! (r factorial)
r_fact <- factorial(r)
r_fact
## [1] 40320

# Calculate N-r
N_r <- N - r

# Putting it together
arrangements <- N_fact/(r_fact * factorial(N_r))
arrangements
## [1] 45
```

There are 45 arrangements for getting eight guilty verdicts in ten trials. Now to define the probability of the judge getting eight heads (and delivering eight guilty verdicts) in ten trials, we will use the binomial formula discussed below.

Applying the Binomial Formula

Now that we have calculated the number of possible arrangements of getting eight guilty verdicts in ten trials, we can determine the likelihood of getting this number of guilty verdicts in ten tosses of a fair coin using the **binomial formula** in Eq. 7.2.

Binomial Formula

$$P\binom{N}{r} = \left[\frac{N!}{r!(N-r)!}\right] p^r \left(1-p\right)^{N-r}$$ **Equation 7.2**

Luckily for us, we have done much of the work already. This is another reason why working with R objects is so handy.

```
# First, let's get the number of arrangements again.
arrangements

## [1] 45

# Next, get the probability of any specific arrangement
## (part 2 of the equation)
prob_arrangement <- prob_8 * (1-prob)^N_r

# Finally, calculate the probability!
prob_8_in_10 <- arrangements * prob_arrangement
prob_8_in_10
## [1] 0.04394531
```

Now we see that the likelihood of tossing eight heads in ten tosses of a fair coin (getting eight guilty verdicts in ten trials) is roughly 0.044. We can use the binomial formula to calculate the likelihood of all other possible outcomes of the ten trials. Doing so would create a **sampling distribution** of all the probabilities associated with the ten trials. To answer our original question of what the observed risk of type I error is of rejecting the null hypothesis that the judge's coin is fair (based on the eight guilty verdicts), we would need to add together the probabilities of getting eight or more (eight, nine, and ten) guilty verdicts out of ten trials. We know that this total risk would equate to roughly 0.055 (0.044 + 0.010 + 0.001), which is a little over the typical threshold of 0.05. Based on this estimate of the risk, you may want to be cautious about confronting the judge about the fairness of his coin!

Most statistical computing environments provide a means of estimating probability distributions, so you do not have to do calculations by hand. R has built-in functions that come preloaded with the **stats** package (in base R) that can give you the same information calculated above in one line of code. To illustrate, we will calculate the exact probability of getting eight heads in ten tosses of a fair coin using the **dbinom()** function. Note that **size** = is the number of trials (ten), **prob** = is the probability of heads or tails (0.5), and *n* = is the number of successes (eight).

```
# Use the dbinom() function
# Calculate probability of getting 8 heads in 10 tosses
## of a fair coin
dbinom(8, size = 10, prob = 0.5)
## [1] 0.04394531
```

We receive the same answer as above!

If we also want to calculate the cumulative probability function for getting eight or more heads in ten tosses of a fair coin, we can use the **pbinom()** function from the **stats** package to accomplish this. Note that rather than inputting the number of successes, we are including the number of failures (in this case, tails or not-guilty verdicts).

```
# Use the pbinom() function to calculate
## cumulative probability
# Getting 8 or more heads in 10 tosses of a fair coin
pbinom(2, size = 10, prob = 0.5)
## [1] 0.0546875
```

We again receive the same answer as when we calculated the cumulative probability when we wrote out the equation.

Application Activities

Problem 1:

You are a criminal justice researcher who studies domestic violence. You just received a dataset containing information on 100 cases of domestic violence, including the victim's sex. You want to see if you can reject the null hypothesis that men and women are equally likely of being a victim of domestic violence. Either by writing out the equation or using **dbinom()**, calculate the observed risk of type I error for 65 cases of domestic violence where the victim was female. Can you reject the null hypothesis that the likelihood is equal for males and females with 95% confidence?

Problem 2:

You are a probation officer who must regularly administer drug tests to your clients. You know from experience that probationers have about a 40% chance of failing a drug test when you administer it to them. Using the **pbinom()** and **dbinom()** functions, calculate the probability of getting 12 positive drug tests out of 15 tests, and then calculate the cumulative probability of 12 *or more* positive drug tests out of 15 tests.

Problem 3:

You are a probation officer and one of your fellow officers discovered that some probationers under your department's supervision are providing one of their friend's urine instead of their own so they can pass a drug test. You want to identify clients on your caseload that may be engaging in this practice. You know that there is a 60% chance of a probationer having a clean urine (passing the drug test). With 95% confidence, how many clean urines would the probationer need to provide before you get suspicious? Write a *while loop* like the one we did above to determine this.

Key Terms

Arrangements The different ways events can be ordered and result in a single outcome. For example, there is only one arrangement for gaining the outcome of ten heads in ten tosses of a coin. There are, however, ten different arrangements for gaining the outcome of nine heads in ten tosses of a coin.

Binomial formula The means of determining the probability that a given set of binomial events will occur in all its possible arrangements.

Independent Describing two events when the occurrence of one does not affect the occurrence of the other.

Multiplication rule The means for determining the probability that a series of events will jointly occur.

Sampling distribution A distribution of all the results of a very large number of samples, each one of the same size and drawn from the same population under the same conditions. Ordinarily, sampling distributions are derived using probability theory and are based on probability distributions.

Functions Introduced in this Chapter

FUNCTION	DESCRIPTION (PACKAGE)
dbinom()	Find probability of events occurring X times (stats)
factorial()	Compute the factorial of a numeric vector (base R)
for()	Initiates a *for loop* (base R)
paste()	Combines a series of string text (base R)
pbinom()	Find cumulative probability of a binomial probability distribution (stats)
while()	Initiates a *while loop* (base R)

Hypothesis Testing Using
the Binomial Distribution

Topics Practiced

Hypothesis testing with the binomial distribution

Parametric and nonparametric assumptions

Two-sided and one-sided hypotheses

Testing equality of group proportions

Confidence intervals

Technical Skills Covered

Conducting a two-sample proportion test

R Packages Required

DescTools, dplyr, ggplot2

MANY PEOPLE INVOLVED in criminology and criminal justice research spend time making predictions about populations in the real world. These predictions tend to be based on a theoretical framework and are formally stated as hypotheses in order to answer a specific research question. Using inferential statistics (see Chap. 6), we can test to what extent our data support these hypotheses and provide empirical evidence to support (or reject) our expectations in R. This chapter uses a simulated dataset of results from a crime reduction intervention for at-risk youth to explore how the binomial distribution allows us to generalize from a sample of 100 participants in a study to the wider population.

Data

Dataset Source: Synthetic data created in R

File Name: Not applicable

Dataset Description: Synthetic intervention data where a sample of 100 at-risk youth are assigned to either a treatment or a control group. The treatment group participates in an experimental crime reduction intervention, so we would expect that they will have a lower incidence of reoffending in comparison to the control group.

Getting Started

1. Install and load the required packages using the `install.packages()` and `library()` functions (see Appendix 1.1).

Hypothesis Testing Using the Binomial Distribution

When we carry out hypothesis testing, we want to be able to understand whether a particular statistic in our sample can be used to generalize to the population parameter that it is thought to represent. In a hypothesis test, our aim is to reject our **null hypothesis**. Our null hypothesis essentially states that there is no association between the two phenomena being examined. It states the *null* of our alternative hypothesis, which is often about some association between our variables. So if our hypothesis states that there is a difference between two groups, for example, our null hypothesis will say that no such difference exists in the population. Before we reject our null hypothesis, we want to be confident that it is, in fact, false for the population we are studying. However, normally we do not have data from the entire population, so we need to make a decision about our null hypothesis without being completely sure about our conclusion. As such, we base our decision on how confident we are. In criminology (and social sciences more generally), we want to be at least 95% confident in our finding.

At 95% confidence, that means we are willing to make a mistake in our conclusions 5% of the time. In statistical jargon, this mistake in hypothesis testing is referred to as a **type I error** or *false-positive* (rejecting the null hypothesis when it is actually true; see Chap. 7). For this reason, we want the observed risk of a type I error in a test of statistical significance to be as small as possible. But how can we calculate that risk in order to define the observed significance level associated with the outcome of a test?

We will consider the evaluation of a (fictitious) intervention scheme aimed at preventing young people from reoffending. Let's assume we take a sample of 100 at-risk young people and randomly assign them into two groups: a treatment group to receive an intervention that is meant to prevent them from committing future offenses and another group that receives no treatment, which is our control group. Now, we want to see whether this intervention worked and whether it can be rolled out to all at-risk youth in our district. To do this, we are going to rely on the **binomial distribution**, which is a sampling distribution for the probability of success (when you only have two possible outcomes). In our example problem, the outcome is dichotomous—success or failure.

Assumptions of Binomial Distribution

The first step in a test of statistical significance is to establish the assumptions on which the test is based and make sure that they are met.

Level of Measurement

First, it is important to establish what the level of measurement is for our variables. For different levels of measurement of our variables, different statistical tests are appropriate. For the binomial test, which is based on the binomial distribution, a nominal-level binary measure is required. Such a binary measure has only two possible outcomes. An example of a binary measure is the outcome of the coin tosses by our judge in Chap. 7—the coin could have landed on heads or tails.

Shape of Population Distribution

We also want to understand the shape of our population distribution. **Parametric tests** make an assumption about the shape of the population distribution. For example, in Chap. 10, we will talk about the normal distribution, and many tests we cover after Chap. 10 carry the assumption that our variable follows such a normal distribution. On the other hand, a **non-parametric test** (also called distribution-free test) does not make a specific assumption regarding the population distribution.

The binomial test is a nonparametric test, so there are actually no assumptions made about the shape of the population distribution.

Sample Assumptions

In statistical tests applied to samples, we want these samples to have high **external validity**, which means they offer a good representation of the population from which they are drawn. Attention should be paid to the method of sampling (e.g., *random samples*, as used in Chap. 6, versus *convenience samples*) to address this assumption.

Assumptions About the Hypotheses

Hypotheses must be stated before the researcher collects outcome data for a study (and conducted any analysis). If hypotheses are stated only after data have been collected and analyzed, the researcher might be tempted to make changes in the hypotheses that unfairly affect the tests of statistical significance that are conducted. This relates directly back to the issue of type I error because we want to leave errors in hypothesis testing to chance (5%) and not increase the chances of a false-positive through our behavior.

You may have a **directional hypothesis** where you specify the direction, or type of relationship, that is expected. For example, we might hypothesize that the young people in our treatment group are going to stop committing offenses at a greater rate than those in our control group. Or it might be a **non-directional hypothesis** where you are concerned only that there is any difference, whether it is positive or negative. For example, we might not actually want to know if our group who received the treatment have lower or greater chance to stop committing offenses than the control group, but instead we want to just know if there is *any* difference between the two, no matter the direction.

It is from the hypothesis of interest (referred to as the alternative hypothesis (H_A)) that you then derive the null hypothesis (H_0). For instance, to answer our question whether the treatment and control group go on to offend equally, for our alternative hypothesis (H_A), we can write "the level of offending in the treatment group relative to offending in the control group changes after the intervention." We are determining this by whether the participant reoffended in the 12-month period they were examined (yes/no). Put in terms of probabilities, there is a 50% chance of success ($P = 0.50$) for the intervention under the null hypothesis. The research hypothesis represents all other possible outcomes ($P \neq 0.50$). Remember that our hypotheses are statements about the populations examined. Accordingly, in stating the hypotheses, we use symbols appropriate for population parameters—in this case, P (representing a proportion) rather than the lowercase p. Stating both our hypotheses, we write:

Hypotheses

H_0: The level of offending in the treatment group relative to offending in the control group does not change after the intervention, $P = 0.50$.

H_A: The level of offending in the treatment group relative to offending in the control group changes after the intervention, $P \neq 0.50$.

Defining Significance Level and Rejection Regions

When we define our significance level, what we really do is specify an acceptable level of type I error. This is denoted by the alpha-level (α), and normally, in the social sciences, it will be set to $\alpha = 0.05$. If we find that the probability of the null hypothesis being true is less than our alpha, then we can reject our null hypothesis. So, for example, if we choose $\alpha = 0.05$ (meaning we want to be at least 95% confident) and we determine the observed probability of the null hypothesis being true is 0.0001, then we can reject it. The thresholds for alpha link back to our discussions about confidence intervals in Chap. 6; there is some degree of ambiguity over what is an acceptable probability and confidence interval. That said, there are rules of thumb which are commonly used, and in social science, this tends to be $\alpha = 0.05$. And just as a reminder, if our p-value is greater than our alpha, we *fail to reject* the null hypothesis, but we cannot say that we accept the null hypothesis.

Hypothesis Testing Using the Binomial Distribution

So, we have our null/alternative hypotheses, we have our α/desired confidence level, and, finally, we have obtained sample data from the experiment to test our hypotheses. How can we now use the binomial distribution to test our hypotheses? Well, in R, we can make use of the `prop.test()` function. This can be used for testing the null hypothesis that the proportions (probabilities of success) in several groups are the same or that they equal certain given values. Essentially, we can compare if the counts of things in two groups are significantly different from one another.

In this scenario, remember that we have a treatment and control group of known at-risk youths. Since this is an experiment in which we try to test the effectiveness of an intervention, we can randomly assign youths to the treatment and control group, respectively. This randomness serves to remove any erroneous (unsystematic) variation caused by factors other than our intervention, and thus, we can be more confident that any variation observed is indeed due to the intervention itself (i.e., the systematic variation we are interested in).

If we have 100 at-risk youths, we can then randomly assign them to the treatment and control groups, giving 50 in each. Let's say that after having done this, we followed up with them all and found that 10 individuals out of the 50 in the treatment group had gone on to reoffend and 28 out of the 50 in the control group had gone on to reoffend. Based on this, you might be tempted to say, "well, of course the treatment worked!" However, we need to remember that there is likely going to be some *random* variation between the two groups which occurs irrespective of our intervention, even when you have randomly assigned them. This is why the test of statistical significance is useful. So let's run `prop.test()`, specifying these figures within the function.

```
prop.test(x = c(10, 28), n = c(50, 50))

##
##  2-sample test for equality of proportions with
    continuity correction
##
## data:  c(10, 28) out of c(50, 50)
## X-squared = 12.267, df = 1, p-value = 0.0004611
## alternative hypothesis: two.sided
## 95 percent confidence interval:
##  -0.5567014 -0.1632986
## sample estimates:
## prop 1 prop 2
##   0.20   0.56
```

There is quite a lot to take in from this output. Some of it is simply useful descriptive information, such as the proportions attributable to each group. As one might expect, we have 20% in one group (10 out of 50 reoffenders in the treatment) and 56% in the other (28 out of 50 reoffenders in the control). You will notice from the help documentation (`?prop.test`) that there are a number of defaults for the function. Some of the output confirms what these defaults were. For instance, the test has used a 95% confidence interval, which, as we have noted above and in previous chapters, is a commonly used threshold in criminology. It has also chosen a two-sided alternative hypothesis. That is, we haven't specified a direction for the hypothesis, only that we expect the groups to be significantly different from one another. We can see that the *p*-value falls below our pre-specified threshold ($\alpha = 0.05$), and thus we can say that it is statistically significant. In other words, there is enough evidence for us to reject the null hypothesis that the level of offending in the treatment group relative to offending in the control group does not change after the intervention. This suggests that at least *something* is happening when we intervene.

But what if we want to test our expectation, namely, that the treatment group which received our intervention went on to offend less often than those who did not get the intervention (control group)? In this circumstance, the direction is pretty important; we wouldn't want to introduce an intervention which makes at-risk youth *more* likely to offend, would we? To specify the direction of the relationship, we can use the **alternative** = argument of the **prop.test()** function. The option we are looking for is **alternative** = **"less"** on the basis that we expect our treatment group to have a smaller probability of offending (success) than the control. Our H_A would be that the level of offending in the treatment group relative to offending in the control group *decreases* with the intervention.

```
prop.test(x = c(10, 28), n = c(50, 50),
          alternative = "less")
##
##  2-sample test for equality of proportions with
    continuity correction
##
## data:  c(10, 28) out of c(50, 50)
## X-squared = 12.267, df = 1, p-value = 0.0002306
## alternative hypothesis: less
## 95 percent confidence interval:
##  -1.0000000 -0.1917075
## sample estimates:
## prop 1 prop 2
##   0.20   0.56
```

We can now see that the alternative hypothesis is no longer two-sided, but instead specified as *less*, as per our expectation. This is specified in the third line of our R output where we can read **alternative hypothesis: less**.

The *p*-value, reported in the line above, has fallen below our threshold ($\alpha = 0.05$), and thus we have sufficient support to reject our null hypothesis (H_0) in favor of our directional alternative hypothesis. In other words, there is evidence to suggest that the at-risk youth in the treatment did indeed offend less than in the control group as a result of our systematic variation (i.e., the intervention) and that this finding is *statistically significant* (i.e., we can generalize from our sample to the population which they represent).

Hypotheses Conclusion

~~H_0: The level of offending in the treatment group relative to offending in the control group does not change after the intervention, $P = 0.50$.~~

H_A: The level of offending in the treatment group relative to offending in the control group changes after the intervention, $P \neq 0.50$. [REJECT NULL]

For the sake of argument, let's say we discovered that the therapist hired to administer a therapy session to those in the treatment group ended up being indicted for posing as a doctor. Now, we are a bit concerned that the treatment group could have done worse than the control group. As such, we may want to test the hypothesis in the other direction. This would mean that we expect the intervention to actually *increase* the amount of reoffending, completely changing our alternative hypothesis. Take a moment to think about whether you expect the *p*-value to have increased or decreased (and thus gone above or below $\alpha = 0.05$) when testing this. When you have thought about this, set the **alternative** = argument of **prop.test()** to **"greater"**, and run the code again, as demonstrated below:

```
prop.test(x = c(10, 28), n = c(50, 50),
          alternative = "greater")
##
##  2-sample test for equality of proportions with
    continuity correction
##
## data:  c(10, 28) out of c(50, 50)
## X-squared = 12.267, df = 1, p-value = 0.9998
## alternative hypothesis: greater
## 95 percent confidence interval:
##   -0.5282925  1.0000000
## sample estimates:
## prop 1 prop 2
##   0.20   0.56
```

What has happened? You will see that the p-value is now extremely high, far above our 0.05 threshold, so we can't reject the null hypothesis, and there is no evidence to support the hypothesis that our intervention *increases* reoffending (as you may have expected given the previous results!).

That said, it is worth emphasizing that we would never normally perform multiple different hypothesis tests in this manner. We have just done this as a demonstration. It's an important underlying premise of hypothesis testing that you state your expectations *before* conducting any analysis. Inspired by other fields, such as medicine, there is a growing movement in criminology to actually publicly preregister your hypotheses before conducting any data collection and analysis, for the very reason that it is sound research practice and ensures complete transparency.

Preregistration of Hypotheses

When you preregister your research, you officially specify your research plan in advance of your study by submitting it to a registry. Preregistration separates *hypothesis-generating (exploratory)* from *hypothesis-testing (confirmatory)* research.

What we were doing above was hypothesis testing. We used our prior knowledge and expectations to generate a hypothesis that was grounded in theory and previous research. We have an intervention which we know was specifically developed to reduce offending in at-risk youth, and so we expect that the group exposed to this intervention will not offend, when compared to the control group who did offend. Phrased specifically in the context of our H_A, this can be written as *the level of offending in the treatment group relative to offending in the control group changes after the intervention, $P \neq 0.50$.*

And we know that to test this, we have to generate our null hypothesis, which would state the case of *no difference* and would look like this: H_0—*the level of offending in the treatment group relative to offending in the control group does not change after the intervention, $P = 0.50$.*

Because we know in advance what question we want to answer, we can preregister this hypothesis, which helps us show an auditable trail of our research, improving it in quality and transparency. It further helps us clearly report our findings and helps others who may wish to build on it.

Exploratory research, on the other hand, is not something we cover here, but there are some handy tips on how to tell the two types apart (see Table 8.1).

Table 8.1	Differences between confirmatory and exploratory research

CONFIRMATORY RESEARCH	EXPLORATORY RESEARCH
Hypothesis testing	Hypothesis generating
Results are held to the highest standards	Results deserve to be replicated and confirmed
Data-independent	Data-dependent
Minimizes false-positives	Minimizes false-negatives in order to find unexpected discoveries
p-values retain diagnostic value	*p*-values lose diagnostic value
Inferences may be drawn to wider population	Not useful for making inferences to any wider population

Confidence Intervals and Hypothesis Testing with Proportions

Another way of thinking about hypothesis tests is in terms of confidence intervals, which we discussed in Chap. 6. Similar to how we worked with confidence intervals there, it is possible to produce confidence intervals for binomial proportions.

The `BinomCI()` function in the `DescTools` package has several methods for calculating confidence intervals for a binomial proportion. With `BinomCI()`, we are interested in building confidence intervals around the proportion of an outcome (termed success even though in this case reoffending might not be a success in the conventional sense, but bear with us) for each group separately. So what you have to specify in this case is the number of successes (in this case, the number of young people who reoffended) and the total number of trials (number of young people in that group).

So, for example, looking at our treatment group (young people who were exposed to the intervention), we know there were 50 young people in the group, and 10 of them reoffended.

```
BinomCI(10, 50)

##      est    lwr.ci    upr.ci
## [1,] 0.2 0.1124375 0.3303711
```

We can see in the outcome the estimated proportion from our sample (`est = 0.2`), which is the same as we could calculate ourselves dividing the successes by the trials (`10/50 = 0.2`). But then we see a value for both lower and upper confidence intervals (`lwr.ci` and `upr.ci`). So how did we reach this value?

The `BinomCI()` function actually allows you to pick few different methods for calculating confidence intervals. If you explore the help file for this function, you can read the following: *wald, wilson, wilsoncc, agresti-coull, jeffreys, modified wilson, modified jeffreys, clopper-pearson, arcsine, logit, witting,* or *pratt.* If we do not specify how to calculate it, the default method implemented is the *Wilson method.* This approach was introduced by Wilson (1927) and is the inversion of the central limit theorem approximation to the family of equal tail tests of $p = p0$. The Wilson interval is recommended by Agresti and Coull (1998), as well as by Brown et al. (2001).

Another thing you can specify is the confidence level. Remember earlier we set our alpha-level and determined how to pick one? Well, we picked 0.05 (meaning we want to be at least 95% confident). So we can explicitly specify this in the `BinomCI()` function.

```
BinomCI(10, 50, conf.level = 0.95)

##       est    lwr.ci    upr.ci
## [1,] 0.2 0.1124375 0.3303711
```

You might see that our results are the same; that is because the default of the `BinomCI()` function is to use a 95% confidence level. If we want to be stricter (less open to type I error of false-positive), we could set this to 99%.

```
BinomCI(10, 50, conf.level = 0.99)

##       est     lwr.ci    upr.ci
## [1,] 0.2 0.09379659 0.3764947
```

You can see that we have a wider confidence interval now, and we say that between 9 and 38% of young people exposed to the treatment will reoffend. But with our original decision of 95%, we estimate that actually between 11 and 33% of young people exposed to the intervention reoffend. How does this compare with our control group? Well, we know in the control group that 28 out of the 50 young people reoffended.

```
BinomCI(28, 50, conf.level = 0.95)

##        est    lwr.ci    upr.ci
## [1,] 0.56 0.4230603 0.688378
```

From our sample then, we can estimate that in the general population of at-risk young people, those who are not exposed to this treatment, we can expect 42% and 69% of them to reoffend. Seems like a large difference. Let's plot this to visualize using **geom_errorbarh()** from the **ggplot()** package.

Let's start by assigning our results to objects, so we can call them later.

```
treatment_group <- BinomCI(10, 50, conf.level = 0.95)
control_group <- BinomCI(28, 50, conf.level = 0.95)
```

Now we can build a plot with two error bar layers, one for each group.

```
ggplot() +
  geom_errorbar(mapping = aes(ymin = treatment_group[2],
                              ymax = treatment_group[3],
                              x = "treatment",
                              colour = "treatment")) +
  geom_point(mapping = aes(y = treatment_group[1],
                           x = "treatment",
                           colour = "treatment")) +
  geom_errorbar(mapping = aes(ymin = control_group[2],
               ymax = control_group[3], x = "control",
               colour = "control")) +
  geom_point(mapping = aes(y = control_group[1],
                           x = "control",
               colou r ="control")) + xlab("Group") +
  ylab("Proportion who reoffended at follow-up") +
  theme_minimal()
```

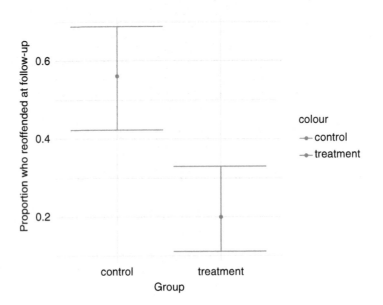

You will notice something interesting from this graph: the confidence intervals of the two groups do not overlap, and the proportion for the treatment is lower than for the control. Given that the aim of our intervention was to reduce reoffending, this is good news. The proportion of young people who reoffended in the treatment group is considerably lower than it is for the control group. Even when constructing 95% confidence intervals, which as we know from Chap. 6 are highly likely to contain the population parameter, there is no overlap between the two.

Why does this matter? Well, because we are pretty sure that the confidence intervals contain the true population parameter, this finding indicates that our two groups are likely to have come from two different populations. Remember that we designed our intervention to *reduce* offending in the treatment group, and remember that the mean for the treatment group is *lower* than the control. This means that our intervention was probably successful. The visualization of the confidence interval provides evidence for us to reject the null hypothesis, namely, that our intervention had no impact on offending, and instead provides evidence to suggest that our intervention worked. However, should the confidence intervals have had considerable overlap, we'd have to conclude that the two probably came from the same population and that our intervention was not successful. This kind of analysis can be tested more specifically using a test of statistical significance in R (see Chap. 11), but hopefully this is a useful demonstration of the link between hypothesis testing and some of the key concepts in previous chapters.

Application Activities

Problem 1:

Imagine you are a prison warden who wants to implement a new cognitive behavioral therapy (CBT) program in your prison. Before rolling out the program to all inmates, you first want to see whether it works to reduce inmate misconduct. You randomly assign 60 inmates to receive the new CBT program (treatment group) and the other 60 to receive business as usual programming (control group). You find that 1 month after you delivered the CBT program, 20 inmates from the treatment group were disciplined for misconduct, compared to 45 inmates in the control group. Use the `prop.test()` function to determine whether there is a statistically significant difference in misconduct between the two groups. Be sure to specify the direction of your hypothesis using the `alternative=` option.

Problem 2:

Using the methods explained in the above section, *Confidence Intervals and Hypothesis Testing with Proportions*, and the `BinomCI()` function, calculate confidence intervals around the proportions of inmates who were disciplined for misconduct in the follow-up period in both the treatment and control groups. Make sure you pick a suitable alpha-level (using `conf.level=` and justifying why you think this is best). Then visualize the proportions and their confidence intervals using `geom_errorbar()`, and draw conclusions about whether you should roll out this CBT program widely in your prison.

Problem 3:

Let's suppose that your prison is very limited in budget and your intervention (the CBT program) will only receive funding if we can be very sure that it works. Thinking about type 1 error (false-positive) and type 2 error (false-negative), which one do you think you want to be more strict about avoiding if you need to be sure that your intervention works? How might you adjust your alpha-level to reflect this? Revisit your work for Problem 1 and Problem 2 using this new confidence level, and discuss how your results might have changed, if at all.

Key Terms

Binomial distribution The probability or sampling distribution for an event that has only two possible outcomes.

Directional hypothesis A research hypothesis that indicates a specific type of outcome by specifying the nature of the relationship that is expected.

External validity The extent to which a study sample is reflective of the population from which it is drawn. A study is said to have high external validity when the sample used is representative of the population to which inferences are made.

Non-directional hypothesis A research hypothesis that does not indicate a specific type of outcome, stating only that there is a relationship or a difference.

Nonparametric tests Tests that do not make an assumption about the distribution of the population, also called distribution-free tests.

Null hypothesis A statement that reduces the research question to a simple assertion to be tested by the researcher. The null hypothesis normally suggests that there is no relationship or no difference.

Parametric tests Tests that make an assumption about the shape of the population distribution.

Type I error Also known as alpha error and false-positive. The mistake made when a researcher rejects the null hypothesis on the basis of a sample statistic (i.e., claiming that there is a relationship) when in fact the null hypothesis is true (i.e., there is actually no such relationship in the population).

Functions Introduced in this Chapter

FUNCTION	DESCRIPTION (PACKAGE)
BinomCI()	Compute confidence intervals for binomial proportions (DescTools)
prop.test()	Test null hypothesis that proportions in groups are the same (base R)

References

Agresti, A., & Coull, B. A. (1998). Approximate is better than "exact" for interval estimation of binomial proportions. *The American Statistician, 52*(2), 119–126.

Brown, L. D., Cai, T. T., & DasGupta, A. (2001). Interval estimation for a binomial proportion. *Statistical Science, 16*(2), 101–117.

Wilson, E. B. (1927). Probable inference, the law of succession, and statistical inference. *Journal of the American Statistical Association, 22*(158), 209–212.

Chi-Square and Contingency Tables

Topics Practiced

Interpreting a two-way contingency table

Tests for association between two categorical variables (chi-square and Fisher's exact tests)

Technical Skills Covered

Produce a two-way contingency table

Conduct chi-square and Fisher's exact tests

Calculate residuals in a two-way contingency table

R Packages Required

dplyr, forcats, gmodels, haven, here

A. Wooditch et al., *A Beginner's Guide to Statistics for Criminology and
Criminal Justice Using R*, https://doi.org/10.1007/978-3-030-50625-4_9

T HIS CHAPTER INTRODUCES methods to explore the relationship between two categorical variables (either measured at the nominal or ordinal levels) using the British Crime Survey data. We will cover how to tabulate and visualize this kind of relationships using a two-way contingency table (also referred to as cross tabulation or cross tabs), but also review the chi-square test (χ^2 test), which is the statistical significance test used to infer association in these cases. The chapter also covers Fisher's exact test and calculation of residuals (difference between observed and expected frequencies).

Data

Dataset Source: British Crime Survey

File Name: bcs_2007_8_teaching_data_unrestricted.dta

Dataset Description: The British Crime Survey is the main victimization survey in England and Wales, which as obtained from the UK Data Service (2009) for years 2007 and 2008. For this chapter, we use a subset of the survey data that have been prepared for teaching and learning purposes by the UK Data Service.

Getting Started

1. Open up your existing R project as outlined in Chap. 2 (see also Appendix 1.3).

2. Install and load the required packages using the `install.packages()` and `library()` functions (see Appendix 1.1).

3. Open the 2007–2008 wave of the British Crime Survey dataset (*bcs_2007_8_teaching_data_unrestricted.dta*) using the `read_dta()` function to import the dataset (Appendix 1.6.9.), specifying the working directory with `here()` (see Appendix 1.3). When doing so, name the data frame `BCS0708` by using the `<-` assignment operator.

4. Use `View(BCS0708)` to make sure the file loaded successfully and to get a feel for the data structure. You can also use `dim(BCS0708)` to see the number of observations and variables.

Contingency Tables (Cross Tabs)

Cross tabulations, also called **contingency tables**, are essentially crossed frequency distributions where you plot the frequency distributions of more than one variable simultaneously. Here we are only going to explore *two-way cross tabulations*. While we are going to conduct a contingency table where we plot the frequency distribution of two variables at the same time, you could have cross tabulations with more than two crossed variables.

Frequency distributions are a useful way of exploring categorical variables that do not have too many categories. By extension, cross tabulations are a useful way of exploring relationships between two categorical variables that do not have too many levels or categories.

We will start by producing a cross tabulation of victimization (bcsvictim variable), a categorical unordered variable, by whether the presence of rubbish (in the United States is referred to as garbage or litter) in the streets is a problem in the area of residence of the survey respondent (rubbcomm variable), another categorical, unordered variable. Broken windows theory would argue that we should see a relationship between the two variables.

Before we use these variables, let's have a close look at them. The `attributes()` function allows us to see the different components of an object. If you can think of an object as a box living in a warehouse (your environment or working memory), you can think of the listed attributes as compartments within your box. Each of these compartments has information about your object. In a **haven** labelled object, typically these attributes include the label (which contains a more informative description of the variable than its name), its original format, its class, and the value labels (that explain the correspondence between numbers used to code the responses and the meaning of those numbers).

```
class(BCS0708$bcsvictim)

## [1] "haven_labelled"

class(BCS0708$rubbcomm)

## [1] "haven_labelled"

attributes(BCS0708$bcsvictim)    # 0-Not victim of crime;
                                 # 1-Victim of crime

## $label
## [1] "experience of any crime in the previous 12 months"
##
## $format.stata
## [1] "%8.0g"
##
## $class
## [1] "haven_labelled"
##
## $labels
## not a victim of crime        victim of crime
##                     0                      1

# 5-point Likert-scale ranging from 1 (very common) to
## 4 (not common)
attributes(BCS0708$rubbcomm)
## $label
## [1] "in the immediate area how common is litter\\rubbish"
##
## $format.stata
## [1] "%8.0g"
##
## $class
## [1] "haven_labelled"
##
## $labels
##      very          fairly         not very         not at
     common          common          common       all common
##         1               2                3                4
##         not coded
##                 5

table(BCS0708$bcsvictim)

##
##    0    1
## 9318 2358

table(BCS0708$rubbcomm)

##
##    1    2    3    4
##  204 1244 4154 5463
```

These columns are both **haven** labelled vectors, and we can see the different labels associated with the various levels in these categorical variables. If, rather than the actual values, you want a frequency distribution with the labels, you can use the **as_factor()** function from the **dplyr** package within your **table()** call.

```
table(as_factor(BCS0708$bcsvictim))

##
## not a victim of crime        victim of crime
##                 9318                   2358

table(as_factor(BCS0708$rubbcomm))

##
##    very          fairly        not very        not at
##    common        common        common          all common
##       204           1244            4154              5463
##    not coded
##         0
```

We can also check whether we have responses for all survey respondents. We have already used **is.na()** in a previous chapter. We can use **sum()** to count the number of **NA** data in a given variable.

```
sum(is.na(BCS0708$bcsvictim))

## [1] 0

sum(is.na(BCS0708$rubbcomm)) # Value of 5 indicates missing

## [1] 611
```

As it is common in survey data, we can see that we lack valid information for some respondents ($n = 611$), but only for one of the variables. It is important to keep in mind that all the statistical tests we cover in this volume rely on *full case analysis* approaches. That is, they exclude from any consideration cases for which we lack valid information. In other words, the analysis is only done on cases for which you have valid information for all respondents (thus the name). Just be mindful that there are more advanced approaches that go beyond the scope of this book for dealing with missing data in a more sophisticated and appropriate manner should that arise in the future.

We can get results from **R** in a variety of ways. You can produce basic tables with some of the core functions in **R**.

```
table(as_factor(BCS0708$bcsvictim),
      as_factor(BCS0708$rubbcomm))

##
##                               very       fairly     not very
##                               common     common     common
##    not a victim of crime      141        876        3173
##    victim of crime             63        368         981
##
##                            not at all common not coded
##    not a victim of crime              4614         0
##    victim of crime                     849         0
```

In this format, we see the observed number of cases for each combination of the two variables.

Previously, we have been using some functions from the **dplyr** package to produce frequency distributions, and you can also use them if you want to explore the relationship between two variables. As we have reviewed in a prior chapter, the **group_by()** function is used to group the tibble by an organizing variable, in this case the <u>rubbcomm</u> variable. This will allow us to perform grouped operations (one of the key assets of the **dplyr** package). After grouping the dataset according to this variable, we are generating a tibble with the **summarize()** function that is going to contain two variable <u>counts</u> that simply count the number of cases in each group, in each level of the <u>rubbcomm</u> variable by using the **n()** function. Then, for the second variable, <u>outcome_1</u>, we are going to compute the mean of positive answers to the victimization question, <u>bcsvictim</u>. This is going to give us the proportion of people that have been victimized within each level of the <u>rubbcomm</u> variable. Last, we are going to use the function **fct_explicit_na()** from the **forcats** package around **as_factor()** so that our missing values get an explicit factor level. See below:

```
results <- BCS0708 %>%
  group_by(fct_explicit_na(as_factor(rubbcomm))) %>%
  summarize(
    count = n(),
    outcome_1 = mean(bcsvictim))


# Auto-print the results stored in the newly created object
results

## # A tibble: 5 x 3
##   `fct_explicit_na(as_factor(rubbcomm))`  count outcome_1
##   <fct>                                   <int>     <dbl>
## 1 very common                               204     0.309
## 2 fairly common                            1244     0.296
## 3 not very common                          4154     0.236
## 4 not at all common                        5463     0.155
## 5 (Missing)                                 611     0.159
```

Here, you can see the proportion of victimized individuals within each of the levels of our categorical, ordered measure of rubbish in the area. We can observe that victimization tends to be higher (31%) in the smaller set of areas in which rubbish in the streets is a very common problem. Also, it is important to note here that we are able to use the **mean()** function in this instance because the variable is binary and because it is coded as *0* and *1*. Otherwise, we would not be using measures of central tendency on a categorical variable.

Storing and Representing Contingency Tables in R

So, as we have seen, there are many ways to create a contingency table in R. But there are also different ways, at least three, to store the underlying data for these tables, and sometimes for particular purposes, you may have to shift from one way to another.

These forms are:

1. *Case Form*. This is basically when you have a data frame with micro data related to cases and information in the two variables you are crossing for each individual case as in our **BCS0708** object.

2. *Frequency Form*. This is when you have a data frame with the variables you are crossing, and another variable often called *freq* or *count* that tells you the observed count on each cell.

3. *Table Form*. This is a table, array, or matrix, whose elements are the frequencies in a n-way table.

So, for example, we could obtain the frequency form for our previous cross tab with the following code:

```
table_df <- as.data.frame(table(BCS0708$bcsvictim,
                                BCS0708$rubbcomm))
str(table_df)

## 'data.frame':    8 obs. of  3 variables:
## $ Var1: Factor w/ 2 levels "0","1": 1 2 1 2 1 2 1 2
## $ Var2: Factor w/ 4 levels "1","2","3","4": 1 1 2 2
##                                              3 3 4 4
## $ Freq: int  141 63 876 368 3173 981 4614 849
```

And the table form, as follows:

```
table_tf <- table(BCS0708$bcsvictim, BCS0708$rubbcomm)


str(table_tf)

## 'table' int [1:2, 1:4] 141 63 876 368 3173 981 4614 849
## - attr(*, "dimnames")=List of 2
## ..$ : chr [1:2] "0" "1"
## ..$ : chr [1:4] "1" "2" "3" "4"
```

Contingency Tables with gmodels

For exploring contingency tables, one of the best packages around is gmodels. This package allows you to produce cross tabulations in a format similar to the one used by commercial statistical packages such as SPSS and SAS. We use the **CrossTable()** function from this package. To save that typing, we use the **with()** function to identify the data frame at the outset rather than having to prefix each variable with the name of the data frame.

The structure of the arguments is quite straightforward. First, you identify the variable that is going to define the rows in your table (rubbcomm) and then the variable that will define the columns (bcsvictim). The default for the **CrossTable()** function is to run a chi-square test. But, before we do this and explain this test, let's just focus on the basic elements of the table (so we will set the default to **FALSE**), and then we specify the format to resemble that of contingency tables in the proprietary software SPSS.

```
with(BCS0708, CrossTable(as_factor(rubbcomm),
  as_factor(bcsvictim),
  prop.chisq = FALSE,
  format = c("SPSS")))
```

```
##
##    Cell Contents
## |-------------------------|
## |                   Count |
## |             Row Percent |
## |          Column Percent |
## |           Total Percent |
## |-------------------------|
##
## Total Observations in Table:  11065
##
## as_factor  |as_factor(bcsvictim)  victim of   Row
## (rubbcomm) |not a victim of crime | crime     | Total   |
## -----------|----------------------|-----------|---------|
## very       |                  141 |        63 |     204 |
## common     |              69.118% |   30.882% |  1.844% |
##            |               1.602% |    2.786% |         |
##            |               1.274% |    0.569% |         |
## -----------|----------------------|-----------|---------|
## fairly     |                  876 |       368 |    1244 |
## common     |              70.418% |   29.582% | 11.243% |
##            |               9.950% |   16.276% |         |
##            |               7.917% |    3.326% |         |
## -----------|----------------------|-----------|---------|
## not very   |                 3173 |       981 |    4154 |
## common     |              76.384% |   23.616% | 37.542% |
##            |              36.040% |   43.388% |         |
##            |              28.676% |    8.866% |         |
## -----------|----------------------|-----------|---------|
## not at all |                 4614 |       849 |    5463 |
## common     |              84.459% |   15.541% | 49.372% |
##            |              52.408% |   37.550% |         |
##            |              41.699% |    7.673% |         |
## -----------|----------------------|-----------|---------|
## Column     |                 8804 |      2261 |   11065 |
## Total      |                      |           |         |
##            |              79.566% |   20.434% |         |
## -----------|----------------------|-----------|---------|
##
##
```

The cells for the central two columns represent the total number of cases in each category, the *row percentages*, the *column percentages*, and the *total percentages*. So you have, for example, 63 people in the category *rubbish is very common* that were victims of a crime; this represents 30.88% of all the people in the *rubbish is very common* category (your row percent), 2.79% of all the people in the *victim of a crime* category (your column percent), and 0.57% of all the people in the sample.

You are only interested in the proportions or percentages that allow you to make meaningful comparisons. Although you can do cross tabs for variables in which a priori you don't think of one of them as the one doing the explaining (your independent variable) and another to be explained (your dependent variable), most often you will already be thinking of them in this way. Here, if you are a fervent believer in broken windows theory, you may think of victimization as the outcome we want to explain and *rubbish in the area* as the feature that may help us to explain variation in victimization.

If you have a dependent variable, you need to request only the percentages that allow you to make comparisons across your independent variable (how common rubbish is) for the outcome of interest (victimization). In this case, with our outcome (victimization) defining the columns, we would request and compare the row percentages only. On the other hand, if our outcome were the variable defining the rows, we would be interested instead in the column percentages. Pay very close attention to this. It is a very common mistake to interpret a cross tab the wrong way if you don't do as explained here.

To reiterate then, there are two rules to producing and reading cross tabs the right way. First, *if your dependent variable is defining the rows, then you ask for the column percentages, but on the other hand, if you decided that you preferred to have your dependent variable defining the columns (as seen here), then you would need to ask for the row percentages.*

Make sure you remember this. But also keep in mind that whether you can treat a variable as explanatory is something that needs to be justified by your research design and that with cross-sectional observational data, such as with the crime survey we are studying here, it is impossible to tell what is explaining (or causing) what.

To avoid confusion when looking at the table, you could as well modify the code to only ask for the relevant percentages. In this case, we will ask for the row percentages. We can control what gets printed in the main console using the different options of the `CrossTable()` function. By default, this function prints all the percentages, but most of them are not terribly useful for our purposes here. So, we are going to modify the default options by asking R not to print the column percentages (not the total).

```
with(BCS0708, CrossTable(as_factor(rubbcomm),
  as_factor(bcsvictim),
  prop.chisq = FALSE,
  prop.c = FALSE,
  prop.t = FALSE,
  format = c("SPSS")))
##
##     Cell Contents
## |-------------------------|
## |                   Count |
## |             Row Percent |
## |-------------------------|
##
## Total Observations in Table:  11065
##
## as_factor  |as_factor(bcsvictim)    victim of     Row
## (rubbcomm) |not a victim of crime | crime       | Total   |
## -----------|----------------------|-------------|---------|
## very       |                  141 |          63 |     204 |
## common     |              69.118% |     30.882% |  1.844% |
## -----------|----------------------|-------------|---------|
## fairly     |                  876 |         368 |    1244 |
## common     |              70.418% |     29.582% | 11.243% |
## -----------|----------------------|-------------|---------|
## not very   |                 3173 |         981 |    4154 |
## common     |              76.384% |     23.616% | 37.542% |
## -----------|----------------------|-------------|---------|
## not at all |                 4614 |         849 |    5463 |
## common     |              84.459% |     15.541% | 49.372% |
## -----------|----------------------|-------------|---------|
## Column     |                 8804 |        2261 |   11065 |
## Total      |                      |             |         |
## -----------|----------------------|-------------|---------|
##
##
```

See? Much less cluttered. Now, we only see the counts and the row percentages. **Marginal** frequencies appear along the right and the bottom. *Row marginals* show the total number of cases in each row: 204 people perceive rubbish as very common in the area where they're living, 1244 perceive rubbish is fairly common in their area, etc. *Column marginals* indicate the total number of cases in each column: 9318 non-victims and 2358 victims.

In the central cells, we see the total number for each combination of categories and now only the row percentage. So, the total in each of those cells is expressed as the percentage of cases in that row. For example, 63 people who perceive rubbish as very common in their area who are also a victim of a crime represent 30.88% of all people in that row ($n = 204$). If we had asked for the column percentages, the 63 people who live in areas where rubbish is very common and area also victims would be divided by the 2261 people in the study who reported being a victim of a crime. As such, *changing the denominator when computing the percentage changes the meaning of the percentage.*

The second rule for reading cross tabulations the right way is as follows: *you make the comparisons across the right percentages (see first rule) in the direction where they do not add up to a hundred.* Another way of saying this is that you compare the percentages for each level of your dependent variable across the levels of your independent variable. In this case, we would, for example, compare what percentage of people who perceive rubbish as common in their area and are victims of crime. We focus on the second column here (being victim of a crime) because typically that's what we want to study and is our outcome of interest (e.g., victimization). We can see rubbish seems to matter a bit. For example, 30.88% of people who live in areas where rubbish is very common have been victimized. By contrast, only 15.54% of people who live in areas where rubbish is not at all common have been victimized in the previous year.

Chi-Square Test and Expected Frequencies

So far, we are only describing our sample. Can we infer the differences we observe in this sample can be generalized to the population from which this sample was drawn? Every time you draw a sample from the same population, the results will be slightly different, and we will have a different combination of people in these cells.

To assess the possibility that the differences we see are simply noise, we carry out a test of statistical significance. This test allows us to examine the null hypothesis that there are no differences in the population. So, our research hypothesis is that there is a relationship between the two variables, while our null hypothesis is that there is not a relationship. We write our hypothesis as follows:

Hypotheses

H_0: Victimization and how common rubbish is in the area are independent (not related to each other).

H_A: Victimization and how common rubbish is in the area are dependent (significantly related to each other).

When examining relationships between categorical variables, we use the chi-square test. You should know what this test does is to contrast the squared average difference between the observed frequencies and the expected frequencies (divided by the expected frequencies). **Expected frequencies** refer to the number of cases you should see in each cell within a contingency table if the two variables we are observing are fully independent, whereas **observed frequencies** relate to what we actually see in our sample. To say another way, expected frequencies is the distribution in the cross tab we would expect if there was no relationship between the two variables.

We can see the expected frequencies for each cell modifying the options of the `CrossTable()` function in the following manner:

```
with(BCS0708, CrossTable(as_factor(rubbcomm),
  as_factor(bcsvictim),
  expected = TRUE,
  prop.c = FALSE,
  prop.t = FALSE,
  format = c("SPSS")
))
##
##    Cell Contents
## |-------------------------|
## |                   Count |
## |         Expected Values |
## |   Chi-square contribution |
## |             Row Percent |
## |-------------------------|
##
## Total Observations in Table:  11065
##
## as_factor  |as_factor(bcsvictim)   victim of   Row
## (rubbcomm) |not a victim of crime | crime     | Total   |
## -----------|----------------------|-----------|---------|
## very       |                  141 |        63 |     204 |
## common     |              162.315 |    41.685 |         |
##            |                2.799 |    10.899 |         |
##            |               36.118% |   30.882% |  1.844% |
## -----------|----------------------|-----------|---------|
## fairly     |                  876 |       368 |    1244 |
## common     |              989.804 |   254.196 |         |
##            |               13.085 |    50.950 |         |
##            |               70.418% |   29.582% | 11.243% |
## -----------|----------------------|-----------|---------|
## not very   |                 3173 |       981 |    4154 |
## common     |             3305.180 |   848.820 |         |
##            |                5.286 |    20.583 |         |
##            |               76.384% |   23.616% | 37.542% |
## -----------|----------------------|-----------|---------|
## not at all |                 4614 |       849 |    5463 |
## common     |             4346.701 |  1116.299 |         |
##            |               16.437 |    64.005 |         |
##            |               84.459% |   15.541% | 49.372% |
## -----------|----------------------|-----------|---------|
## Column     |                 8804 |      2261 |   11065 |
## Total      |                      |           |         |
## -----------|----------------------|-----------|---------|
##
##
## Statistics for All Table Factors
##
##
## Pearson's Chi-squared test
## ------------------------------------------------------------
## Chi^2 =  184.0443      d.f. = 3      p =  1.180409e-39
##
##
##
##        Minimum expected frequency: 41.68495
```

So, you can see, for example, that although 63 people lived in areas where rubbish was very common and experienced a victimization in the past year, under the null hypothesis of no relationship, we should expect this value to be 41.69. There are more people in this cell than we would expect under the null hypothesis. Therefore, we would conclude that there is a significant relationship between victimization and the presence of rubbish (reject the null hypothesis).

Hypotheses Conclusion

H_0: ~~Victimization and how common rubbish is in the area are independent (not related to each other).~~

H_A: Victimization and how common rubbish is in the area are dependent (significantly related to each other). [REJECT NULL]

The *chi-square test* (1) compares these expected frequencies with the ones we actually observe in each of the cells, (2) then averages the differences across the cells, and (3) produces a **chi-square statistic** (a standardized value, χ^2). We examine this χ^2 value in relation to the chi-square distribution to see how probable/improbable it is.

If this absolute value is large, it will have a small p-value associated with it, and we will be in a position to reject the null hypothesis. We would conclude then that observing such a large chi-square statistic is improbable if the null hypothesis is true. In practice, we don't actually do any of this. Phew! (Not that I'm bitter that my statistics professor in college made me compute every chi-square test by hand... okay, maybe a little bitter.) Nowadays (normally, anyways), the computer does it for us. We just run the chi-square test in our software and look at the p-value in much the same way we have done for other tests. But it is helpful to know what the test is actually doing.

Asking for the expected frequencies with `CrossTable()` automatically prints the results of the chi-square test. In this case, you get a chi-square value of 184.04, with 3 degrees of freedom (df). The df being obtained by the number of rows minus one times the number of columns minus one– $(4 - 1)*(2 - 1)$. The probability associated with this particular value is nearly zero (1.180e-39). This value is considerably lower than the standard alpha level of 0.05. So, these results would lead us to conclude that there is a statistically significant relationship between these two variables.

We are able to reject the null hypothesis that these two variables are independent in the population from which this sample was drawn. In other words, this significant chi-square test means that we can assume that there was indeed a relationship between our indicator of broken windows (rubbish) and victimization in the population of England and Wales in 2007/2008.

If you don't want to use `CrossTable()`, you can rely on the base `chisq.test()` function from base R, which will give you the same chi-square value.

```
chisq.test(BCS0708$rubbcomm, BCS0708$bcsvictim)
##
##   Pearson's Chi-squared test
##
## data:  BCS0708$rubbcomm and BCS0708$bcsvictim
## X-squared = 184.04, df = 3, p-value < 2.2e-16
```

Remember that the chi-square is simply a test of independence and, like any other significance tests, provides limited information. As geographers like to say, "everything is related to everything else." These tests are only checking for full independence only, and they say nothing about the strength of the association. In a later chapter, we study statistics that allow you to make inferences about the strength of the relationship that you may have detected as statistically significant.

Equally, the test says nothing about whether all the cells deviate greatly from independence or whether the results are being driven by differences between the observed and expected frequencies in one or just a few cells.

Fisher's Exact Test and Monte Carlo Approximations

Notice that R is telling us that the minimum expected frequency is 41.68. Why? The chi-square test, for it to work, assumes the cell counts are sufficiently large. Precisely what constitutes *sufficiently large* is a matter of some debate. One rule of thumb is that all expected cell counts should be above 5. If we have small N cells, one alternative is to rely more on *Fisher's exact test* rather than the chi-square test. We don't have to request it here. Our cell Ns are large enough for chi-square to work fine. But, if needed, we could obtain Fisher's exact test with the following code:

```
with(BCS0708, fisher.test(rubbcomm, bcsvictim))
```

You will most likely get an error message telling you to increase the size of the workspace. When this happens, you may try following the recommendation provided (increasing the size of the workspace for the calculation) and using a hybrid approximation of the exact probabilities.

```
fisher.test(BCS0708$rubbcomm, BCS0708$bcsvictim,
            workspace = 2e+07, hybrid = TRUE)
##
##   Fisher's Exact Test for Count Data hybrid using
    asym.chisq. iff
##   (exp=5, perc=80, Emin=1)
##
## data:  BCS0708$rubbcomm and BCS0708$bcsvictim
## p-value < 2.2e-16
## alternative hypothesis: two.sided
```

The *p*-value is still considerably lower than our alpha level of 0.05. So, we can still reach the conclusion that the relationship we observe can be generalized to the population.

Another less extreme solution (if cell Ns are too small) is to use a *p*-value using *Monte Carlo simulation*. This is a way of proceeding that is similar in philosophy to resampling techniques. To obtain such a chi-square test, you could use the `chisq.test()` function and pass an argument requiring that the *p*-value is obtained via resampling simulation.

```
mytable.1 <- table(BCS0708$rubbcomm, BCS0708$bcsvictim)


chisq.test(mytable.1, simulate.p.value = TRUE)

##
## Pearson's Chi-squared test with simulated p-value (based
## on 2000 replicates)
##
## data:  mytable.1
## X-squared = 184.04, df = NA, p-value = 0.0004998
```

Remember that we didn't really need Fisher's test or the simulated *p*-values in this case, but there may be occasions when you need it, as suggested above.

Residuals

If we look at the observed and expected frequencies in the previous cross tabulations, we will see that there are differences in pretty much all the cells. The difference in each cell between the expected and the observed count is called a **residual**. You can possibly notice as well that some differences (residuals) are bigger than others. For example, earlier we saw how there are about 21 more people that live in areas where rubbish is very common and experience victimization than expected under the null hypothesis. Clearly, when you see large differences, you should expect that the cell in question may be playing a particularly strong role in driving the relationship.

But what should we consider *large*? How can we conclude that a residual is particularly important? A statistic that helps in this regard is the *adjusted standardized residuals*, which behaves like a *z*-score (something we cover in a later chapter). These residuals give you an idea of the difference between the expected and the observed counts in a standardized scale. When the null hypothesis is true, there is only about a 5% chance that any particular standardized residual exceeds 2 in absolute value. Whenever you see differences that are greater (in absolute value) than 2, that's telling you that the difference between expected and observed frequencies in that particular cell is significant and is driving the results of your chi-square test. Values above +3 or below −3 are taken as hints of convincing evidence of a true effect in that cell. We can request R to print these residuals with the following code:

```
with(BCS0708, CrossTable(as_factor(rubbcomm),
  as_factor(bcsvictim),
  expected = TRUE,
  prop.chisq = FALSE,
  prop.c = FALSE,
  prop.t = FALSE,
  asresid = TRUE,
  format = c("SPSS")
))
##
##      Cell Contents
## |-------------------------|
## |                   Count |
## |         Expected Values |
## |             Row Percent |
## |            Adj Std Resid |
## |-------------------------|
##
## Total Observations in Table:  11065
##
## as_factor  |as_factor(bcsvictim)   victim of    Row
## (rubbcomm) |not a victim of crime  crime      | Total  |
## -----------|-----------------------|----------|--------|
## very       |                   141 |       63 |    204 |
## common     |               162.315 |   41.685 |        |
##            |               69.118% |  30.882% | 1.844% |
##            |                -3.736 |    3.736 |        |
## ----------|-----------------------|----------|--------|
## fairly     |                   876 |      368 |   1244 |
## common     |               989.804 |  254.196 |        |
##            |               70.418% |  29.582% |11.243% |
##            |                -8.494 |    8.494 |        |
## ----------|-----------------------|----------|--------|
## not very   |                  3173 |      981 |   4154 |
## common     |              3305.180 |  848.820 |        |
##            |               76.384% |  23.616% |37.542% |
##            |                -6.436 |    6.436 |        |
## ----------|-----------------------|----------|--------|
## not at all |                  4614 |      849 |   5463 |
## common     |              4346.701 | 1116.299 |        |
##            |               84.459% |  15.541% |49.372% |
##            |                12.605 |  -12.605 |        |
## ----------|-----------------------|----------|--------|
## Column     |                  8804 |     2261 |  11065 |
## Total
## ----------|-----------------------|----------|--------|
##
##
## Statistics for All Table Factors
##
##
## Pearson's Chi-squared test
## ------------------------------------------------------------
## Chi^2 =  184.0443     d.f. =  3     p =  1.180409e-39
##
##
##
##        Minimum expected frequency: 41.68495
```

You can see here, looking at the column identifying the outcome of interest (victimization), that the adjusted standardized residual is lower than −12 for the *not at all common* category. That is the largest residual for the outcome of interest. The expected count under the null hypothesis here is much higher than the observed count.

Application Activities

Problem 1:

Using `CrossTable()`, produce a cross tabulation and compute the chi-square to study the relationship between ethnicity (ethgrp2) and victimization (bcsvictim) with the **BCS0708** dataset. Write a null and alternative hypothesis. Interpret your results with respect to the null hypothesis and make sure to include the appropriate percentages in your description by adding comments to your syntax.

Problem 2:

Using `CrossTable()`, produce a cross tabulation and compute the chi-square to study the relationship between fear of crime (homealon) and gender (sex). Write a null and alternative hypothesis. Interpret your results with respect to the null hypothesis and make sure to include the appropriate percentages in your description by adding comments to your syntax.

Problem 3:

Using `CrossTable()`, produce a cross tabulation and compute the chi-square to study the relationship between respondents' views on the causes of crime (causem) and whether the respondents are employed (work). Write a null and alternative hypothesis. Interpret your results with respect to the null hypothesis and make sure to include the appropriate percentages in your description by adding comments to your syntax.

Key Terms

Chi-square statistic The test statistic resulting from applying the chi-square formula to the observed and expected frequencies for each cell. This statistic tells us how much the observed distribution differs from that expected under the null hypothesis.

Contingency table A tabular way of viewing the relationship between categorical variables (also referred to as cross tabs).

Expected frequency The number of observations one would predict for a cell in a contingency table if the null hypothesis were true.

Marginal The value in the margin of a table that totals the scores in the appropriate column or row.

Observed frequency The observed result of the study, recorded in a cell of a contingency table.

Residual An index of the relative deviation of the observed frequency from the expected frequency for a cell of a contingency table. It is useful for guiding the interpretation of an association between two nominal variables.

Functions Introduced in this Chapter

FUNCTION	DESCRIPTION (PACKAGE)
chisq.test()	Produces the chi-square test (base **R**)
CrossTable()	Produces contingency tables (**gmodels**)
fct_explicit_na()	Provides missing values an explicit factor level (**forcats**)
fisher.test()	Produces Fisher's exact test (base **R**)
n()	Count observations within summarize(), mutate(), filter() (dplyr)
read_dta()	Imports a *.dta* Stata file (**haven**)
with()	Evaluates an expression, often to specify data you want to use (base **R**)

Reference

Home Office, Research, Development and Statistics Directorate, BMRB, Social Research. (2009). British crime survey, 2007-2008 (3rd ed.) [data file]. UK Data Service. SN: 6066. Retrieved from https://doi.org/10.5255/UKDA-SN-6066-1.

The Normal Distribution and Single-Sample Significance Tests

Topics Practiced

Characteristics of the normal distribution

Single-sample significance testing

Technical Skills Covered

Conducting single-sample z- and t-tests

Writing functions

R Packages Required

stats, tigerstats

A. Wooditch et al., *A Beginner's Guide to Statistics for Criminology and
Criminal Justice Using R*, https://doi.org/10.1007/978-3-030-50625-4_10

IN THIS CHAPTER, we focus on characteristics of the normal distribution and single-sample significance tests that are used for variables measured at the ratio and interval levels. Specifically, this chapter reviews percentages under the normal curve, application of the 68-95-99.7 rule, and how to conduct a significance test in **R** for the following: (1) comparing a sample mean to a *known* population (single-sample z-test for means), (2) comparing a sample mean to an *unknown* population (single-sample t-test), and (3) comparing a sample proportion to a population proportion (single-sample z-test for proportions). In doing so, the chapter walks through criminal justice-related examples, lays out the null and alternative hypotheses for presented examples, and shows the user how to make a determination about the null hypothesis for the aforementioned tests from **R** output. Additionally, you will learn how to write your own functions in **R**.

Data

Dataset Source: Synthetic data created in **R**

File Name: Not applicable

Dataset Description: Synthetic data containing information about IQ scores of prisoners in the United States.

Getting Started

1. Install and load the required packages using the `install.packages()` and `library()` functions (see Appendix 1.1).

The Normal Distribution

As we have already introduced in Chap. 6, the most widely used distribution in statistics is the **normal distribution**. It is sometimes referred to as the *Gaussian distribution* for the reason that two mathematicians, Carl Friedrich Gauss and Robert Adrian, independently identified the bell-shaped distribution when studying measurement error. Since the normal distribution is symmetrical, we already know something about the underlying distribution—50% of estimates are located above the mean and 50% are located below the mean. Let's walk through an example of examining a distribution that we know is normally distributed to see if this holds true. We are going to rely on a simulated dataset of intelligence quotient (IQ) scores, which are normally distributed in the US population ($\mu = 100$; SD = 15). We do this by generating a dataset of simulated IQ scores for the approximately 1.5 million individuals who are incarcerated in US prisons. Then, we are going to test whether approximately half of our population of IQ is above 100 (the mean).

In the code below, the dataset we generate will be put in an object named `PrisonerIQ` by using the `data.frame()` function we learned in an earlier chapter. You will also see that we are creating an ID for each prisoner, which is stored in the <u>prisoner id</u> variable. The function `rnorm()` from the `stats` packages in base **R** will create our IQ distribution, which is based on the Gaussian standard distribution and the mean/SD that we specify in our code ($\mu = 100$; SD = 15). Since IQ is an integer, we nest our `rnorm()` argument within the `round()` function and tell **R** to round IQ so it has *0* decimals (essentially, we want whole numbers) and to store this in a variable named <u>IQ</u>.

Next, we are going to rely on the `which()` function (as specify within it our data frame and variable name) to select a subset of prisoners who have an IQ higher than 100. Notice that we specify the name of the data frame (`PrisonerIQ`), and to the right of it, we have brackets that contain our `which()` function. The comma within the brackets is important here and its location. Our `which()` function is to the left of the comma, indicating to **R** that we are selecting rows (if it were on the other side, it would be selecting columns).

Last, we calculate the proportion in our subset versus in the total population by drawling on the `nrow()` function—dividing the number of prisoners with an IQ higher than 100 by the total number of prisoners in the population. (Your results may be slightly different than ours, but you should see that close to 0.50 of your population should have an IQ higher than the mean.)

```
PrisonerIQ <- data.frame(
  prisoner_id = 1:1500000,
  IQ = round(rnorm(1500000, mean = 100, sd = 15), 0))

IQ_Over_100 <- PrisonerIQ[ which(PrisonerIQ$IQ>100) ,]

nrow(IQ_Over_100)/nrow(PrisonerIQ)

## [1] 0.4867627
```

Perhaps one of the most useful characteristics of a normal distribution is that the percentage of cases between its mean and points at a measured distance from the mean is always fixed. This measure is referred to as the **standard deviation unit**. A **z-score** is used to represent standard deviation units for the standard normal distribution. z-scores range from −4 standard deviations below the mean (left side of the bell curve) to +4 standard deviations above the mean (right side of the bell curve).

In base **R**, the `scale()` function will create z-scores for a given variable based on its mean. In the example below, we create a new column, named *z_scoreIQ*, that contains the calculated z-scores for our *IQ* variable. For it to be easier for you to visualize, let's change the IQ of the first prisoner so their IQ is 115. Based on a distribution with an approximate mean of 100 and standard deviation of 15, that prisoner should have a z-score that is close to the value 1—indicating that their IQ is 1 standard deviation above our population mean.

```
PrisonerIQ[1:5,] # View the first 5 prisoner IQs

##   prisoner_id  IQ
## 1           1 102
## 2           2  87
## 3           3 123
## 4           4  88
## 5           5  86

# Change the IQ of prisoner #1
PrisonerIQ$IQ[1] <- 115

# Create a variable storing z-scores of IQs
PrisonerIQ$z_scoreIQ <- scale(PrisonerIQ$IQ)

# Check to make sure prisoner #1 has a z-score around 1
PrisonerIQ[1,]

##   prisoner_id  IQ z_scoreIQ
## 1           1 115  1.001205
```

Now, suppose an official on the parole board is writing a report on a young prisoner who is coming up for parole. She finds that the young man has an IQ of 124. She wants to give the board a good sense of what this means in terms of how this young man's IQ compares to all other prisoners. A good way of doing that would be to state what proportion of prisoners have an IQ lower than him. This can be done with the `pnormGC()` function in the `tigerstats` package. We just need to provide the prisoner's IQ, the mean of the population, and the standard deviation of the population. For region (referring to what region of the normal distribution), we are going to specify **below** since we are interested in the proportion of prisoners with an IQ below 124. Since the mean and standard deviation of our population are not perfectly 100 and 15, respectively, we are going to compute it and put it in the function.

```
m<-mean(PrisonerIQ$IQ)

sd<-sd(PrisonerIQ$IQ)

pnormGC(124, region="below", mean=m, sd=sd,graph=TRUE)
```

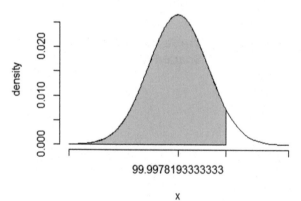

Normal Curve, mean = 100 , SD = 14.98
Shaded Area = 0.9454

```
## [1] 0.9454046
```

And we find that it is 0.9453, so he has a higher IQ than over 94% of the prison population. Pretty smart!

The 68-95-99.7 Rule

Hypothesis testing using the normal distribution is useful because it allows us to convert a given score into a standardized value, referred to as a z-score, and use that information to estimate the probability of that value occurring based on the standard normal distribution. A z-score indicates how far away a score is from the mean based on the standard normal distribution.

In statistics, the empirical rule associated with the normal distribution is the **68-95-99.7 rule**. This states that 68% of the cases in the distribution should fall within 1 standard deviation of the mean (so within a z-score of -1 and $+1$); 95% of the cases in the distribution should fall within 2 standard deviations of the mean (so within a z-score of -2 and $+2$); and 99.7% of the cases in the distribution should fall within 3 standard deviations of the mean (so within a z-score of -3 and $+3$). In the real world, you will likely not find a distribution where this rule is exact.

We can draw on the **pnormGC()** function again to demonstrate this rule by asking the function to tell us the proportion of prisoners that have an IQ between 85 and 115 (minus/plus 1 standard deviation from the mean). We are now going to specify **between** as the region since we are interested in the proportion of prisoners with an IQ between two given values.

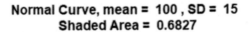

```
pnormGC(bound=c(85, 115),region="between",
    mean=100,sd=15,graph=TRUE)
```

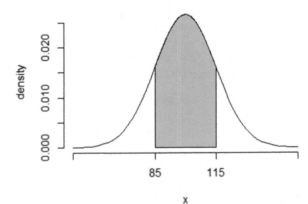

```
## [1] 0.6826895
```

The shaded region on the grade is, indeed, close to 0.68!

Single-Sample *z*-Tests for Means

Let's continue with our example of the official on the parole board. She knows that the prison where she works is low security and, as such, tends to have a lot more white-collar criminals than prisons normally do on average. She wants to know whether the prisoners at her prison have an average IQ that is significantly different than prisoners in all prisons in the United States. The population characteristics for the United States, as discussed above, are known. The mean score for the population is 100, and the standard deviation of the population mean is 15. She conducts an IQ assessment of just those prisoners at the small prison where she is currently working ($n = 233$). She finds that the mean IQ at her prison is 103 (SD = 18), and she would like to know with 99% confidence whether this average IQ is significantly different from the mean of all US prisoners. Because the population parameter of the US population is known, a **single-sample *z*-test** for a known population is appropriate.

Let's set up our null and alternative hypotheses. We just want to test whether they are different, so this will be a non-directional hypothesis.

Hypotheses

H_0: The mean IQ of the population from which our sample of prisoners was drawn is the same as the mean IQ of the US population (mean = 100).

H_A: The mean IQ of the population from which our sample of prisoners was drawn is not the same as the mean IQ of the US population (mean ≠ 100).

So that other prisons can easily compare the IQ of their prisoners to that of all prisoners, we are going to create our own function that they can use, named z_test(). To run the test using the function, the user will have to input the sample mean (named in our function as xbar), the standard deviation of the sample (named sd), the number of prisoners in the sample (named n), and the population mean to which the sample mean should be compared (named mu). Once our function is defined, we can input our estimates into the function to have it return the *z*-score of the sample IQ in relation to the population. Note that we are also going to use the concatenates function in base R, cat(), which will combine our string text to label our *z*-score in the output and the computed *z*-score together.

```
# Specifying inputs in the order that the user needs
## to enter them
z_test<-function(xbar, sd, n, mu) {

    # Equation for one-sample z-test
    z <- (xbar-mu) / (sd / sqrt(n))

    return(cat('z =', z))  # Report z-score to the user

} # End function

# Test it with our example by supplying estimates
z_test(103, 18, 233, 100)
## z = 2.544056
```

You will see that our function conducted the *z*-test and provided the corresponding *z*-score for our example. Now that we have the function providing the *z*-score, let's modify it so it also provides the *p*-value. It relies on the **pnorm()** function in the **stats** package from base R and the **abs()** function in base R (provides absolute value) to compute the probability value. We are going to use \n in our concatenate function, so the *p*-value is reported a different row from *z*-score. Since our hypothesis is non-directional, we multiply the **pnorm()** function by *2* since we are concerned with both sides of the distribution.

```
z_test<-function(xbar, sd, n, mu) {
    z <- (xbar-mu) / (sd / sqrt(n))

    p<-2 * pnorm(-abs(z))  # Added code for p-value
            return( cat('z =', z,
                    '\np-value =', p))  # Added code to return
                                        ## p-value

}

# Test it with our example again
z_test(103, 18, 233, 100)

## z = 2.544056
## p-value = 0.01095734
```

Our function reported our z-score from the z-test, and it now provides the p-value associated with that z-score. The p-value is 0.0109. At the 99% confidence level, we *fail to reject the null hypothesis* since 0.0109 is greater than 0.01. Therefore, we would conclude that the average IQ of prisoners at the given prison is the same as that of all the prisoners.

Hypotheses Conclusion

H_0: The mean IQ of the population from which our sample of prisoners was drawn is the same as the mean IQ of the US population (mean = 100). [FAIL TO REJECT]

H_A: ~~The mean IQ of the population from which our sample of prisoners was drawn is not the same as the mean IQ of the U.S. population (mean ≠ 100).~~

Single-Sample z-Tests for Proportions

Suppose that you were asked to evaluate a new prison education program. The foundation sponsoring the effort sought to achieve a program success rate of 75% among the 100,000 prisoners enrolled in the program. Success was defined as completion of a 6-month course supported by the foundation. Managers of the program claim that the success rate is actually much greater than the criteria set by the foundation. However, a recent newspaper exposé claims that the success rate of the program is actually much lower than 75%. You are able to collect information on 150 prisoners, selected using independent random sampling. You find that 85% of your sample successfully completed the course. What conclusions can you make about the claims of managers and the newspaper exposé based on your sample results? Our research hypothesis is non-directional. Managers of the program claim that the program has a success rate of greater than 0.75% ($P > 0.75$). The newspaper exposé claims that the success rate is much lower than 75% ($P < 0.75$). Accordingly, we want to be able to examine both of these potential outcomes in our test. The null hypothesis is that the rate of success for the program is 75% ($P = 0.75$). To examine this, we are going to conduct a single-sample z-test for proportions.

Hypotheses

H_0: The success rate of the program is 75% ($P = 0.75$).

H_A: The success rate of the program is not 75% ($P \neq 0.75$).

Let's set up our null and alternative hypotheses. We just want to test whether there is a difference, so this will be a non-directional hypothesis.

To conduct our single-sample z-test for proportions, let's create a function like we did in the prior section. The user inputs will be the proportion successes of the sample (p), the proportion successes of the population (P), and the sample size (n).

```
prop_z_test<-function(p, P, n) { # Specifying inputs

    Numerator<-(p - P)

    PQ<- P * (1-P)
    Denominator<-sqrt(PQ / n)  # Standard error

    z<- Numerator /
        Denominator

  return(z)  # Return the z-value to the user
}

# Let's test it using the values from our problem
prop_z_test(0.85, 0.75, 150)

## [1] 2.828427
```

If you run the test and you get a z-value of 2.828427, then congrats! You wrote your function correctly. This p-value is statistically significant, so we would reject our null hypothesis and conclude that the success rate is not 75%.

Hypotheses Conclusion

H_0: The success rate of the program is 75% ($P = 0.75$).

H_A: The success rate of the program is not 75% ($P \neq 0.75$). [REJECT NULL]

Single-Sample t-Tests for Means

When you are comparing a sample mean to a known population, you should use the z-distribution. However, when you are comparing a sample mean to an unknown population, you should use the t-distribution (which has a larger variance than the normal distribution/z-distribution), a

single-sample *t*-test. Therefore, rather than using *N* in the denominator, we use *n – 1* (the degrees of freedom).

To illustrate this, let us turn to a practical example. Suppose that the study described in the prior section also examined the average test scores for those prisoners who had completed the program. The foundation set a standard of success of 65 on the test. Program managers say that prisoners who have completed the program achieve average scores much higher than this. The newspaper exposé again claims that the average scores are considerably lower than those expected by the foundation. In this case, you are able to take an independent random sample of 51 prisoners who have completed the test. You find that the test mean for the sample is 60 and the standard deviation is 15 (using the *n – 1* formula). What conclusions about the larger population of prisoners can you draw based on your sample results at the 95% confidence level? Let's first set up our hypotheses…

Hypotheses

H_0: The mean test score for prisoners who have completed the program is 65 ($\mu = 65$).

H_A: The mean test score for prisoners who have completed the program is not 65 ($\mu \neq 65$).

We are now going to take the code from our `z_test()` function we created earlier in the chapter and are going to modify it. First, change the name of the function to `single_t_test`. Second, change `sqrt(n)` in the equation to `sqrt(n - 1)`. And third, change all instances of the letter `z` to `t`.

Applying the *t*-formula to our example, we use the mean of the sample, 60, as <u>xbar</u>; <u>sd</u> is our sample standard deviation of 15; <u>n</u> is the number of cases for our sample (51); and <u>mu</u> is defined by the null hypothesis as 65.

```
single_t_test<-function(xbar, sd, n, mu) { # Specifying inputs

    # Equation for one-sample z-test
    t <- (xbar-mu) / (sd / sqrt(n - 1))

    return(cat('t =', t))   # Report z-score to the user
}
# Test it with our example
single_t_test(60, 15, 51, 65)
## t = -2.357023
```

This observed *t*-value is statistically significant, so we would reject the null hypothesis and conclude that the mean test score for prisoners who have completed the program is not 65 ($\mu \neq 65$).

Hypotheses Conclusion

~~H₀: The mean test score for prisoners who have completed the program is 65 ($\mu = 65$).~~

H_A: The mean test score for prisoners who have completed the program is not 65 ($\mu \neq 65$). [REJECT NULL]

If we want to calculate our **confidence intervals** around the sample mean, you will want to use the *t*-distribution as well. With a 95% confidence level and 50 degrees of freedom, the critical value of *t* is 2.009.

Application Activities

Problem 1:

Modify the `z_test()` function we created so you can conduct a 1-tailed test to see whether the sample mean is more than the population mean. Instead of the function reporting the *z*-score on the first row, have it provide the sample mean and population mean being compared, along with an appropriate label such as *Sample vs Population Mean:*. Using the same data as the example, what is your null hypothesis and what are your conclusions about the null hypothesis from the test?

Problem 2:

Similar to the `z_test()` function we wrote, modify the `prop_z_test()` function to have it also return the following: (1) the *p*-value associated with the *z*-score and (2) the 95% confidence intervals of the proportion (hint: add and subtract the **Denominator * 1.96**).

Problem 3:

Add to the `single_t_test()` function by modifying and incorporating the code below so it also reports the lower and upper 99% confidence interval. Then, test out your revised function using the same example data. Note that the critical value for *t* at the 99% confidence interval and 50 degrees of freedom is 2.678.

```
# The sample mean plus/minus critical t (2.009) *
## standard deviation (15) / sample size (n - 1)

# Upper 95% CI
60 + 2.009 * (15 / sqrt(51 - 1))

## [1] 64.26173

# Lower 95% CI
60 - 2.009 * (15 / sqrt(51 - 1))

## [1] 55.73827
```

Key Terms

68-95-99.7 rule Empirical rule that states that 68% of the cases in a normal distribution should fall within 1 standard deviation of the mean (so within a z-score of -1 and $+1$); 95% of the cases in the distribution should fall within 2 standard deviations of the mean (so within a z-score of -2 and $+2$); and 99.7% of the cases in the distribution should fall within 3 standard deviations of the mean (so within a z-score of -3 and $+3$). In the real world, you will likely not find a distribution where this rule is exact.

Confidence interval An interval of values around a statistic (usually a point estimate). If we were to draw repeated samples and calculate a 95% confidence interval for each, then in only 5 in 100 of these samples would the interval fail to include the true population parameter. In the case of a 99% confidence interval, only 1 in 100 samples would fail to include the true population parameter.

Normal distribution A bell-shaped frequency distribution, symmetrical in form. Its mean, mode, and median are always the same. The percentage of cases between the mean and points at a measured distance from the mean is fixed.

Single-sample t-test A test of statistical significance that is used to examine whether a sample is drawn from a specific population with a known or hypothesized mean. In a t-test, the standard deviation of the population to which the sample is being compared is unknown.

Single-sample z-test A test of statistical significance that is used to examine whether a sample is drawn from a specific population with a known or hypothesized mean. In a z-test, the standard deviation of the population to which the sample is being compared is either known or—as in the case of a proportion—is defined by the null hypothesis.

Standard deviation unit A unit of measurement used to describe the deviation of a specific score or value from the mean in a z distribution.

z-score Score that represents an observation in standard deviation units from the mean.

Functions Introduced in this Chapter

FUNCTION	DESCRIPTION (PACKAGE)
cat()	Combines/concatenates character values and prints them (base **R**)
function()	Creates a user-specified function (base **R**)
pnorm()	Probability of random variable following normal distribution (**stats**)
pnormGC()	Compute probabilities for normal random variables (**tigerstats**)
prop_z_test()	Single-sample *z*-test for proportions we created in this chapter
return()	Used in functions to tell **R** what to return/print for the user (base **R**)
scale()	Mean centers or rescales a numeric variable (base **R**)
single_t_test()	Function created in this chapter for single-sample *t*-tests for means
which()	Provides the position of the elements such as in a row (base **R**)
z_test()	Function created in this chapter for a single-sample *z*-test

Comparing Two-Sample Means or Proportions

Topics Practiced

Comparing means or proportions in two samples

Technical Skills Covered

Conducting *F*-test to compare two sample variances

Conducting independent sample *t*-test (two means)

Conducting dependent sample *t*-tests (two means)

Conducting *z*-test for two sample proportions

R Packages Required

dplyr, haven, here, labelled, skimr, tidyverse

A. Wooditch et al., *A Beginner's Guide to Statistics for Criminology and
Criminal Justice Using R*, https://doi.org/10.1007/978-3-030-50625-4_11

IN CRIMINAL JUSTICE RESEARCH, we are often interested in comparing the means or proportions in two samples of data, either two different groups, the same group across time (before/after), or two related samples (e.g., comparing twins). In this chapter, we will walk through using the independent sample *t*-test for two sample means, dependent sample *t*-test for two sample means, or *z*-test to compare means and proportions in R using data from the *National Youth Survey*, which is a nationally representative survey of 1725 American adolescents, aged 11–17, to gauge adolescents' attitudes and behaviors on various topics, including school performance, family life, deviance, drug use, and peer influence.

Data

Dataset Source: National Youth Survey (NYS)

File Name: nys_1_ID.dta; nys_2_ID.dta

Dataset Description: The nys_1_ID.dta and nys_2_ID.dta datasets are, respectively, subsets of waves 1 and 2 of the National Youth Survey (Elliott, 2008a, 2008b). Conducted in 1976 and 1977, the respondents for this survey are a nationally representative sample of American adolescents, aged 11–17. The datasets contain responses from 1725 adolescents and are composed of a series of questions that gauge adolescents' attitudes and behaviors on various topics, including school performance, family life, deviance, drug use, and peer influence.

Getting Started

1. Open your existing R project as outlined in Chap. 2 (see also Appendix 1.3).

2. Install and load the required packages using the `install.packages()` and `library()` functions (see Appendix 1.1).

3. Open the National Youth Survey datasets (*nys_1_ID.dta* and *nys_2_ ID.dta*) using the `read_dta()` function to import the datasets (see Appendix 1.6.7), specifying the working directory with `here()` (see Appendix 1.3). When doing so, respectively name the data frames `nys_1` and `nys_2` by using the `<-` assignment operator.

4. Use `View(nys_1)` and `View(nys_2)` to make sure the files loaded successfully and to get a feel for the data structure.

5. And because we are never very good at figuring out that scientific notation stuff, we are going to turn it off with this code: `options(scipen=999)`.

Comparing Two Independent Sample Means

If we are interested in comparing the means from two independent samples, such as comparing the mean recidivism risk score between males and females who are on probation in Washington, D.C., we would use an **independent sample *t*-test** (which is also referred to as an *unpaired t-test*). Since we are interested in mean differences, the dependent variable must be ratio or interval and normally distributed unless N is large, and the independent variable (the two groups you are comparing) must be binary. In this next example, we are comparing males and females on their alcohol usage, so our independent variable satisfies the two-group requirement without a need for recoding our variable. We are conducting an independent sample *t*-test because the two samples are not related/dependent.

For this example, we are interested in whether there is a significant difference between males and females in the mean number of times they reported being drunk in the prior year. Let's write out our null and alternative hypothesis.

Hypotheses

H_0: There is no significant difference in frequency of getting drunk between males and females in the prior year.

H_A: There is a significant difference in frequency of getting drunk between males and females in the prior year.

In our `nys_1` data frame, the variable measuring this is aptly named <u>drunk</u>. Before running our *t*-tests, we first need to check whether our grouping variable needs any recoding. To do this, we will use some of the lessons learned in Chaps. 2, 4, and 5. Specifically, let's use the `summarize()` function from `dplyr` to examine the variable for gender (<u>sex</u> variable). We also rely on the `n()` function to obtain frequencies.

```
# Examining distribution of the gender variable
nys_1 %>% group_by(sex) %>% summarize(n = n())

## # A tibble: 2 x 2
##           sex       n
##     <dbl+lbl> <int>
## 1 1 [Male]      918
## 2 2 [Female]    807
```

The output above shows us that there are 918 males and 807 females in our data frame. Importantly, this also shows us how each value is coded and labeled. Males are given a value of 1, and females are given a value of 2. You may want to recode this variable and add/remove value labels. Let's create a dummy variable named <u>female</u> to add to our `nys_1` data frame, where a value of 1 indicates a female and 0 indicates a male.

```
# First, recode sex variable and store it in a new variable
nys_1$female <- recode(nys_1$sex, '2' = 1, '1' = 0)

# Next, label the values
nys_1 <- nys_1 %>% add_value_labels(female=
    c("Female"=1, "Male"=0))

# Check they were added correctly by getting frequencies
count(nys_1, female)

## # A tibble: 2 x 2
##        female       n
##     <dbl+lbl> <int>
## 1 0 [Male]      918
## 2 1 [Female]    807
```

Now, let's take a look at our dependent variable. Since we have coded our grouping variable, we will also want to examine the dependent variable by group (<u>female</u>). We see from the output that our missing values have already been defined.

```
# Use skim() function from skimr package to examine
## drunk variable
skim(nys_1, drunk)
```

Data summary

NAME	NYS_1
Number of rows	1725
Number of columns	26
Column type frequency:	
numeric	1
Group variables	None

Variable type: numeric

SKIM_VARIABLE	N_MISSING	COMPLETE_RATE	MEAN	SD	P0	P25	P50	P75	P100	HIST
drunk	6	1	1.24	10.48	0	0	0	0	250	▮____

```
# skimr
nys_1 %>% group_by(female) %>% skim(drunk)
```

Data summary

NAME	PIPED DATA
Number of rows	1725
Number of columns	26
Column type frequency:	
numeric	1
Group variables	female

Variable type: numeric

SKIM_VARIABLE	FEMALE	N_MISSING	COMPLETE_RATE	MEAN	SD	P0	P25	P50	P75	P100	HIST
drunk	0	3	1	1.61	11.75	0	0	0	0	250	▮____
drunk	1	3	1	0.82	8.82	0	0	0	0	240	▮____

It is clear that most youth in the sample did not report getting drunk at all in the year prior to the interview. Male youth also reported being drunk slightly more often than the females in the sample. It *appears* that there may be a difference between males and females, but is this a statistically significant difference?

Test for Equality of Variance

Before we can run our *t*-test, we need to test whether the variances of getting drunk by sex are equal because it affects how to specify our *t*-test. We use a **test for equality of variance** via the *F*-test.

Use *F*-test to compare variances. Notice that the dependent variable comes first and then your grouping variable.

```
var.test(nys_1$drunk~nys_1$female)

##
##  F test to compare two variances
##
## data:  nys_1$drunk by nys_1$female
## F = 1.7729, num df = 914, denom df = 803,
    p-value < 0.00000000000000022
## alternative hypothesis: true ratio of variances is
    not equal to 1
## 95 percent confidence interval:
##  1.549899 2.026885
## sample estimates:
## ratio of variances
##            1.772941
```

This function gives us a lot of information, but the most important pieces you will want to note for our purposes are the alternative hypothesis and the *F*-statistic and associated *p*-value. R tells us that the alternative hypothesis for this test is that the variances do not have a ratio of 1; in other words, they are *not* equal. Since our *p*-value is very small, we easily reject the null hypothesis that the variances are equal in favor of the alternative hypothesis that they are not. This is an important step in that it lets us know that we should set `var.equal` to FALSE when we conduct our independent sample *t*-test.

Independent Sample *t*-Test for Two Means

Now we are going to conduct our independent sample *t*-test, setting `var.equal = FALSE` based on the information we obtained from our `var.test()` in the prior section.

```
# Run the t-test with var.equal option set to FALSE
t.test(nys_1$drunk~nys_1$female, var.equal = FALSE)

##
##  Welch Two Sample t-test
##
## data:  nys_1$drunk by nys_1$female
## t = 1.5994, df = 1677.3, p-value = 0.1099
## alternative hypothesis: true difference in means
   is not equal to 0
## 95 percent confidence interval:
##  -0.1800974  1.7716968
## sample estimates:
## mean in group 0 mean in group 1
##        1.614208        0.818408
```

Remember that you can save your test results in an object if you need to refer to it later. For example:

```
t_test_results <- t.test(nys_1$drunk~nys_1$female,
      var.equal = FALSE)

# Print independent t-test results
t_test_results

##
##  Welch Two Sample t-test
##
## data:  nys_1$drunk by nys_1$female
## t = 1.5994, df = 1677.3, p-value = 0.1099
## alternative hypothesis: true difference in means is
   not equal to 0
## 95 percent confidence interval:
##  -0.1800974  1.7716968
## sample estimates:
## mean in group 0 mean in group 1
##        1.614208        0.818408
```

Note that the **t.test()** function gives us all kinds of helpful output that helps us in our interpretation. You will want to pay extra special attention to the alternative hypothesis that is provided with the output, the t-statistic, and p-value and the 95% confidence interval. From the output, we know male youth got drunk an average of 1.6 times the year before, whereas females got drunk an average of 0.8 times. The p-value is greater than the standard threshold of 0.05 ($p = 0.1099$); therefore, we *fail to reject the null* *hypothesis*. We conclude that the true difference in means is not significantly different from 0. In other words, we find based on this test that there is *no significant difference in frequency of getting drunk between males and females in the prior year.*

Hypotheses Conclusion

H_0: There is no significant difference in frequency of getting drunk between males and females in the prior year. [FAIL TO REJECT]

H_A: ~~There is a significant difference in frequency of getting drunk between males and females in the prior year.~~

Comparing Two Independent Sample Proportions

You can compare independent sample *proportions* using the z-test. The z-test comparing two proportions is equivalent to the chi-square test of independence, and the `prop.test()` function formally calculates the chi-square test.

For this example, we are interested in whether the proportion of male youth who hit another student last year (hit_stdt variable) is significantly *higher* than the proportion of female youth who hit another student (female variable). Let's write out our null and alternative hypothesis (note that this is a directional hypothesis).

Hypotheses

H_0: The proportion of males who have hit another student is not greater than the proportion of females who have hit another student.

H_A: The proportion of males who have hit another student is greater than the proportion of females who have hit another student.

Since both variables of interest in the dataset are counts (*how many times[...]*) but we are interested in comparing proportions, we are going to recode the variable, so it is binary. Make sure to create a new variable rather than writing over an existing variable. Remember, you can use multiple methods for recoding, including from the **tidyverse** package and base **R**.

Create a binary variable indicating whether youth hit another student.

```
# Tidyverse method
nys_1 <- nys_1 %>% mutate(hit_stdt_binary = case_when(
  hit_stdt == 0 ~ 0,
  hit_stdt > 0 ~ 1)) # if the value is > 0, code as 1

# Base R method
nys_1$hit_stdt_binary<-nys_1$hit_stdt # Create new variable
# Code any cases over 0 as 1
nys_1$hit_stdt_binary[nys_1$hit_stdt > 0] <- 1
```

Now, let's take a look at the proportions for both males and females (female variable). Get the total number of youths who reported hitting a student and the proportion for each group.

```
nys_1 %>%
  group_by(female) %>%
  summarize(N = n(),
            Sum = sum(hit_stdt_binary, na.rm = TRUE),
            Prop = mean(hit_stdt_binary, na.rm = TRUE))

## # A tibble: 2 x 4
##        female      N   Sum  Prop
##     <dbl+lbl> <int> <dbl> <dbl>
## 1 0 [Male]      918   574 0.629
## 2 1 [Female]    807   247 0.308
```

We see the proportion is much higher for males than females. Let's now conduct the z-test to assess whether this difference is statistically significant. We need to include the number of youth who reported hitting another student for both groups, in addition to the number of youth in each group to run the **prop.test()** from the **stats** package in base R.

```
# Create a vector of the number of youth reporting hitting
## another student
n_hit_stdts <- c(574, 247) # Males, Females

# Then, create a vector of the number of youth in each group.
# It's important to keep the same order as above.
n_cases <- c(918, 807) # Males, Females
```

Now, run the test of proportions. Note the alternative option is set to *greater*. The default is non-directional, but we specified a one-directional hypothesis.

```
prop.test(x = n_hit_stdts, n_cases,
          alternative = "greater")

##
##   2-sample test for equality of proportions with
     continuity correction
##
## data:  n_hit_stdts out of n_cases
## X-squared = 174.16, df = 1, p-value < 0.00000000000000022
## alternative hypothesis: greater
## 95 percent confidence interval:
##   0.2805847 1.0000000
## sample estimates:
##     prop 1     prop 2
## 0.6252723 0.3060719
```

Looking at the super small p-value ($p < 0.00000000000000022$), we see that we can *reject the null hypothesis*. In other words, it appears that there is a higher proportion of male youth who have hit another student compared to female youth.

Hypotheses Conclusion

H$_0$: ~~The proportion of males who have hit another student is not greater than the proportion of females who have hit another student.~~

H$_A$: The proportion of males who have hit another student is greater than the proportion of females who have hit another student. [REJECT NULL]

Comparing Two Dependent Sample Means

If we are interested in comparing the means of two groups that are related to one another, we want to run a **dependent sample *t*-test**. You may also hear this be referred to as a *paired sample t-test* (it's the same thing) because responses are actually paired together based on some sort of relationship. Sometimes, this can be a hard concept when you are first learning *t*-tests… to get a better understanding of dependent samples, let's think of things that we would pair together. It would be logical, for example, to pair twins. You could compare my low GRE score *before* I took a GRE prep-course to my low score *after* I took the prep-course (too bad for its test-retest reliability!). If I went to a fancy pants restaurant, I would want to get wine pairings where they select one wine for each course that would best complement the dish.

If you are still having trouble deciding whether an independent or dependent sample *t*-test is appropriate, imagine selecting one person (or whatever the unit of analysis) from your first sample, we will refer to as Sample A. Then, ask yourself, is there *one* person (one and only one) in Sample B that is making sense to pair them with? For instance, if you wanted to compare boys and girls and you selected John from Sample A (all males), is there only *one* girl in Sample B to pair John with? Normally, that answer is no. John is not related to any one girl in Sample B, so you would conduct an independent sample *t*-test. But, when would it be appropriate to pair John? For example, imagine we wanted to examine if there is significant difference in test scores between fraternal twins of different sexes. In that case, it would make sense to *pair* John with his sister Mary in Sample B.

Now that you feel a little bit more confident about the concept of pairing respondents, let's get back to our NYS example. Since the NYS has multiple waves of data (fixed sample, where the same person was surveyed across multiple time periods), we are able to compare a given youth's behavior at one point in time (Wave 1) to their behavior at another time (Wave 2). In this section, we'll compare the behaviors of youth from Wave 1 to Wave 2 with our research question being, *do youth report a significantly different number of instances stealing something over $50 in Wave 2 as compared to Wave 1?* Let's write out our null and alternative hypothesis (non-directional).

Hypotheses

H_0: There is no significant difference in the number of times a youth reported stealing something worth more than $50 in Wave 1 and with the number of times they reported in Wave 2.

H_A: There is a significant difference in the number of times a youth reported stealing something worth more than $50 in Wave 1 and with the number of times they reported in Wave 2.

Notice that our hypothesis specifies that we are pairing each youth's Wave 1 response with their Wave 2 response. If a youth was surveyed at Wave 1 but not at Wave 2 (or vice versa), they are not included in our sample. Cases without pairs will be dropped automatically when we run our analysis. Since we are interested in paired mean differences, the dependent variable must be stored in two separate variables, and the level of measurement needs to be interval or ratio (and it is ratio in our example).

As such, let's view our Wave 2 dataset.

```
# View NYS wave 2 data
View(nys_2)
```

By viewing Wave 2, you can see that each field has a unique case identification number (CASEID variable). These case identification numbers are consistent throughout the waves of data. Since we want to examine the differences between Wave 1 and 2 responses, we need to merge our waves together using this CASEID variable. Use the merge() function from base R to combine the data from Waves 1 and 2 into one data frame called nys_merged. We'll merge them based on their common CASEID field. So, imagine that you were part of the NYS sample. We are pairing your survey result from Wave 1 with your survey result in Wave 2.

```
# Merging waves of data together
nys_merged <-merge(nys_1, nys_2, by="CASEID")
```

View your new dataset. Now that the values from Wave 1 and Wave 2 are in the same dataset, we'll begin to conduct our dependent sample t-test on the nys_merged data frame. Remember that we are interested in whether there is a difference of means across the two waves in the number of times youth reported stealing something worth more than $50. For Wave 1, the dependent variable is thftg50, and in Wave 2, the dependent variable is thftg50_w2. Recall that for dependent sample t-tests, you will want to specify TRUE for the paired option, indicating these are paired samples.

```
# Lets run the dependent samples t-test
# Specify TRUE for the paired option
t.test(nys_merged$thftg50_w2, nys_merged$thftg50,
        paired= TRUE)

##
##  Paired t-test
##
## data:  nys_merged$thftg50_w2 and nys_merged$thftg50
## t = 1.7707, df = 1648, p-value = 0.07679
## alternative hypothesis: true difference in means is
    not equal to 0
## 95 percent confidence interval:
##   -0.004178788  0.081801589
## sample estimates:
## mean of the differences
##                0.0388114
```

According to our results, we *fail to reject the null hypothesis* since our *p*-value is higher than our 0.05 alpha level threshold ($p = 0.07679$). We can conclude that there is not a significant difference in thefts of items totaling more than $50 between the paired Waves 1 and 2 responses.

Hypotheses Conclusion

H_0: There is no significant difference in the number of times a youth reported stealing something worth more than $50 in Wave 1 and with the number of times they reported in Wave 2. [FAIL TO REJECT]

~~H_A: There is a significant difference in the number of times a youth reported stealing something worth more than $50 in Wave 1 and with the number of times they reported in Wave 2.~~

Application Activities

Problem 1:

Using the **t.test()** function from the **stats** package and the **nys_1** data frame, explore whether there is a significant difference in average age (age) between youth who stole something over $50 in the prior year and those who have not (thftg50). Don't forget to use the **var.test()** function to test for equality of variances of your dependent variable before running your *t*-test. Write your null and alternative hypotheses, and explain what you conclude with respect to the null hypothesis and why.

Problem 2:

Using the recoding steps above, create a new variable, called hit_any, that collapses three variables from the **nys_1** data frame: hit_prnt (number of times hit parents), hit_tchr (number of times hit teacher), and hit_stdt (number of times hit another student). Recode hit_any so it is binary, where if the youth hit a parent, teacher, or another student, they are coded as 1, while youth who did not hit a teacher or parent are coded as 0. Then, use the **prop.test()** function to determine whether there is a significant difference in age between those youth who hit a parent, teacher, or student and those who did not. Write your null and alternative hypotheses, and explain what you conclude with respect to the null hypothesis and why.

Problem 3:

Use a dependent sample *t*-test (**t.test()** function where **paired = TRUE**) to find out if youth report more instances of using marijuana in Wave 2 as compared to Wave 1 (marijuan and marijuan_w2 in our **nys_merged** data frame). Write your directional null and alternative hypotheses, and explain what you conclude with respect to the null hypothesis and why.

Problem 4:

Using Wave 1 of the NYS (`nys_1`), conduct the appropriate *t*-test to find out if youth who have a GPA of *Mostly C's*, *Mostly D's*, or *Mostly F's* (gpa) report a significantly higher number of times cheating on an exam (cheat) in comparison to youth whose GPA is *Mostly A's* or *Mostly B's*. Recode your independent variable as necessary using the **mutate()** function from **dplyr** or base R method using the **<-** assignment operator. To do this, you must group together those students who got *Mostly C's*, *Mostly D's*, or *Mostly F's* to code them as 0, and code students who got *Mostly A's* or *Mostly B's* as 1. It may be helpful to first view how the gpa variable is coded using the **attributes()** function. Write your directional null and alternative hypotheses, and explain what you conclude with respect to the null hypothesis and why.

Key Terms

Dependent sample *t*-test A test of statistical significance that is used when two samples are not independent.

Independent sample *t*-test A test of statistical significance that examines the difference observed between the means of two unrelated samples.

Test for equality of variance An *F*-test used to assess the null hypothesis that the two population variances are equal.

Functions Introduced in this Chapter

FUNCTION	DESCRIPTION (PACKAGE)
add_value_labels()	Add value labels to a variable (`labelled`)
merge()	Merge datasets by common row or column names (base **R**)
recode()	Replaces values of a integer/factor variable
t.test()	Performs one and two sample *t*-tests on vectors of data (base **R**)
var.test()	Performs an *F*-test to compare the variances of two samples from normal populations (base **R**)

References

Elliott, D. S. (2008a). National youth survey [United States]: Wave I, 1976 [Data file]. Ann Arbor, MI: Inter-university Consortium for Political and Social Research [distributor]. Retrieved from https://doi.org/10.3886/ICPSR08375.v2.

Elliott, D. S. (2008b). National youth survey [United States]: Wave II, 1977 [Data file]. Ann Arbor, MI: Inter-university Consortium for Political and Social Research [distributor]. Retrieved from https://doi.org/10.3886/ICPSR08424.v2.

Analysis of Variance (ANOVA)

Topics Practiced

Comparing means (ratio/interval variable) among three or more groups

Technical Skills Covered

Conducting one-way ANOVA

Conducting ANOVA post-hoc tests

R Packages Required

car, DescTools, dplyr, ggplot2, here, tidyverse

© The Editor(s) (if applicable) and The Author(s), under exclusive license to
Springer Nature Switzerland AG 2021
A. Wooditch et al., *A Beginner's Guide to Statistics for Criminology and
Criminal Justice Using R*, https://doi.org/10.1007/978-3-030-50625-4_12

IN THE PREVIOUS CHAPTER, you learned to compare the means of a numeric variable between two groups. But what if you want to compare a ratio or interval variable between more than two groups? If you are interested in comparing across more than two groups, you cannot run multiple *t*-tests because it increases the risk of a type I error (mistakenly concluding an intervention is effective or efficacious). In these instances, you will want to conduct a one-way analysis of variance (ANOVA). In this chapter, you will walk through how to conduct ANOVA and the appropriate post-hoc tests by comparing frequencies of stop and searches conducted by the police between neighborhoods across different local authorities in London.

Data

Dataset Source: Data on stop and searches carried out in London in 2019 come from the *data.police.uk* open-data website (data.police.uk, 2019). It is linked with the indices of multiple deprivation, available from the London Datastore (MHCLG, 2019; https://data.london.gov.uk/dataset/indices-of-deprivation), and also the current political party representing the local authority.

File Name: stop_search_london.csv

Dataset Description: Stop and search data represent individual stop and search records, including date and time, street-level location, ethnicity, gender, age of the person stopped, and outcome. These data were aggregated to neighborhood level to get the number of stop and search incidents in each neighborhood (Lower Super Output Area) in this year. It is linked with the indices of multiple deprivation. The index of multiple deprivation (IMD) is the official measure of relative deprivation in England and is part of a suite of outputs that form the indices of deprivation (IoD).

Getting Started

1. Open your existing R project as outlined in Chap. 2 (see also Appendix 1.3).

2. Install and load the required packages using the `install.packages()` and `library()` functions (see Appendix 1.1).

3. Open the stop-question-frisk dataset (*stop_search_london.csv*) using the `read_csv()` function to import the dataset (see Appendix 1.6.3), specifying the working directory with `here()` (see Appendix 1.3). When doing so, name the data frame `sqf` by using the `<-` assignment operator.

Conducting One-Way ANOVA

If you are interested in comparing a ratio/interval variable across more than two groups, then you would rely on the ANOVA test. In this instance, it is not appropriate to conduct multiple *t*-tests because of a **multiple comparisons problem**. By running multiple comparisons, you increase the likelihood that you find significant differences by random chance (referred to as type I error). Imagine you throw a six-sided die with numbers from 1 to 6. What is the probability of getting a 1? One in six (1/6). Now, imagine that we throw the die six times. What is the probability of getting a 1 at least once? Well, the probability is no longer one in six; it would be the probability of getting a 1 given roll of the die multiplied by the number of times rolled. As the number of comparisons (tests) increase, the chances that we get a false-positive increase also (meaning that we would be more likely to mistakenly conclude an intervention is effective or efficacious). To get around this issue, instead of running multiple *t*-tests, we will run a **one-way analysis of variance** test (referred to as **ANOVA**) that allows us to explore whether there are significant differences across the three or more groups being compared.

In this chapter, we will explore the number of stop, question, and frisk (referred to as stop and search in the United Kingdom) between neighborhoods conducted by the police across different local authorities in London. Let's start by taking a look at the dataset.

```
head(sqf)

##   x x_2   lsoa11cd                    lsoa11nm         district_name total_sqf
## 1 1   1 E01000006 Barking and Dagenham 016A Barking and Dagenham       26
## 2 2   2 E01000007 Barking and Dagenham 015A Barking and Dagenham       76
## 3 3   3 E01000008 Barking and Dagenham 015B Barking and Dagenham      197
## 4 4   4 E01000009 Barking and Dagenham 016B Barking and Dagenham      246
## 5 5   5 E01000010 Barking and Dagenham 015C Barking and Dagenham     1027
## 6 6   6 E01000011 Barking and Dagenham 016C Barking and Dagenham        4
##   political_control deprivation_lvl log_total_sqf crime_score
## 1            Labour               5      1.414973        -0.1
## 2            Labour               3      1.880814         0.8
## 3            Labour               2      2.294466         0.4
## 4            Labour               3      2.390935         0.9
## 5            Labour               3      3.011570         1.2
## 6            Labour               3      0.602060         0.5
```

We can see that our unit of analysis is the neighborhood, denoted by Lower Super Output Area (LSOA) (the <u>local authority district name 2019</u> variable). For each neighborhood, we can see the total number of stop and searches alongside other variables such as the local authority in which they were conducted, as well as the neighborhood's relative ranking in the English index of multiple deprivation, both for the overall score and also for the crime-based score (broken into deciles). So what do you think? How does stop and search vary between a neighborhood's level of deprivation across London? Well, first, let us visualize these differences by relying on the **ggplot()** function from the **ggplot2** package to calculate a series of box plots. We first specify our dataset name (**sqf**); **x** is going to be our independent variable/deprivation index (<u>deprivation lvl</u>), and **y** is going to be our dependent variable/count of stop and frisks (<u>total sqf</u>).

```
# Fill the color in accordance to deprivation level
ggplot(sqf, aes(x = deprivation_lvl, y = total_sqf,
       fill = deprivation_lvl)) +
# Outline thickness of the box in the box plot
  geom_boxplot(outlier.size = 0.5) +
# Don't need a key for the deprivation index so set to fals
  guides(fill=FALSE) +
  xlab("Index of Multiple Deprivation Decile") +
# Label our axes
  ylab("Number of Stop and Searches in 2019") +
  # Theme with white background and black gridlines
  theme_bw()
```

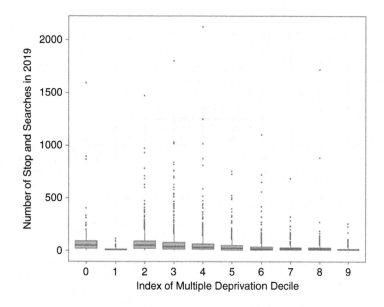

Wait… that doesn't look quite right. This is an ordinal variable, so we should arrange them in a proper order. Remember the **factor()** function from Chap. 2.

```
sqf$deprivation_lvl <- factor(sqf$deprivation_lvl,
    levels = c("1 (most deprived)", "2", "3", "4",
               "5", "6", "7", "8", "9", "10 (least deprived)"),
    ordered = TRUE)
```

Now, let's try this again. This time let's use a log scale on the y-axis to not be so affected by outliers. You can do this by adding the function **scale_y_log10()** to your **ggplot** code. Let's also rotate our x-axis labels so we can better read them.

```
ggplot(sqf, aes(x = deprivation_lvl,
       y = total_sqf, fill = deprivation_lvl)) +
  geom_boxplot(outlier.size = 0.5) +
  guides(fill=FALSE) +
  xlab("Index of Multiple Deprivation Decile") +
  ylab("Number of Stop and Searches in 2019") +
  theme_bw() +
      # Rotate Labels
  theme(axis.text.x = element_text(angle = 45, hjust = 1)) +
  scale_y_log10()    # Logging number of SQFs
```

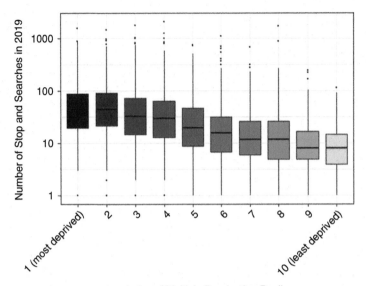

Index of Multiple Deprivation Decile

What you see here is that the box plot also displays the number of stop and searches in the neighborhoods that are in each one of these deciles of the index of multiple deprivation. Looking at the results, we can clearly see that there seem to be some differences in the means across deprivation levels. The greater the ranking on the deprivation deciles, it seems there are more stop and searches conducted by police in the area. There are a lot of categories here. Let's explore these data more. How about we look at the political party (political control variable) as the independent variable instead this time?

```
ggplot(sqf, aes(x = political_control, y = total_sqf,
      fill = political_control)) +
  geom_boxplot(outlier.size = 0.5) +
  guides(fill=FALSE) +
  xlab("Political Control in Local Authority for the
      Neighborhood") +
  ylab("Number of Stop and Searches in 2019") +
  theme_bw() +
  scale_y_log10()
```

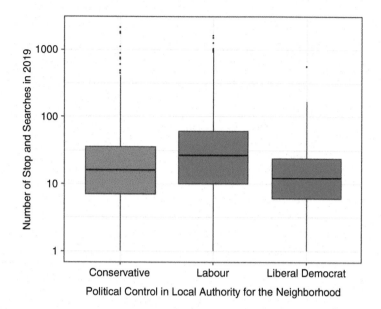

Political Control in Local Authority for the Neighborhood

This is interesting; it seems like the areas with *Labour* (centrist/moderate political views) control have more stop and searches, followed by *Conservative* and *Liberal Democrat*. But how precise are these point estimates for the means as measures of the population parameters? How much trust can we place in them as indicative of the true level of stop and searches in the various political party-controlled areas?

I want you to pay attention to the column in our table that provides you with the sample size for each of the political parties.

```
table(sqf$political_control)

##
##      Conservative              Labour Liberal Democrat
##              1234                3146              313
```

Notice anything worth thinking about here? Do you think that the estimates of stop and searches for neighborhoods controlled by each of these political parties will be equally precise? Remember back in the prior chapters when you learned about sampling variability, sampling distributions, and confidence intervals. Do you think that (given the different size of the samples for the different political groups) the confidence interval will be equally wide for each of them?

So what is the mean for each one of these? Well, let's see....

```
sqf %>%
  group_by(political_control) %>%
  summarize(mean = mean(total_sqf))
## # A tibble: 3 x 2
##   political_control   mean
##   <fct>              <dbl>
## 1 Conservative        42.2
## 2 Labour              57.2
## 3 Liberal Democrat    22.1
```

We have now examined the means for the number of stop and searches for the political groups and have seen how the *Labour* group seems to have the highest average level of stop searches. But we have discussed in this book that point estimates are problematic because they do not communicate sampling variability. Let's consider the use of ANOVA to understand how we can discuss these differences in a more generalizable way. Are these differences statistically significant? In other words, can we infer that they exist in the population from which the sample was drawn? For this, we can run ANOVA and an *F*-test.

How does this test work? We run ANOVA because we want to decide if the sample means are different enough for us to be able to reject the null hypothesis that they are different in the population. Clearly, if they are very different between themselves in the sample, we will be in a stronger position to do this. That should be clear; if you want to talk about differences in the population, observing big differences across the means in the sample gets you closer to that.

What ANOVA does is to contrast the variability between the groups with the variability within the groups to produce a ratio: *variance of means between the groups/variance within groups*. If there is more variability between the groups than within the groups, the more confidence we can have in a conclusion that the population means are not equal. Likewise, if there is more variation within the groups than between the groups, we will be on weaker ground to conclude that the population means are different.

So that's how ANOVA gets its name—it is a ratio of variability. To be more precise, a ratio of variances. The observed value is then compared to a probability distribution—the **F-distribution**. We have talked about the normal distribution and the *t*-distribution; the *F*-distribution is just another family of probability distributions. But the idea remains the same in relation to the *t*-test. If you obtain large absolute values for *F*, you will be more confident that the observed differences are inconsistent with the null hypothesis. These values will have a low probability of being observed if the null hypothesis is true (if all the population means are equal), and therefore we will be able to reject this null hypothesis.

Before we run our ANOVA, let's write out our hypotheses.

Hypotheses

H_0: There is no difference in mean number of stop, question, and frisks conducted among the types of political parties in power.

H_A: There is a difference in mean number of stop, question, and frisks conducted among the types of political parties in power.

Now, to run the ANOVA test, we use the `aov()` function.

```
stopsearch_1 <- aov(total_sqf ~ political_control, data=sqf)

summary(stopsearch_1)

##                    Df   Sum Sq Mean Sq F value   Pr(>F)
## political_control   2   477210  238605   21.13 7.32e-10
   ***
## Residuals        4690 52960745   11292
## ---
## Signif. codes:  0 '***' 0.001 '**' 0.01 '*' 0.05 '.'
   0.1 ' ' 1
```

Assuming that we met all of ANOVA's assumptions, we would conclude that because our result is statistically significant, there are some significant differences in stop and frisk practices by the political control of the area. The probability of observing our F-value with these data if the null hypothesis were true is also very low (7.32e–10 or 0.000000000732).

As such, we would reject the null hypothesis:

Hypotheses Conclusion

H_0: ~~There is no difference in mean number of stop, question, and frisks conducted among the types of political parties in power.~~

H_A: There is a difference in mean number of stop, question, and frisks conducted among the types of political parties in power. [REJECT NULL]

Done, right? Well, not quite. Remember the steps in the hypothesis testing process. Before running the test, we need to think and check the assumptions of the test that should precede running the test.

Assumptions of ANOVA

The ANOVA F-test makes the following assumptions:

- *Independence Assumption*: The groups must be independent of each other (this assumption would be violated if, for example, we compare a subject's performance before some treatment, again during the treatment, and then after the treatment: for this, you would need something called *repeated measures ANOVA*, which is beyond the scope of the current text).

- *Randomization Condition*: Were the groups created through randomization, or in the case of surveys, are the data from each group a representative sample of that group? As with the *t*-test, we are assuming simple random selection, which is not the case when the survey uses a complex survey design (but as we said, we will ignore this for convenience).

- *Equal Variance Assumption* (also called the lovely names of homogeneity of variance or homoskedasticity): To check this assumption, you need to check that the groups have similar variances (we'll discuss this in greater length in the next section of the chapter). But it is important that you know statisticians have discussed the degree to which this assumption matters, or in other words, to what degree ANOVA is *robust* to violations of this assumption. Is ANOVA robust (will give us results we can trust) when this assumption is violated? Andy Field and his coauthors (2012) discuss this at length on page 413. His view is that "when sample sizes are unequal, ANOVA is not robust to violations of homogeneity of variance." As such, we should proceed accordingly.

- *Normal Population Assumption*: Like the *t*-test, we need to assume that the normal model is reasonable for the populations underlying each of the treatment groups.

Homogeneity of Variance

Let's start by discussing why we care about the spread of the groups (checking homogeneity of variance). Remember that ANOVA contrasts variability between the groups with variability within each group. If the variability within the groups varies, we are making this pooled variance larger, reducing the *F* statistic, and making it less likely that we can reject the null hypothesis. So, when you have this problem, the ANOVA test will usually be a conservative test that will reject your null hypothesis less often than it should.

Look at the box plots we produced. Does it look as if the spreads change systematically by political party? Do the boxes with the wider IQR also have the wider spread? This sort of systematic trend may be more concerning than random differences in spread across the groups.

We can also run a test that will check the homogeneity of variance. This is the **Levene's test**. We can run this test with the `leveneTest()` function in the `car` package.

```
leveneTest(sqf$total_sqf, sqf$political_control,
        center = median)
## Levene's Test for Homogeneity of Variance
   (center = median)
##          Df F value      Pr(>F)
## group     2  15.194 2.645e-07 ***
##        4690
## ---
## Signif. codes:  0 '***' 0.001 '**' 0.01 '*' 0.05 '.'
   0.1 ' ' 1
```

In this case, the test is statistically significant (F = 15.194, p < 0.001), suggesting that the variances are different in the population. However, you need to keep in mind that with the large samples of some of the groups, this result is unsurprising, but this does create an issue since one-way ANOVA assumes equal variances ⊗. We discuss this issue further below.

We can further explore this assumption by plotting the results from the ANOVA model we already ran. Plotting the results of this ANOVA model allows us to inspect some plots that are useful for diagnosing problems.

```
# Running this would result in three consecutive plots
plot(stopsearch_1)

# Alternatively, if you don't want to run ANOVA first and
## store the results in an object
plot(aov(total_sqf ~ political_control, data=sqf))
```

As Andy Field and his colleagues (2012) suggest, the more important of these plots are the first two (to assess equal spread and normality). If you don't want to print the three diagnostic plots, you need to use more specific instructions so that R knows which one you want. Let's just get the plot we need for assessing equal spread by accessing the model fitted values with the **fitted()** function and check for heteroscedasticity in the model residuals (whether errors are correlated) with the **resid()** function.

```
plot(fitted(aov(total_sqf ~ political_control, data=sqf)),
    resid(aov(total_sqf ~ political_control, data=sqf)),
    xlab = "Fitted values",
    ylab = "Residuals",
    main = "Residuals vs Fitted")
```

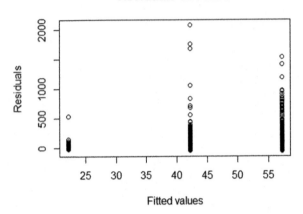

This plot can be used to further explore homogeneity of variances. It is a plot of residuals versus fitted values. We already know the Levene's test is significant and that the variances cannot be assumed to be the same in the population. This plot helps us visualize how. The lines correspond to the levels of the variable in the order which they sit, if it is an ordered factor (ordinal), then in the natural order. If not, then in alphabetical order.

In this sort of situation (when we have unequal variance), you expect plots such as this in which the vertical lines do not have the same length (a longer collection of points suggests more variance and a shorter collection of points less variance). If we had equal variance, they would look the same. When they are not the same, we should be particularly concerned with any systematic patterning (i.e., some sort of funneling visual effect suggesting a systematic shortening or expanding of the lines as we move right to left in the x-axis).

Dealing with Unequal Variance: Welch's ANOVA
If you find that you have violated the equality of variance assumption of the one-way ANOVA, don't worry; you can use **Welch's ANOVA**! Unlike one-way ANOVA, this test does not have the assumption that the variances

across groups are equal. And you can even use Welch's ANOVA when variances are equal because the results should be very similar to the one-way ANOVA. You can run Welch's ANOVA using the **oneway.test()** function.

```
oneway.test(total_sqf ~ political_control, data=sqf)

##
##   One-way analysis of means (not assuming equal variances)
##
## data:  total_sqf and political_control
## F = 73.456, num df = 2.0, denom df = 1347.4,
    p-value < 2.2e-16
```

In this case, the substantive conclusion is unsurprisingly the same. You reject the null hypothesis given the low *p*-value associated with the observed Welch's *F*-value.

One key thing to remember with Welch's ANOVA is that the normality assumption still holds. If your data are not normally distributed, there is still hope! There are several options presented in the next section.

Checking Normality and Dealing with Normality Issues

The *F*-tests require the underlying errors to follow a normal distribution. Strictly speaking, we need to check whether the normal model is reasonable for the population underlying each group. We should start by looking at the side-by-side box plots for indications of skewness. If they are all or mostly skewed in the same direction, the normal condition will fail. We also need to look at outliers within each group (particularly with smaller samples). You may also find it useful to compare the density estimates.

```
ggplot(na.omit(sqf[,c("political_control", "total_sqf")]),
       aes(x = total_sqf, fill = political_control)) +
  geom_density(alpha = .3) +
  theme_bw()
```

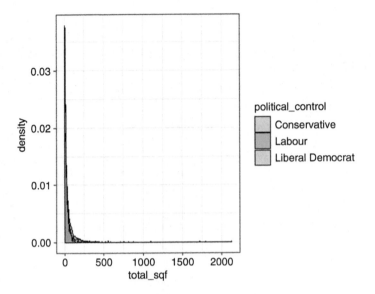

We can also use a normal probability plot (Q-Q plot) of the residuals. **Q-Q plot** (or quantile-quantile plot) draws the correlation between a given sample and the normal distribution. A 45-degree reference line is also plotted. Q-Q plots are used to visually check the normality of the data. Alternatively, we can specifically ask for it.

```
qqnorm(resid(aov(total_sqf ~ political_control, data=sqf)),
    main="Normal Q-Q P lot")
qqline(resid(aov(total_sqf ~ political_control, data=sqf)),
    col = 2)
```

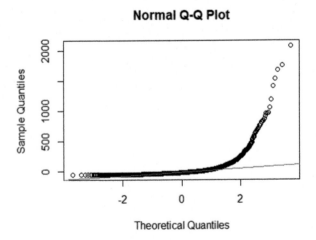

Normal scores-check for skewness, kurtosis, outliers in residuals

As before, we are concerned here with clear departures from the red line. How do you interpret a Q-Q plot? It takes practice and some subjective judgment; it's kind of an art. These are common patterns and possible interpretations:

- All but a few points fall on a line: *outliers in the data.*
- Left end of pattern is below the line, and right end of pattern is above the line: *long tails at both ends of the data distribution.*
- Left end of pattern is above the line, and right end of pattern is below the line: *short tails at both ends of the data distribution.*
- Curved pattern with slope increasing from left to right: data distribution is *skewed to the right.*
- Curved pattern with slope decreasing from left to right: data distribution is *skewed to the left.*
- Staircase pattern (plateaus and gaps): data have been rounded or are discrete.

The `qqPlot()` function of the `car` package assists the interpretation by drawing a confidence interval around the expected values.

```
qqPlot(stopsearch_1)
```

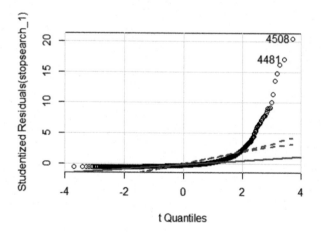

```
## [1] 4481 4508
```

We can see that there is some departure from normality, which we would expect with a count variable.

Data Transformation

Sometimes, when non-normality is an issue, **data transformation** (transforming your variable) may be a way of solving the problem. You create a new transformed variable based on the original one that will now meet the normality assumption. This is something that can also sort out issues with extreme observations (outliers). The idea behind transformations is that "you do something to every score to correct for distributional problems, outliers or unequal variances" (Field et al., 2012). There's nothing dodgy about it. It's not like we are cheating, because the same transformation will be applied to all scores. But it changes the units of measurement, which can make interpretation a bit more obscure. Of course, you always have the option of un-logging using the `exp()` (exponentiate) function. Another thing to remember is that if the variable you are logging has cases that take on the value 0, then you need to add 1 when doing the log—`log(VarName + 1)`.

There are many different potential transformations: log transformations, square root transformations, reciprocal transformations, reverse score transformations, etc. How do you choose? Trial and error. That is, you have got to work and work until you find one that solves your problem. And sometimes, none of the transformations give you an ideal solution.

We will illustrate the process of trial and error for normalizing `total_sqf` (as much as we can). Let's look again at the distribution of the variable.

```
ggplot(sqf, aes(x = total_sqf)) +
  geom_density()
```

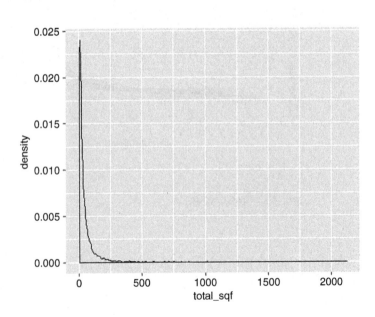

We can see that the distribution follows a Poisson distribution, which is to be expected as these are count data.

Let's see what happens when we apply a logarithmic transformation (often used with skewed data).

```
ggplot(na.omit(sqf[,c("political_control", "total_sqf")]),
    aes(x = log10(total_sqf), fill = political_control)) +
    geom_density(alpha = .3) +
    theme_bw()
```

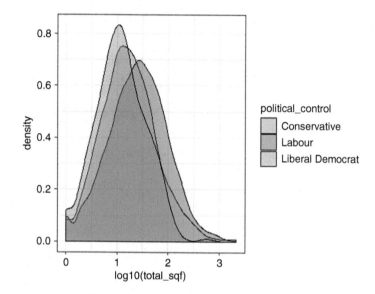

This looks much closer to the normal distribution we know and love. Here, I will discuss power transformations. We define a simple power transformation as the replacement of a variable X by X^p. Often, powers in the range from −2 to 3 are useful. The power −1 is in fact the reciprocal or inverse transformation. This family of transformations was first used by a seminal paper by Box and Cox in 1964, which is why you will find the literature refers to them as the Box-Cox (BC) transformations in their honor.

How do you select the right power transformation? Again, trial and error. The **symbox()** function in the **car** package is useful for finding a transformation to approximate symmetry by trial and error. The following code will produce a series of box plots comparing the distribution of our variable (total sqf) for various power transformations:

```
symbox(sqf$total_sqf)
```

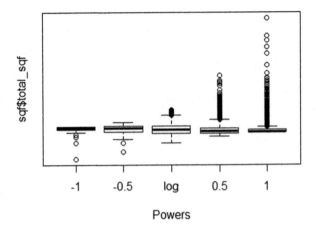

We can see that the most symmetrical of all is the log transformation, so we picked well! Let's create a new variable with this transformation:

```
sqf$log_total_sqf <- log10(sqf$total_sqf)
```

Now we can see the two variables side-by-side.

```
qqPlot(sqf$log_total_sqf)
```

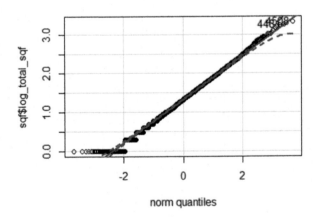

```
## [1] 4508 4481
qqPlot(sqf$total_sqf)
```

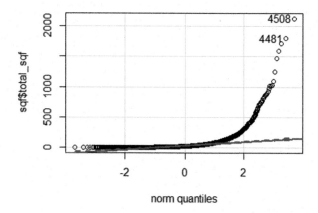

```
## [1] 4508 4481
```

As we said, the normal probability plots using this function display a (blue) straight line (which is how a normally distributed probability should look like in these plots) and then the dots (in black here) show the actual distribution of data. You can see that the variable in which we took the log10 of stop and searches (the first plotted, <u>log total sqf</u> variable) is much closer to the line.

If we were happy with our transformations, we could then run ANOVA as if the data were normal; only, instead of comparing means on stop and frisks, we would be comparing means on whatever transformation we have made, log10 of stop and searches (which to many mortals may sound rather obscure).

It looks as if the larger group (*Labour*) is the one with more variance. Again, in this sort of scenario, the ANOVA *F*-test will be more conservative (it may lead you to reject the null hypothesis in more occasions than it is warranted). Despite this, we found a significant effect; so in practical terms, it does not look as if the homogeneity of variance was such a big deal (it made our test more conservative, right, but we still manage to reject the null hypothesis).

Nonparametric ANOVA: The Kruskal-Wallis Test

Another option you have when dealing with non-normal data is the **Kruskal-Wallis test**. This is the nonparametric equivalent to ANOVA. It is also similar to the Mann-Whitney U test, but Mann-Whitney U is only for an independent variable with two groups.

The Kruskal-Wallis test is computed a bit differently than the parametric one-way ANOVA because the test compares mean ranks between groups (e.g., ranks scores from high to low) rather than comparing means. Since we had some concerns about the distribution of our stop and frisk variable (total sqf), let's see if our overall conclusion would change if we applied the Kruskal-Wallis Test.

```
kruskal.test(total_sqf ~ political_control, data=sqf)

##
##  Kruskal-Wallis rank sum test
##
## data:  total_sqf by political_control
## Kruskal-Wallis chi-squared = 168.89, df = 2,
    p-value < 2.2e-16
```

In this case, we still get a significant result, and our decision to reject the null hypothesis would stay the same.

ANOVA Post-Hoc Tests

So we are fairly certain there's bound to be differences in the number of stop and searches across areas under control of different political parties that may be reflective of those we see in our sample. In our sample (see below), the mean value of stop and searches across groups is different. The Liberal Democrat group (22.1) has the lowest number of stop and searches and the Labour group the highest (57.2), and the Conservative areas have an average of 42.2 stop and searches per neighborhood (see section on the size of the effect).

However, all that the tests described above tell you is that there are significant differences across these categories. What the ANOVA results don't do is to tell you which of those differences are significant, nor can you use the size of the F-value to tell you how different the means are. In other words, we don't know if, for example, the apparent difference between stop and frisk for the Conservative and the Liberal group is significant or not. Alternatively, the differences could be driven by Conservative versus Liberal or Liberal versus Labour. We know that some of these differences are significant, but we don't know which ones. We can, however, run post-hoc (after the fact) comparisons that would give us answers to these, although this would only make sense if the ANOVA (or equivalent) test has already detected some differences.

Bonferroni Correction

There are different methods that have been proposed for doing post-hoc multiple comparisons. All of these methods try to take into account the problem of multiple comparisons and the way they modify the probability of finding a significant result, but they do it in a different way. In this section, we will illustrate one of these methods, the **Bonferroni Correction**. The `pairwise.t.test()` function asks for multiple *t*-tests adjusting for the fact you are running multiple comparisons. The first variable identifies your dependent variable, then you identify the categorical predictor (independent variable), and then you select the particular multiple comparisons adjustment you are choosing.

```
pairwise.t.test(sqf$total_sqf, sqf$political_control,
                p.adjust.method="bonferroni")

##
##  Pairwise comparisons using t tests with pooled SD
##
## data:  sqf$total_sqf and sqf$political_control
##
##                   Conservative Labour
## Labour            8.1e-05      -
## Liberal Democrat  0.0086       8.2e-08
##
## P value adjustment method: bonferroni
```

What you see printed in this matrix are the *p*-values for each of the comparisons. Whenever that value is below the alpha level you have set out, say our conventional .05, then you can conclude that this particular comparison/difference is significant. So here, we can say that:

- Labour areas have significantly more stop searches than Conservative areas ($p < 0.001$).

- Labour areas have significantly more stop searches than Liberal Democrat areas ($p < 0.001$).

- Conservative areas have significantly more stop searches than Liberal Democrat areas ($p < 0.01$).

It is important to note, however, that a criticism of this test is that it overcorrects for type I errors. Additionally, there are many more post-hoc comparisons tests that you can run. In the next several sections, we will discuss two other common ANOVA post-hoc tests: Tukey HSD and Scheffe's tests.

Tukey's HSD

You could also try the **Tukey's Honest Significant Difference (HSD)** method. This way, you create a set of confidence intervals on the differences between the means of the levels of a factor with the specified family-wise probability of coverage. The intervals are based on the studentized range statistic, Tukey's HSD method. This is similar to the Bonferroni Correction, but Tukey HSD is more powerful when examining differences across a large number of means, whereas Bonferroni is more powerful when examining differences across a small number of means. You can run Tukey's HSD in R with the following code:

```
TukeyHSD(stopsearch_1)

##   Tukey multiple comparisons of means
##     95% family-wise confidence level
##
## Fit: aov(formula = total_sqf ~ political_control, data = sqf)
##
## $political_control
##                        diff      lwr       upr      p adj
## Labour-Conservative    15.00015   6.63197  23.368333 0.0000798
## Liberal
## Democrat-Conservative -20.06250 -35.82941  -4.295599 0.0080672
## Liberal
## Democrat-Labour       -35.06265 -49.82838 -20.296930 0.0000001
```

You can see the *p*-values (should be similar to the ones from the pairwise Bonferroni), as well as confidence intervals for the difference in means for each category pair.

Scheffé's Test

Finally, you can use **Scheffé's test**. This statistic is used to build confidence intervals using the prespecified alpha (α) value. In general, Scheffé's method accounts for family-wise error rate by weighting the test statistic by the mean squared error (MSE), the between-samples DF (k−1), and group sizes (if inequal):

$$C = \sqrt{(k-1) F\, MSE \left(\frac{1}{n_i} + \frac{1}{n_j} \right)}$$ **Equation 12.1**

As such, Scheffé's test controls for the overall confidence level and is normally preferred to be used with unequal sample sizes.

You can run the test using the `ScheffeTest()` function from the `DescTools` package.

```
ScheffeTest(stopsearch_1)

##
##   Posthoc multiple comparisons of means : Scheffe Test
##     95% family-wise confidence level
##
## $political_control
##                            diff      lwr.ci      upr.ci     pval
## Labour-Conservative    15.00015   6.260463  23.739840  0.00015 ***
## Liberal
## Democrat-Conservative -20.06250 -36.529379  -3.595625  0.01173 *
## Liberal
## Democrat-Labour       -35.06265 -50.483904 -19.641403    2e-07 ***
##
## ---
## Signif. codes:  0 '***' 0.001 '**' 0.01 '*' 0.05 '.' 0.1 ' ' 1
```

Again, we generate confidence intervals and *p*-values for each pairwise comparison.

Eta Squared (Size of Effect)

Of course, it is not enough to say there is a difference, but we also want to talk about the *size* of this difference. You can use the following programming code to get what is called eta squared (discussed in detail below):

```
summary.lm(stopsearch_1)

##
## Call:
## aov(formula = total_sqf ~ political_control, data = sqf)
##
## Residuals:
##     Min      1Q  Median      3Q     Max
##   -56.18  -41.18  -27.18    0.82 2080.82
##
## Coefficients:
##                           Estimate  Error t value Pr(>|t|)
##                           Std.
## (Intercept)                 42.181  3.025  13.944  < 2e-16 ***
## political_controlLabour     15.000  3.569   4.202 2.69e-05 ***
## political_controlLiberal
## Democrat                   -20.063  6.725  -2.983  0.00287 **
## ---
## Signif. codes:  0 '***' 0.001 '**' 0.01 '*' 0.05 '.' 0.1 ' ' 1
##
## Residual standard error: 106.3 on 4690 degrees of freedom
## Multiple R-squared:  0.00893,    Adjusted R-squared:  0.008508
## F-statistic: 21.13 on 2 and 4690 DF,  p-value: 7.32e-10
```

The summary function is simply invoking the results we obtained earlier when we ran the ANOVA and created the `stopsearch_1` object. You get loads of numbers there. But the only part you are interested is what the output labels as *R-squared* (0.00893). In the context of ANOVA, this is usually called **eta squared**. This value is also referred to as the *percent of variance explained*. This is simply the proportion of the total sum of squares that is accounted for by the between sum of squares. The larger the proportion of total variance that is accounted for by the between sum of squares, the stronger the relationship between the independent and the dependent variable. When the means of the groups defined by your dependent variable are the same, eta squared will be 0. That would mean no relationship exists between your independent and dependent variable. The largest value eta squared can take is 1, meaning that all the variability in your independent variable can be explained by your dependent variable.

Taking the square root of eta squared gives you the correlation between the independent and the dependent variable. Eta (the correlation) is a measure of effect size (the substantive impact of your dependent variable on your independent variable). In this case, that value (square root of 0.00893) is around 0.0945. That suggests that while statistically significant, political party of the area has a very, very small effect on the number of stop and searches conducted in the area.

Application Activities

Problem 1:

Initially, we visually explored the index of multiple deprivation variable (deprivation_lvl)/the role of being in the higher or lower deciles and what that might mean for the number of stop and searches (total_sqf) in an area, but we did not conduct an ANOVA. Using the `leveneTest()` function, determine whether equal variances are assumed. Then, use the results of Levene's test to inform whether you conduct a one-way ANOVA (`aov` function) or Welch's ANOVA (`oneway.test` function) to assess the relationship. Write your null and alternative hypothesis, then conduct the appropriate ANOVA test, and interpret your results with respect to the null hypothesis.

Problem 2:

In the `sqf` dataset, there is a crime indicator variable (crime_score), similar to the overall index of multiple deprivation but relating specifically to crime-related issues for each neighborhood (specifically, it measures the risk of personal and material victimization at local level). Transform this variable to create groups—low, medium, and high crime areas—and name the new variable <u>crime group</u>. Hint: use the `cut()` function, like this: `sqf$crime_group <- cut(sqf$crime_score, 3)`. Follow the same steps as the prior question, and determine whether there is a significant difference in stop and searches (<u>total sqf</u>) by the area's crime level (<u>crime group</u>).

Key Terms

Bonferroni Correction A post-hoc pairwise comparison of means that controls the type I error rate by dividing the selected α-level by the number of pairwise comparisons made.

Data transformation An adjustment of data to a different unit or scale (normally to deal with normality issues).

Eta squared The proportion of the total sum of squares that is accounted for by the between sum of squares. Eta squared is sometimes referred to as the percent of variance explained.

F-distribution A continuous probability distribution used as the null distribution in ANOVA.

Kruskal-Wallis test A nonparametric test of statistical significance for multiple groups, requiring at least an ordinal scale of measurement.

Levene's test A test of the equality of variances.

Multiple comparisons problem The problem associated with heightened chance of obtaining a false-positive (type I error) increase as the number of comparisons increase.

One-way analysis of variance (ANOVA) A parametric test of statistical significance that assesses whether differences in the means of several samples (groups) can lead the researcher to reject the null hypothesis that the means of the populations from which the samples are drawn are the same.

Q-Q plot Used to check for normality of data, plots the correlation between the sample and a normal distribution.

Scheffé's test A multiple comparisons test that accounts for family-wise error rate by weighting the test statistic by the mean squared error, between-samples degrees of freedom, and group sizes.

Tukey's Honest Significant Difference (HSD) A parametric test of statistical significance, adjusted for making pairwise comparisons. The HSD test defines the difference between the pairwise comparisons required to reject the null hypothesis.

Welch's ANOVA ANOVA test for when the equality of variances assumption (homoscedasticity) is not met.

Functions Introduced in this Chapter

FUNCTION	DESCRIPTION (PACKAGE)
aov()	Fit an analysis of variance model (base **R**)
cut()	Divides by the specified interval (base **R**)
fitted()	Extract fitted values from objects when modeling functions (base **R**)
guides()	Used to customize plot legend when using **ggplot()** (**ggplot2**)
kruskal.test()	Performs a Kruskal-Wallis rank sum test (base **R**)
leveneTest()	Computes Levene's test for homogeneity of variance across groups (**car**)
log10()	Computes common (i.e., base 10) logarithms (base **R**)
oneway.test()	Tests if 2+ samples from normal distributions have the same means (base **R**)
pairwise.t.test()	Pairwise comparisons between group levels (base **R**)
qqnorm()	Produces a normal Q-Q plot of the variable (base **R**)
qqline()	Adds a reference line to Q-Q plot produced by **qqnorm()** (base **R**)
qqPlot()	Draws theoretical quantile-comparison plots for variables (**car**)
resid()	Extract residuals from objects returned by modeling functions (base **R**)
scale_y_log10()	Log scales the y-axis on your chart (**ggplot2**)
ScheffeTest()	Scheffé's test for pairwise and otherwise comparisons (**DescTools**)
summary.lm()	Summary method for class **lm** (base **R**)
symbox()	Transforms **x** to a series of selected powers and displays box plots (**car**)
theme_bw()	The traditional dark-on-white **ggplot** theme (**ggplot2**)
TukeyHSD()	Implements Tukey's Honest Significant Difference method (base **R**)

References

DATA.POLICE.UK. (2019). Metropolitan Police Service, stop and search data set [Data file]. Retrieved March 30, 2020, from https://data.police.uk/data/.

Field, A., Miles, J., & Field, Z. (2012). *Discovering statistics using R*. Sage publications.

Ministry of Housing, Communities & Local Government (MHCLG). (2019). Indices of deprivation [Data file]. Retrieved March 30, 2020, from https://data.london.gov.uk/dataset/indices-of-deprivation.

Measures of Association for Nominal and Ordinal Variables

Topics Practiced

Strength of relationship between nominal- and ordinal-level variables

Technical Skills Covered

Calculate measures of association

Nominal: Phi, Cramer's V, Goodman-Kruskal lambda and tau

Ordinal: Goodman-Kruskal gamma, Kendall's tau(b) and (c), Somers' D

R Packages Required

DescTools, GoodmanKruskal, haven, here, stats

© The Editor(s) (if applicable) and The Author(s), under exclusive license to
Springer Nature Switzerland AG 2021
A. Wooditch et al., *A Beginner's Guide to Statistics for Criminology and
Criminal Justice Using R*, https://doi.org/10.1007/978-3-030-50625-4_13

T HROUGHOUT THIS BOOK, we have covered various ways of measuring the relationships among variables. We have already discussed tests of statistical significance and how they help us infer differences in a population based on a sample from the population. However, tests of statistical significance do not tell us about the *strength* of associations among variables. In criminal justice research, we often want to detect not only whether a relationship exists among variables but the *size* of this relationship as well. Determining the size of the relationship among variables makes the interpretation of our results much more meaningful and useful in real-life applications. In this chapter, we focus on how to use various measures of association for nominal- and ordinal-level variables in R by relying on data from the Seattle Neighborhoods and Crime Survey, which aimed to test multilevel theories of neighborhood social organization and crime using telephone surveys of 2,220 Seattle, WA residents.

Data

Dataset Source: Seattle Neighborhoods and Crime Survey

File Name: Seattle_Neighborhoods_Crime_RandomSample.dta

Dataset Description: The Seattle Neighborhoods and Crime Survey was conducted in 2002–2003 and aimed to test multilevel theories of neighborhood social disorganization and crime (Matsueda, 2010). The survey was conducted with 2,220 Seattle, WA, residents over the phone, and residents were asked about their demographics, neighborhood characteristics, neighbors, routine activities, victimization, and more. There were three separate samples drawn for the study (and for which data are available). This chapter uses the random sample in the walk-through.

Getting Started

1. Open your existing R project as outlined in Chap. 2 (see also Appendix 1.3).

2. Install and load the required packages using the `install.packages()` and `library()` functions (see Appendix 1.1).

3. Open the Seattle Neighborhoods and Crime Survey dataset (*Seattle_Neighborhoods_Crime_RandomSample.dta*) using the `read_dta()` function to import the dataset (see Appendix 1.6.7), specifying the working directory with `here()` (see Appendix 1.3). When doing so, name the data frame `seattle_df` by using the `<-` assignment operator.

Use `View(seattle_df)` to make sure the file loaded successfully.

Measures of Association for Nominal Variables

There are a number of paths we can take when trying to understand the relationship between two nominal-level variables. The chi-square test for independence covered in Chap. 9 is a way to determine *whether* the two variables are related. Once you know they are significantly related to one another, the measures discussed below are ways of determining *how related* they are. In other words, what is the *strength of the relationship* between the two nominal variables?

The following nominal measures of association are discussed below: *Phi*, Cramer's V, Goodman-Kruskal *tau*, and Goodman-Kruskal *lambda*. Before we get into how to calculate these measures in R, let's just provide a quick overview of what measures to use when.

- *Phi:* Used for 2×2 tables to obtain a measure of association ranging from 0 to 1 with higher values indicating a stronger relationship.

- *Cramer's V:* Used to obtain a measure of association ranging from 0 to 1 with higher values indicating a stronger relationship for tables larger than 2×2.

- *Goodman-Kruskal lambda:* It uses modal probabilities to measure the percentage improvement in predictability of the dependent variable given the independent variable, similar conceptually to R^2 in regression. It has a standardized scale ranging from 0 to 1.0 (higher values indicating a stronger association).

- *Goodman-Kruskal tau:* This measure is the same as lambda (discussed above), but tau is based on assignment probabilities specified by marginal/conditional proportions.

Phi

The first measure of association we will cover is **Phi (φ)**, which builds off of the chi-square statistic by measuring the strength of association between two *binary* variables. You may recall that the chi-square statistic is influenced by the sample size under observation. The *phi* coefficient adjusts the chi-square statistic by taking into account the sample size. We can obtain the *phi* coefficient by dividing the chi-square value by the sample size and taking the square root of the result. Alternatively, the `Phi()` function from the `DescTools` collection of packages provides a way of asking R to do the hard work of calculating these statistics for you. To illustrate, we will ask R to calculate the *phi* measure of association for the relationship between the respondent's sex (QDEM3) and whether they reported their most recent physical victimization incident to the police (Q58E). We are first going to make sure our variables are coded correctly, and also make sure there is a significant relationship between the two variables (using a crosstabs nested within the `chisq.test()` function) since we would only assess the strength of the relationship if we know that one exists between the two variables.

```r
# Create copies of the variables,
## rename them so it's easier to remember

table(seattle_df$QDEM3)

##
##    1    2
## 1145 1075

seattle_df$sex <- factor(seattle_df$QDEM3,
    levels = c(1, 2), labels = c("female", "male"))

# Reported victimization to police?

table(seattle_df$Q58E)
##
##   -1    0    1    8    9
## 1582  379  255    2    2

seattle_df$reported_to_police <- factor(seattle_df$Q58E,
    levels = c(0,1), labels = c("no", "yes"))

# Make sure a significant relationship exists
chi<-table(seattle_df$sex,  seattle_df$reported_to_police)
chisq.test(chi)
##
##   Pearson's Chi-squared test with Yates'
##   continuity correction
##
## data:  chi
## X-squared = 5.8156, df = 1, p-value = 0.01588
```

We used the **factor()** function from base **R** to create a factor variable named <u>sex</u> and <u>reported to police</u>, and our chi-square test confirmed that there is a significant relationship between the two binary variables ($p < 0.05$).

To calculate the *phi* coefficient for the association between these two variables, we can use the **Phi()** function.

```
# Calculate the phi coefficient

Phi(seattle_df$sex, seattle_df$reported_to_police)

## [1] 0.09903062
```

We get a *phi* value of roughly 0.1, out of a possible range of 0 and 1. While there is no precise interpretation for values of *phi*, we know that values closer to 1 indicate a stronger association between the two variables. Clearly, our value is closer to 0 than 1! We can conclude from this result that there is likely a weak association between a respondent's sex and whether they reported their victimization to the police.

Cramer's V

You conduct a **Cramer's V** test to measure the strength of association on tables larger than 2×2. If you do conduct a Cramer's V test on a 2×2 table, you will get the same value as *phi*. A benefit of Cramer's V is that it is not sensitive to sample size, so it is useful to get a better understanding of the relationship between the two variables when you believe the chi-square test was statistically significant due to a large sample size. We illustrate this using the `CramerV()` function from the `DescTools` package.

```
# Cramer's V test for the same relationship detailed above:

CramerV(seattle_df$sex, seattle_df$reported_to_police)

## [1] 0.09903062
```

Let's calculate Cramer's V again, this time for the variables indicating respondents' sex (sex) and how often residents are worried about being attacked in their neighborhood (Q52). This example is an appropriate use of Cramer's V since we are examining a table larger than 2×2.

```
# Make a copy of the Q52 variable
# Q52: How often do you worry about being attacked
## in your neighborhood

table(seattle_df$Q52)

##
##    1    2    3    4    8    9
## 1584  354  167   98   12    5

seattle_df$worry_attacked <- factor(seattle_df$Q52,
   levels = c(1, 2, 3, 4),
   labels = c("Less than once a month" ,"once
             a month", "about once a week",
             "everyday"))

# Run a chi-square test to make sure there is a significant
## relationship
# Save the result in the object "chi2"

chi2 <- table(seattle_df$worry_attacked, seattle_df$sex)

chisq.test(chi2)

##
##   Pearson's Chi-squared test
##
## data:  chi2
## X-squared = 38.092, df = 3, p-value = 0.00000002702

# Conduct the Cramer's V test of association on the
## contingency table
# You can use the object "chi2" for convenience

CramerV(chi2)

## [1] 0.1314953
```

The Cramer's V statistic resulted in a value of 0.131, indicating a relatively *small* relationship between residents' sex and how often they worry about being attacked in their neighborhood.

Goodman and Kruskal's Lambda and Tau

Another measure of association for nominal variables are Goodman and Kruskal's *lambda* and *tau*. These statistics do not rely on the chi-square statistic like *phi*. The **Goodman and Kruskal's tau (τ)** statistic also provides us with a standard score between 0 and 1, which we can interpret as the **proportional reduction in errors (PRE)** made by using the information from one measure to define the values of another measure. On the other hand, **Goodman and Kruskal's lambda (λ)** uses information about the modal value of the dependent variable within categories of the independent variable (and overall). To use these measures of association, you need to define your independent and dependent variables a priori. For these examples, we will use functions from two other package called `GoodmanKruskal`. Specifically, we will use the `GKtau()` function to obtain the *tau* statistic and the `Lambda()` function from the `DescTools` package to obtain *lambda*.

Continuing in our exploration of sex differences, this time around we want to understand the relationship between sex (<u>sex</u>) and gun ownership (<u>Q65</u>) in our sample of Seattle residents. Because sex is an attribute, we will specify sex as the independent variable and the dichotomous measure of gun ownership as the dependent variable. Note that in statistics, the character x is often used to denote an independent variable or predictor, while y is typically used to denote a dependent variable or outcome. This will be important for our interpretation of results below.

```
# First, take a look at your gun ownership variable

table(seattle_df$Q65)

##
##    0    1    8    9
## 1966  213    2   39

# Create a new object called "own_gun"

seattle_df$own_gun <- factor(seattle_df$Q65,
    levels = c(0, 1),
    labels = c("no" , "yes"))

# Let's make sure there is a significant relationship
## between the two

chisq.test(table(seattle_df$own_gun, seattle_df$sex))

##
##  Pearson's Chi-squared test with Yates'
    continuity correction
##
## data:  table(seattle_df$own_gun, seattle_df$sex)
## X-squared = 62.5, df = 1, p-value = 0.000000000000002665
```

To calculate *tau*, you need to apply the `GKtau()` function to a contingency table of your independent and dependent variable. The independent variable should be listed first, followed by the dependent variable. Make sure you put these in the right order! If you are ever unsure about the correct syntax, the online R help files or user forums will almost always provide the answer.

```
# Calculate tau for respondent's sex and whether they
## own a gun

GKtau(seattle_df$sex, seattle_df$own_gun)

##                 xName                 yName Nx Ny tauxy tauyx
## 1 seattle_df$sex seattle_df$own_gun  2  3 0.026 0.029

# Calculate lambda for the same relationship

Lambda(seattle_df$sex, seattle_df$own_gun)

## [1] 0.08148734
```

Remember, these values are constrained between 0 and 1. In the result for *tau*, the column that reads *tauxy* gives us what we are interested in for this measure. The *tauyx* column provides the reverse measure of association (how well does the dependent variable predict values of the independent variable). According to both the *tau* and *lambda* results, it appears that knowing a respondent's sex is not really predictive of whether they reported owning a gun. In other words, the association is relatively small or weak.

Conducting Measures of Association for Ordinal Variables

We are not limited to working with nominal-level variables in understanding the associations between variables. Oftentimes in criminal justice research, we work with survey data that are filled with ordered response categories. This next section briefly outlines how we can conduct measures of association for these pairs. Let's get a basic understanding of these variables before learning how to calculate them in R.

- *Goodman-Kruskal Gamma:* Provides a value between −1 and +1, indicating how much knowledge of the independent variable reduces error in predicting the dependent variable. Values closer to −1 and +1 indicate stronger negative and positive relationships, respectively.

- *Kendall's τ_b and τ_c:* Both measures provide a value between −1 and +1 to indicate stronger negative or positive relationships, respectively. Both measures differ from gamma in that they use information on tied pairs in addition to concordant and discordant pairs. τ_c is used for asymmetric tables (unequal number of columns and rows), while τ_b is used for symmetric tables.

- *Somers' D:* Provides a value between −1 and +1, indicating how much known information from the independent variable improves the prediction of the dependent variable. Values closer to −1 and +1 indicate better prediction ability.

Goodman-Kruskal Gamma

Sometimes you may want to calculate a measure of association for a pair of ordinal-level variables. Four common measures of association include *gamma*, Kendall's τ_b and τ_c, and Somers' *D*. These measures all use what are termed *concordant pairs* and *discordant pairs* of observations to estimate how strongly associated two variables are. What these terms mean is that each pair of observations on two variables of interest in a dataset is compared on their relative ranks. **Concordant pairs of observations** are those observations where they track with each other—that is, the rankings are consistent for both variables. **Discordant pairs of observations** are observations that do not track with each other—one observation may be ranked low on one variable and high on the other, and vice versa for the other observation. In other words, their rankings are inconsistent. If a pair of observations has the same rank on the variables of interest, this is referred to as a *tie*, or a **tied pairs of observations**.

Information on discordant and concordant pairs can be used to then calculate each of our measures of association. In this next example, we will calculate **gamma (γ)** to show how associated two variables are from our dataset. Note that *gamma* can be interpreted as a PRE measure similar to *tau* and *lambda* above, meaning that the *gamma* coefficient will indicate how much information on our independent variable reduces our error in predicting our dependent variable of interest. *Gamma* can take on values ranging from −1 to +1, where a value of 0 indicates no relationship at all, a negative value indicates a negative relationship, and a positive value a positive relationship. The closer the value is to either −1 or +1 is indicative of how strong the relationship is between the variables.

Let's calculate the *gamma* coefficient for two of our survey measures. We are interested in testing the association between two measures commonly used to gauge community informal social control. The first variable, Q20A, is based on a survey question asking respondents how likely it is that their neighbors would do something about a group of neighborhood children skipping school. The second variable, Q20B, asks respondents how likely it is that neighbors would do something if children were spray painting graffiti on a neighborhood building. We will recode our variables as necessary and then use the `GoodmanKruskalGamma()` function from the `DescTools` package to estimate *gamma*. When recoding Q20A, though the values are not labelled, we know from checking the codebook that this variable is ranked such that values of 1 are equal to *very likely* and values of 4 are *very unlikely*. Remember always refer to the codebook for your dataset when recoding variables, and you can also use the `attributes()` function.

```
# First, check and recode your variables if necessary.
table(seattle_df$Q20A)

##
##    1    2    3    4    8    9
## 432  701  784  207   87    9

seattle_df$intv.truancy <- factor(seattle_df$Q20A,
    levels = c(1, 2, 3, 4),
    labels = c("very likely",
    "likely", "unlikely",
    "very unlikely"))

# Review everything was coded correctly
table(seattle_df$intv.truancy)
##
##    very likely          likely       unlikely very unlikely
##            432             701            784           207

class(seattle_df$intv.truancy)

## [1] "factor"

# Now do the same for the graffiti variable...
table(seattle_df$Q20B)

##
##    1    2    3    4    8    9
## 1198  761  177   43   35    6

seattle_df$intv.graff<- factor(seattle_df$Q20B,
    levels = c(1, 2, 3, 4),
    labels = c("very likely",
    "likely", "unlikely",
    "very unlikely"))

table(seattle_df$intv.graff)

##
##    very likely          likely       unlikely very unlikely
##           1198             761            177            43

class(seattle_df$intv.graff)

## [1] "factor"

# Assess the relationship between these two variables
GoodmanKruskalGamma(seattle_df$intv.truancy,
   seattle_df$intv.graff, lconf.leve = .95)

##     gamma     lwr.ci     upr.ci
## 0.6315274 0.5898587 0.6731960

# We can also run it using a table saved as an R object
x <- table(seattle_df$intv.truancy,
           seattle_df$intv.graff)
gamma_neighbor_intervene <- GoodmanKruskalGamma
                            (x, conf.level =.95)
```

Because we specified the `conf.level` option, we get a 95% confidence interval around the *gamma* coefficient in addition to the coefficient itself. The value we receive is 0.63, which, in addition to the confidence interval that does not overlap with 0, indicates a fairly strong statistically significant and positive association between the two variables.

Kendall's τ_b and τ_c

Kendall's τ_b and **Kendall's τ_c** measures have similar interpretations to *gamma*, but they also use information on tied pairs. You will need to know the dimensions of your contingency table when making a decision on which *tau* to use—*tau_b* is able to deal with tables where the number of rows is the same as the number of columns. Alternatively, *tau_c* should be applied to a table where the number of rows and columns are not equal. Both measures have a possible value between −1 and +1. We will use the *tau_b* measure on our previous example using the function `KendallTauB()` from the `DescTools` package. We will also use the `kendall` method in the `cor.test()` function from the `stats` package to determine if the two variables are significantly related.

```
# First, change variables to numeric vectors

seattle_df$intv.truancy <- as.numeric
    (seattle_df$intv.truancy)
seattle_df$intv.graff <- as.numeric
    (seattle_df$intv.graff)

# Make sure there is a significant relationship

cor.test(seattle_df$intv.truancy, seattle_df$intv.graff,
    method = "kendall")

##
##  Kendall's rank correlation tau
##
## data:  seattle_df$intv.truancy and seattle_df$intv.graff
## z = 21.452, p-value < 0.00000000000000022
## alternative hypothesis: true tau is not equal to 0
## sample estimates:
##       tau
## 0.4168616

# Use the tau-b measure on our table "x" from the
## last example
# You should receive the same answer as in the cor.test()
## results

KendallTauB(x, conf.level = .95)

##     tau_b    lwr.ci    upr.ci
## 0.4168616 0.3849656 0.4487576
```

You can see from this value that our knowledge about the independent variable (in this example, the likelihood of neighbors intervening in children spraying graffiti) reduces our errors in predicting our dependent variable by about 42%. This measure is also statistically significant, as evident from the *p*-value obtained through the `cor.test()`, and from the fact that the 95% confidence interval around the estimate obtained through `KendallTauB()` does not overlap with 0.

So far we have conducted measures on symmetrical tables, but we may be interested in the relationship between two *asymmetric* variables. Let's now look at the association between the variable Q10D from our dataset, which measures how often the respondent has helped a neighbor with a problem, and the variable measuring the respondent's perception of the likelihood a neighbor would try to stop kids from vandalizing property with graffiti. We will use the `StuartTauC()` function from `DescTools` to estimate this measure.

```
# Recode the variable Q10D

table(seattle_df$Q10D)
##
##    -1    1    2    3    8    9
##     1  476 1372  364    5    2

seattle_df$nbrs_helped <- factor(seattle_df$Q10D,
    levels = c(1, 2, 3),
    labels = c("often", "sometimes", "never"))
# Check your recoded variable

table(seattle_df$nbrs_helped)

##
##      often sometimes     never
##        476      1372       364

# Let's look at a crosstabs of the two variables and
## save it in the object "y"

y <- table(seattle_df$intv.graff, seattle_df$nbrs_helped)

y

##
##      often sometimes never
## 1      316       733   145
## 2      121       493   145
## 3       25       101    51
## 4       10        25     8

# Now conduct the Kendall's tau-c test using the
## StuartTauC function
# Using the table saved above in the object "y"

StuartTauC(y, conf.level=.95)

##        tauc     lwr.ci     upr.ci
## 0.1223570 0.0900816 0.1546324
```

You can see that this value is much closer to 0, indicating a weak, albeit significant, relationship between these two variables. If you were really interested in which survey measures did a better job of predicting a respondent's perception of their neighbor's likelihood of exerting this type of informal social control, you may want to search for a different variable from your survey.

Somers' *D*

The final measure of association commonly used for ordinal variables is **Somers' *D***. This measure differs slightly from the *tau* measures, in that it uses information on tied pairs on the independent variable only, rather than both the independent and dependent variables. This means that prior to using this measure, you must define which is your independent and which is your dependent variable.

We will use the `SomersDelta()` function from the `DescTools` package to demonstrate this measure. We will examine the relationship between the respondents' perception of their neighbor's willingness to exert informal social control (via intervening when kids are skipping school) and how likely the respondent would miss their neighborhood if they had to move away (Q7). We will specify the measure of perceived neighbor's likelihood of intervening as the independent variable (intv.graff defined above) and the likelihood that the respondent would miss their neighborhood as the dependent variable.

```
# Recode the variable Q7

seattle_df$miss_neigh <- factor(seattle_df$Q7,
        levels = c(1, 2, 3, 4),
        labels = c("very likely", "likely",
                   "unlikely", "very unlikely"))

# Check our newly coded variable

table(seattle_df$miss_neigh)

##
##    very likely         likely       unlikely very unlikely
##           1094            760            244           102

# To run Somers' D, first save the contingency table
## in the R object "z"

z <- table(seattle_df$intv.graff, seattle_df$miss_neigh)

# Now run the Somers' D measure

SomersDelta(z, direction = "row", conf.level = 0.95)

##     somers    lwr.ci    upr.ci
## 0.1867064 0.1502957 0.2231171
```

The `direction` option tells R which variable should be considered the independent variable. The function defaults to *row*, so if you excluded this option, the function would still provide you with a value. In this case, our value is positive, but fairly close to 0, indicating the respondents' perception of their neighbors' willingness to intervene is a poor predictor of how much they would miss their neighborhood if they had to move. Moreover, the confidence interval around the estimate does not overlap with 0, indicating that, despite the small relationship, this association is statistically significant. Now you can try practicing these different measures of association below.

Application Activities

Problem 1:

Using all three methods of association we covered so far, *phi*, *tau*, and *lambda*, and the functions `Phi()`, `GKtau()`, and `Lambda()`, find the measure of association between respondents' race (choose one of Q70_1, Q70_2, Q70_3, or Q70_5) and different types of crime prevention measures taken by neighborhood residents (choose one of Q64A, Q64B, Q64C, Q64D, Q64E, Q64F). Remember that you can obtain more information on how variables are coded using the `attributes()` function. Then, interpret your results using comments in your script file.

Problem 2:

Using the `GoodmanKruskalGamma()`, `KendallTauB()`, and `SomersDelta()` functions, find the *gamma*, *tau_b*, and *Somers' D* measures of association between the variables Q22B and Q22C, which measure respondents' perceptions about potential street codes of violence in their neighborhood. Then, interpret your results using comments in your script file.

Problem 3:

Find *Somers' D* for the relationship between the measure of how safe the respondent thinks their neighborhood is from crime (Q54) and how much they worry about their safety (Q55A). Remember to define your independent and dependent variable when using the function `SomersDelta()`. Then, interpret your results using comments in your script file.

Problem 4:

Using the `StuartsTauC()` function, find Kendall's *tau_c* of the relationship between variable Q19D, which asks respondents to indicate how much they agree that people in their neighborhood are willing to help their neighbors, and Q16A, which asks respondents how effective they think small groups of neighbors would be in solving neighborhood problems. Then, interpret your results using comments in your script file.

Key Terms

Concordant pairs of observations Pairs of observations that have consistent rankings on two ordinal variables.

Cramer's V A measure of association for two nominal variables that adjusts the chi-square statistic by the sample size. V is appropriate when at least one of the nominal variables has more than two categories.

Discordant pairs of observations Pairs of observations that have inconsistent rankings on two ordinal variables.

Gamma (γ) PRE measure of association for two ordinal variables that uses information about concordant and discordant pairs of observations within a table. Gamma has a standardized scale ranging from −1.0 to 1.0.

Goodman and Kruskal's lambda (λ) PRE measure of association for two nominal variables that uses information about the modal category of the dependent variable for each category of the independent variable. Lambda has a standardized scale ranging from 0 to 1.0.

Goodman and Kruskal's tau (τ) PRE measure of association for two nominal variables that uses information about the proportional distribution of cases within a table. Tau has a standardized scale ranging from 0 to 1.0. For this measure, the researcher must define the independent and dependent variables.

Kendall's τ_b PRE measure of association for two ordinal variables that uses informa-

tion about concordant pairs, discordant pairs, and pairs of observations tied on both variables examined. τ_b has a standardized scale ranging from −1.0 to 1.0 and is appropriate only when the number of rows equals the number of columns in a table.

Kendall's τ_c A measure of association for two ordinal variables that uses information about concordant pairs, discordant pairs, and pairs of observations tied on both variables examined. τ_c has a standardized scale ranging from −1.0 to 1.0 and is appropriate when the number of rows is not equal to the number of columns in a table.

Phi (φ) A measure of association for two nominal variables that adjusts the chi-square statistic by the sample size. Phi is appropriate only for nominal variables that each have two categories.

Proportional reduction in error (PRE) The proportional reduction in errors made when the value of one measure is predicted using information about the second measure.

Somers' D PRE measure of association for two ordinal variables that uses information about concordant pairs, discordant pairs, and pairs of observations tied on the independent variable. Somers' D has a standardized scale ranging from −1.0 to 1.0.

Tied pairs of observations Pair of observations that have the same ranking on two ordinal variables.

Functions Introduced in this Chapter

FUNCTION	DESCRIPTION (PACKAGE)
GKtau()	Conducts the Goodman-Kruskal *tau* measure of association (GoodmanKruskal)
GoodmanKruskalGamma()	Conducts Goodman-Kruskal *gamma* measure of association (DescTools)
KendallTauB()	Conducts the Kendall tau_b measure of association (DescTools)
Lambda()	Conducts the *lambda* measure of association (DescTools)
Phi()	Conducts the *phi* measure of association (DescTools)
SomersDelta()	Conducts the Somers' *D* measure of association (DescTools)
StuartTauC()	Conducts the Kendall tau_c measure of association (DescTools)
cor.test(…method = "kendall")	Conducts a Kendall's *tau* correlation test (stats)

Reference

Matsueda, R. L. (2010). Seattle neighborhoods and crime survey, 2002-2003 [Data file]. Ann Arbor, MI: Inter-university Consortium for Political and Social Research [distributor]. Retrieved from https://doi.org/10.3886/ICPSR28701.v1.

Bivariate Correlation

Topics Practiced

Exploring bivariate relationships between two ratio-/interval-level variables

Exploring bivariate relationships between two ordinal-level variables

Technical Skills Covered

Conduct a Pearson's correlation

Conduct a Spearman's (rho) rank-order correlation

Conduct a Kendall's rank correlation

R Packages Required

dplyr, GGally, ggplot2, gmodels, grid, here, tibble, tidyverse

A. Wooditch et al., *A Beginner's Guide to Statistics for Criminology and
Criminal Justice Using R*, https://doi.org/10.1007/978-3-030-50625-4_14

THIS CHAPTER COVERS how to measure the strength of the relationship between two ratio-/interval- and two ordinal-level variables. The walk-through starts out by visually examining the bivariate relationship between the two variables of interest using a scatterplot. This is important because it will inform us whether we measure the strength of the relationship using a Pearson's correlation (parametric test for a linear relationship) or a Spearman's rho/Kendall's tau correlation (nonparametric test for a nonlinear relationship). The chapter draws on a dataset used by Patrick Sharkey et al. (2017) to study the effect of nonprofit organizations on crime.

Data

Data Source: For this chapter, we will rely on the data used by Patrick Sharkey (a Professor of Sociology and Public Affairs at Princeton University) and his colleagues to study the effect of nonprofit organizations on crime.

File Name: sharkey.csv

Dataset Description: From the 1990s to the 2010s, the rate of homicides declined by nearly 50% across more than one-third of the largest US cities. In the book *Uneasy Peace*, Prof. Sharkey argues that one of the factors that contributed to this crime decline was the role played by nonprofit community organizations to bring peace and services to deteriorated neighborhoods. The dataset combines data from many different sources on a sample of 264 US cities across 44 states (crime data from Uniform Crime Reports, demographic data from the US Census, and data on nonprofits from the National Center for Charitable Statistics). In this chapter, we will use the replication data from one of the papers that Prof. Sharkey published to study this question (Sharkey, 2018). We can find this dataset in the Harvard Dataverse (Sharkey et al., 2017).

Getting Started

1. Open your existing R project as outlined in Chap. 2 (see also Appendix 1.3).

2. Install and load the required packages using the `install.packages()` and `library()` functions (see Appendix 1.1).

3. Load the dataset (*sharkey.csv*) using the `read_csv()` function to import the dataset (see Appendix 1.6.3), specifying the working directory with `here()` (see Appendix 1.3). Alternatively, you can load the dataset from the Dataverse website (see Appendix 1.6.10). The web address is https://dataverse.harvard.edu/api/access/datafile/:persistentId?persistentId=doi:10.7910/DVN/46WIH0/ARS2VS. When doing so, name the data frame `sharkey` by using the `<-` assignment operator.

4. And if you dislike scientific notation as much as we do, you can turn it off in R by using `options(scipen=999)`.

Visualizing Bivariate Relationships

We are first going to examine the bivariate relationship between the variables of interest using a **scatterplot**. (You may want to review Chap. 3 and Appendix 4 if you would like to add more customizations to the scatterplot.) The purpose of doing this is because, if we want to examine whether two continuous variables are significantly related to each other, we need to determine whether the variables have a **linear relationship** as it determines what statistical test we need to conduct. For instance, two variables could have a positive linear relationship (as one variable increases, the other increases), or there can be a negative linear relationship (as one variable increases, the other decreases). The extent to which two variables move together is referred to as **covariation**.

There are many more variables in our dataset than we are going to need, so let's do some filtering and selection. Let's just focus on a single year, 2012, which is the most recent in the dataset and just a few select variables. We are going to place them in a data frame named, `df`. To do this, we are using the `filter()` and `select()` functions from the `dplyr` package. Then, we are going to remove the dataset from R using the `rm()` function.

```
df <- filter(sharkey, year == "2012")

df <- select(df, place_name, state_name, black, lesshs,
            unemployed, fborn, in carceration,
            log_viol_r, largest50)
rm(sharkey)
```

So, now we have a more manageable dataset that we can use for this walk-through. We can view the number of cities located in each of the 44 states (see place_name variable) in the sample using the **table()** function.

```
table(df$place_name)
```

The variables we have extracted contain information on the demographic composition of those cities (percent black population, percent without high school degree, percent unemployed, percent foreign born), some criminal justice ones (incarceration rate and the rate of sworn full-time police officers). We also have measures of the violence rate and a binary indicator that tell us if the city is one of the 50 largest in the country (1 on this variable indicating one of the 50 largest).

The first step in exploring relationships should always be using graphs because a Pearson's correlation requires that the two variables demonstrate a linear relationship. For assessing relationships between quantitative variables, we use scatterplots. Let's look at the scatterplot between the log of the violence rate (log_viol_r) and unemployment (unemployed) using the **ggplot()** function in the **ggplot2** package.

```
ggplot(df, aes(x = unemployed, y = log_viol_r)) +
  # Jitter adds a little random noise
  # This makes points less likely to overlap one
  ## another in the plot
  geom_point(alpha=.2, position="jitter")
```

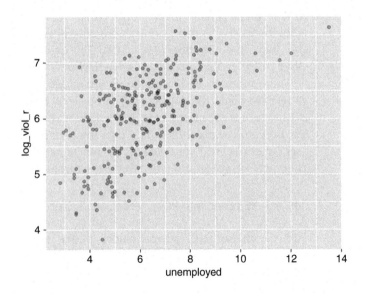

What do you think when looking at this scatterplot? Is there a linear relationship between violence and unemployment? Does it look as if cities that have a high score on the x-axis (unemployment) also have a high score on the y-axis (violent crime)?

It may be a bit hard to see but I would think there is certainly a trend. In this sample, cities with more unemployment seem to have more violence. Notice, for example, how at high levels of unemployment, there aren't places with low levels of violence. We can see this if we plot the conditional means. The conditional means are simply the means for one of the variables at the various values of the other one. In this case, we will look at the means of violence for various levels of unemployment.

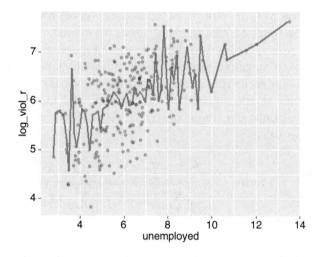

We can see here that the red line, the conditional means, fluctuates quite a lot (given that the sample of cities at each value of unemployment is small and that makes the estimate noisy). But all in all, we can see something of a trend. The line seems to be moving upward, that is, indicating a positive relationship. High values on the y-axis tend to correspond to high values on the x-axis and vice versa. Therefore, the two variables have a linear relationship and we can conduct a Pearson's correlation.

Pearson's Correlation Coefficient

Now, you may be interested in assessing the strength of the relationship between the two continuous measures. The scatterplot you conducted reveals that a linear relationship exists; thus, you can conduct a **Pearson's correlation**. This test tells you whether the two variables are significantly related to one another (whether they covary), and a p-value is provided to determine this. A Pearson's correlation test also provides a **Pearson's r** value, which provides the strength of the relationship between the two variables. A Pearson's r value ranges from -1 (as one variable increases, the other decreases) to 1 (as one variable increases, the other increases too), and values that are closer to 1 or -1 suggest a stronger relationship. Note that this test establishes a correlation exists; it does not assess whether one variable causes an effect on the other.

What the Pearson's correlation test does is examine how much each case deviates from the mean of each of the two variables and then multiplies these deviations.

$$\text{Covariation of scores} = \sum_{i=1}^{N} \left(X_{1i} - \bar{X}_1\right)\left(X_{2i} - \bar{X}_2\right)$$ **Equation 14.1**

However, the size of the covariation between two measures depends on the units of measurement used. To permit comparison of covariation across variables with different units of measurement, we must standardize the covariation between the two variables according to the variability within each. This is done by taking the square root of the product of the sums of the squared deviations from the mean for the two variables. Pearson's r is, then, the ratio between the covariation of scores and this value.

$$\text{Pearson's } r = \frac{\sum_{i=1}^{N}\left(X_{1i} - \bar{X}_1\right)\left(X_{2i} - \bar{X}_2\right)}{\sqrt{\left[\sum_{i=1}^{N}\left(X_{1i} - \bar{X}_1\right)^2\right]\left[\sum_{i=1}^{N}\left(X_{2i} - \bar{X}_2\right)^2\right]}}$$ **Equation 14.2**

The formula is implemented in base R with the `cor()` function (just provides Pearson's r value) and `cor.test()` function (provides Pearson's r value, confidence intervals, p-value, etc.). Let's explore the relationship between the violence rate and unemployment with a Pearson's correlation. First, let us write out our hypotheses and then we can run the test in R.

Hypotheses

H_0: There is no correlation between the violence rate and unemployment.

H_A: There is a correlation between the violence rate and unemployment.

Conduct Pearson's correlation.

```
cor(df$log_viol_r, df$unemployed)

## [1] 0.5368416

cor.test(~ log_viol_r + unemployed,
        data=df,
        method = "pearson",
        conf.level = 0.95)

##
##  Pearson's product-moment correlation
##
## data:  log_viol_r and unemployed
## t = 10.3, df = 262, p-value < 0.00000000000000022
## alternative hypothesis: true correlation is not equal to 0
## 95 percent confidence interval:
##  0.4449525 0.6175447
## sample estimates:
##       cor
## 0.5368416
```

The `cor()` function is convenient over `cor.test()` when we want to use the correlation coefficient as an input for something else. Both give a positive correlation of 0.54. The fact that it is positive indicates that high values in one variable are associated with high values in the other. The coefficient gives us also an indication of the strength of the relationship. Jacob Cohen (1988) suggests that within the social sciences, a correlation of 0.10 may be defined as a small relationship; a correlation of 0.30, a moderate relationship; and a correlation of 0.50, a large relationship. As with all rules of thumb, this should be taken with a grain of salt, and we would need to be aware of the specific context of application.

The `cor.test()` function printed a 95% confidence interval for the coefficient (0.44–0.62), which is informative of sampling variation. It also provides a statistical test that this value is different from zero, which in this case is highly significant.

Given that the linearity assumption of Pearson's correlation is met, and our results are statistically significant, we can reject the null hypothesis. We conclude that there is a statistically significant relationship between the violence rate and unemployment.

> **Hypotheses Conclusion**
>
> H_0: ~~There is no correlation between the violence rate and unemployment.~~
>
> H_A: There is a correlation between the violence rate and unemployment. [REJECT NULL]

Outliers and Nonlinear Relationships

Pearson's r correlation coefficient will be misleading in situations where you have serious outliers or whenever you are dealing with nonlinear relationships. Let's see this in practice. We are going to add an influential outlier to our data frame to start with.

If you want to add cases to a data frame, you have several possible ways of doing it. Perhaps the most convenient is to use the **add_row()** function from the **tibble** package.

```
# For convenience, we will first further reduce the
## number of variables
df_1 <- select(df, unemployed, log_viol_r)

df_1 <- add_row(df_1, unemployed = 20, log_viol_r = 1)
```

You will notice that we now have 265 observations in our data frame. Let's plot this.

```
ggplot() +
  geom_point(data=df_1, aes(x = unemployed, y = log_viol_r),
                           alpha=.2) +
  geom_line(data=df_1, aes(x = round(unemployed/0.12)*0.12,
            y = log_viol_r), stat='summary', fun.y=mean,
            color="red", size=1)
```

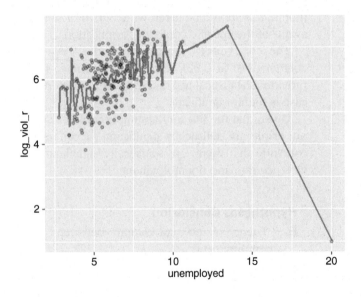

Now, we have a fictitious city with a very high level of unemployment and the lowest level of violence. Let's see what that does to our correlation coefficient.

```
cor.test(~ log_viol_r + unemployed,
         data=df_1,
         method = "pearson",
         conf.level = 0.95)

##
##  Pearson's product-moment correlation
##
## data:  log_viol_r and unemployed
## t = 4.4884, df = 263, p-value = 0.00001074
## alternative hypothesis: true correlation is not equal to 0
## 95 percent confidence interval:
##  0.1510944 0.3751766
## sample estimates:
##       cor
## 0.2667366
```

Pearson's *r* value is about half of what it was before. Just a single observation has managed to do that. That is oftentimes why the log of a variable is used for a parametric test (see the **log()** function in Chap. 1).

Let's now look at the relationship between the log of the violence rate (log_viol_r) and the percentage residents with less than a high school degree (lesshs variable). If we observe this scatterplot, we can see that when we move until the population reaches about 15% with less than a high school degree, the level of violence goes up quickly. But once that level of low education is reached, the relationship seems to flatten. Additional increases in the level of low educational achievement do not seem to lead to any further increases in violence.

Clearly, there is a relationship here. It is simply that is not a relationship that can be captured by a straight line. Here, we need at least one angle to explain the pattern of data.

```
ggplot(df, aes(x = lesshs, y = log_viol_r)) +
  geom_point(alpha=.2, position="jitter") +
  geom_smooth()
```

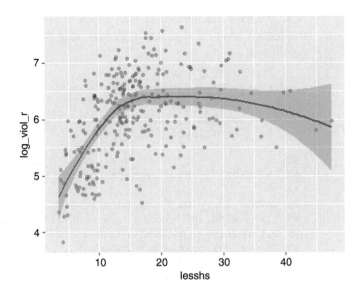

So, what is the correlation here?

```
cor.test(~ log_viol_r + lesshs,
         data=df,
         method = "pearson",
         conf.level = 0.95)

##
##  Pearson's product-moment correlation
##
## data:  log_viol_r and lesshs
## t = 6.8081, df = 262, p-value = 0.00000000006727
## alternative hypothesis: true correlation is not equal to 0
## 95 percent confidence interval:
##  0.2800879 0.4856982
## sample estimates:
##       cor
## 0.387705
```

Is this a good summary of what we observe? What would happen if we split the sample in two?

```
# Split the data according to the level of
## educational achievement

df_a <- filter(df, lesshs <=15)
df_b <- filter(df, lesshs > 15)


# Compute correlation for cities with higher levels of
## achievement

cor.test(~ log_viol_r + lesshs,
         data=df_a,
         method = "pearson",
         conf.level = 0.95)

##
##   Pearson's product-moment correlation
##
## data:  log_viol_r and lesshs
## t = 9.2127, df = 140, p-value = 0.0000000000000004247
## alternative hypothesis: true correlation is not equal to 0
## 95 percent confidence interval:
##   0.5002494 0.7074811
## sample estimates:
##        cor
## 0.6143512

# Compute correlation for cities with lower levels of
## achievement

cor.test(~ log_viol_r + lesshs,
         data=df_b,
         method = "pearson",
         conf.level = 0.95)

##
##   Pearson's product-moment correlation
##
## data:  log_viol_r and lesshs
## t = -0.66973, df = 120, p-value = 0.5043
## alternative hypothesis: true correlation is not equal to 0
## 95 percent confidence interval:
##   -0.2362225  0.1180171
## sample estimates:
##         cor
## -0.06102407
```

What we observe is that our summary was somehow inappropriate in representing the full pattern of data. In this case, splitting the sample helps to see the correlation when the percent of residents with high school degree is low. As this percentage increases, the level of violence goes up quickly. But then, in fact, what we see is a flat relationship, a straight line with an insignificant coefficient.

Nonparametric Alternatives to Pearson's *r*: Kendall's Tau and Spearman's Rho

Kendall's tau and Spearman's correlation are the nonparametric version of Pearson's correlation, so they should be used if the assumption of linearity cannot be met. **Kendall's tau** and **Spearman's (rho) rank correlation** are similar in that they calculate a correlation coefficient by ranking the data, and like Pearson's *r*, higher absolute values indicate a stronger relationship. Kendall's tau is more accurate in comparison to Spearman's rho when you have a small sample size.

In R, we can ask the `cor.test()` for Kendall's tau and Spearman's correlation coefficients. Again, both focus on the rank order of cases and are used when the two variables do not have a linear relationship.

```
cor.test(~ log_viol_r + unemployed,
        data=df_1,
        method = "kendall",
        conf.level = 0.95)

##
##  Kendall's rank correlation tau
##
## data:  log_viol_r and unemployed
## z = 8.3925, p-value < 0.00000000000000022
## alternative hypothesis: true tau is not equal to 0
## sample estimates:
##       tau
## 0.345979

cor.test(~ log_viol_r + unemployed,
        data=df_1,
        method = "spearman",
        conf.level = 0.95)

## Warning in cor.test.default(x = c(7.2830276, 6.79316,
##                                   6.478019, 5.949461,
:
## Cannot compute exact p-value with ties

##
##  Spearman's rank correlation rho
##
## data:  log_viol_r and unemployed
## S = 1574389, p-value < 0.00000000000000022
## alternative hypothesis: true rho is not equal to 0
## sample estimates:
##       rho
## 0.4923882
```

Notice how both of them give you a higher coefficient than Pearson's r in the case where we added a fictitious outlier. The correlation coefficient is represented by tau for Kendall's rank (ranges from 0 to 1) and by Spearman's rho value (ranges −1 to 1) for Spearman's rank.

Correlation Matrix

It is often convenient to examine correlations between variables you want to explore. For this, graphical displays for a correlation matrix are particularly convenient. There are multiple ways of generating these in R. We could, for example, use the **ggcorr()** function from the **GGally** package that takes all the quantitative variables in a data frame to produce such a plot. And note that R gives you a warning that it is excluding variables from the plot that are not the appropriate level of measurement.

```
ggcorr(df)

## Warning in ggcorr(df): data in column(s) 'place_name',
    'state_name', 'high_vio',
## 'high_unem' are not numeric and were ignored
```

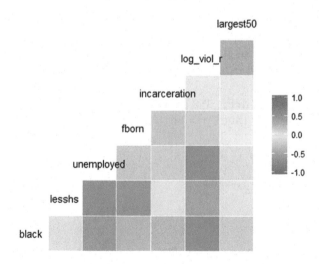

The **ggcorr()** function admits a number of arguments to control the appearance of the visualization.

```
ggcorr(df, label = TRUE, label_size = 3, label_round = 2,
       label_alpha = TRUE)

## Warning in ggcorr(df, label = TRUE, label_size = 3,
## label_round = 2, label_alpha = TRUE): data in column(s)
## 'place_name', 'state_name', 'high_vio', 'high_unem'are
## not numeric and were ignored
```

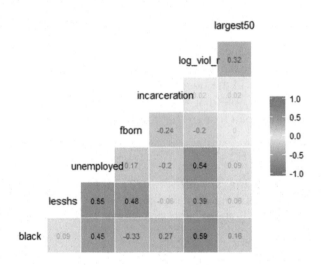

And one could use standard indexing in R to select just some of the columns in our data frame. So, let's get rid of largest50, which is a binary categorical indicator and column 9 in our data frame.

```
ggcorr(df[, 3:8], label = TRUE, label_size = 3,
       label_round = 2, label_alpha = TRUE)
```

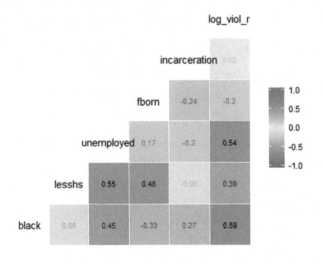

We can also use a Spearman method, if we prefer.

```
ggcorr(df[, 3:8], method = c("pairwise", "spearman"),
    label = TRUE, label_size = 3, label_round = 2,
    label_alpha = TRUE)
```

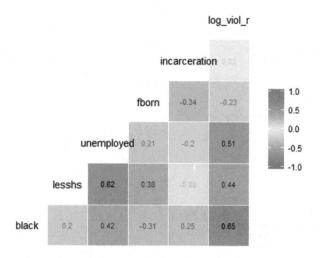

Another convenient way to plot multiple correlations is the **ggpairs()** function from the **GGally** package.

```
ggpairs(df, columns=3:8)
```

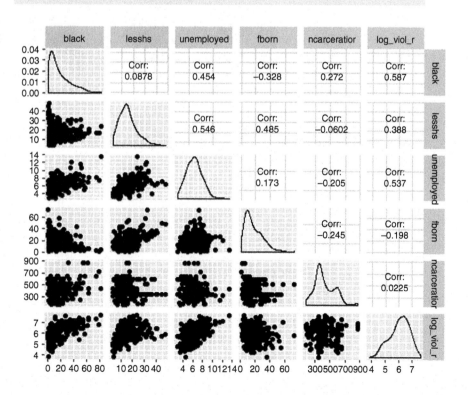

With `ggpairs()`, not only do we get the correlation matrix, but we also see the paired scatterplots for each pair of variables, as well as the univariate distribution (in the diagonal axis) for each of the variables we are plotting. We can also name the variables in the plot by name if we prefer. Let's just select three of them.

```
ggpairs(df, columns = c("black", "unemployed", "lesshs",
                        "log_viol_r"))
```

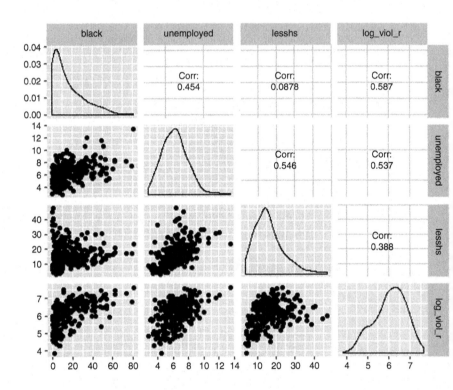

Correlations for Categorical Variables?

Sometimes people use Pearson's *r* to explore relationships between some types of categorical variables and argue that this is an okay approach, typically when the measures are dichotomous or ordinal (not with categorical, unordered variables with more than three levels because in these cases Pearson's *r* just cannot apply). More often than not, however, you should be using the measures of association we have discussed for categorical variables. It is not advisable to use Pearson's *r* with categorical or ordinal-level variables. In more advanced applications, particularly in psychometric work or latent variable modeling, you may need to compute correlations between categorical variables. There is a whole family of these correlation coefficients developed for those areas (tetrachoric, polychoric, biserial, and polyserial correlations). These materials go beyond the scope of this volume, but both the **polycor** and the **psych** package provide solutions for this.

Application Activities

Problem 1:

Using the <u>state name</u> variable, create a binary indicator to identify cities in Southern states and those not in Southern states. You can use any of the functions provided so far for generating new variables to do this. The list of Southern states is as follows: Alabama, Arkansas, Delaware, Florida, Georgia, Kentucky, Louisiana, Maryland, Mississippi, North Carolina, Oklahoma, South Carolina, Tennessee, Texas, Virginia, and West Virginia (use the state_name variable). Produce the appropriate correlation between log violence (<u>log viol r</u>) and unemployment (<u>unemployed</u>) using the appropriate combination of **cor()**, **group_by()**, and **summarize()** for the year 2012 for Southern and Northern cities. Is the correlation different for Southern and Northern cities?

Problem 2:

Use the same approach employed in the previous problem to explore how the correlation between the log violence rate (<u>log viol r</u>) and percentage of population that is black (<u>black</u>) has evolved during the whole study period for Southern and Northern cities. In the **cor()** function, you will have to pass the **use = "complete.obs"** argument so that the correlations are computed despite the existence of missing data. Are there any discernible patterns? Create appropriate visualization for the resulting tibble.

Problem 3:

Use **GGpairs()** to produce a visualization of the correlation between the percent of the population that is black (<u>black</u>), unemployment (<u>unemployed</u>), the percentage of residents with less than a high school degree (<u>lesshs</u>), and violence rate (<u>log viol r</u>) variables for the 50 largest cities and then for the rest of the sample (non-50 largest) by using the <u>largest50</u> variable.

Key Terms

Covariation A measure of the extent to which two variables vary together relative to their respective means. The covariation between the two variables serves as the numerator for the equation to calculate Pearson's r.

Kendall's tau Measures the strength and direction of two rank-ordered variables on a standardized scale between 0 and 1.0, whereby higher values indicate a stronger relationship.

Linear relationship An association between two variables whose joint distribution may be represented in linear form when plotted on a scatter diagram.

Pearson's correlation coefficient See *Pearson 's r.*

Pearson's *r* A commonly used measure of association between two variables. Pearson's *r* measures the strength and direction of linear relationships on a standardized scale from −1.0 to 1.0.

Scatterplot A graph whose two axes are defined by two variables and upon which a point is plotted for each subject in a sample according to its score on the two variables.

Spearman's correlation coefficient See *Spearman 's rho.*

Spearman's rho *(r_s)* A measure of association between two rank-ordered variables. Spearman's rho measures the strength and direction of linear relationships on a standardized scale between −1.0 and 1.0.

Functions Introduced in this Chapter

FUNCTION	DESCRIPTION (PACKAGE)
add_row()	Add rows to a data frame (`tibble`)
cor()	Produces the correlation of two variables (base **R**)
cor.test()	Obtains correlation coefficient (base **R**)
ggcorr()	Visualize a correlation matrix (`GGally`)
ggpairs()	Makes a matrix of plots, e.g. correlations, scatterplots (`GGally`)
rm()	Remove object from **R** environment (base **R**)

References

Cohen, J. (1988). *Statistical power analysis for the behavioral sciences.* Hillsdale, NJ: Lawrence Erlbaum.

Sharkey, P., Torrats-Espinosa, G., & Takyar, D. (2017). Community and the crime decline: The causal effect of local nonprofits on violent crime. *American Sociological Review, 82*(6), 1214–1240.

Sharkey, P. (2018). Replication data for, "Sharkey, P., Torrats-Espinosa, G., & Takyar, D. (2017). Community and the crime decline: The causal effect of local nonprofits on violent crime. American Sociological Review, 82(6), 1214-1240." Retrieved March 30, 2020, from https://doi.org/10.7910/DVN/46WIH0, Harvard Dataverse, V2, UNF:6:kGD4YDh/xSMtgVJ6knZnmA== [fileUNF].

Ordinary Least Squares
Regression

Topics Practiced

Modeling linear relationships between two ratio or interval variables using OLS regression

Meeting model assumptions

Building models and interpreting output

Assessing model fit

Technical Skills Covered

Using `ggplot()` to examine linear relationships

Conducting OLS regression

Making predictions from a fitted model

R Packages Required

`arm`, `car`, `ggplot2`, `here`, `tidyverse`

© The Editor(s) (if applicable) and The Author(s), under exclusive license to
Springer Nature Switzerland AG 2021
A. Wooditch et al., *A Beginner's Guide to Statistics for Criminology and
Criminal Justice Using R*, https://doi.org/10.1007/978-3-030-50625-4_15

THIS CHAPTER PROVIDES an introduction to ordinary least squares (OLS) regression analysis in R. This is a technique used to explore whether one or multiple variables (the independent variable or X) can predict or explain the variation in another variable (the dependent variable or Y). OLS regression belongs to a family of techniques called generalized linear models, so the variables being examined must be measured at the ratio or interval level and have a linear relationship. The chapter also reviews how to assess model fit using regression error (the difference between the predicted and actual values of Y) and R^2. While you learn these techniques in R, you will be using the Crime Survey for England and Wales data from 2013 to 2014; these data derive from a face-to-face survey that asks people about their experiences of crime during the 12 months prior to the interview.

Data

Dataset Source: The Crime Survey for England and Wales (CSEW) from 2013 to 2014 sweep teaching dataset

File Name: csew1314_teaching.csv

Dataset Description: The CSEW is a face-to-face survey that asks people about their experiences of crime during the 12 months prior to the interview. Respondents are also asked about their perceptions of crime and their attitudes toward crime-related issues, such as the police and criminal justice system. It includes all 35,371 cases and 127 select variables from the survey. It contains derived scalar variables, which measure key concepts such as confidence in the police, worry about crime, and so on. The dataset also includes construct variables (derived from other CSEW variables using principal components analysis) that all tap into the same concepts such as one variable that indicates how worried a respondent is about crime, derived using five related measures on *worrying about crime* in the dataset.

Getting Started

1. Open up your existing R project as outlined in Chap. 2 (see also Appendix 1.3).

2. Install and load the required packages using the `install.packages()` and `library()` functions (see Appendix 1.1).

3. Import the dataset, *csew1314_teaching.csv*, using the `read_csv()` function to import the dataset (see Appendix 1.6.3), specifying the working directory with `here()` (see Appendix 1.3). When doing so, name the data frame `df`.

OLS Regression Model Assumptions

In this chapter, we begin to talk about regression modeling and introduce you to **ordinary least squares regression** (OLS regression). This form of analysis has been one of the main techniques of data analysis in the social sciences for many years, and it belongs to a family of techniques called *generalized linear models*. Regression is a flexible model that allows you to *explain* or *predict* a given **dependent variable** (*Y*), variously called your outcome or response, as a function of a number of what is called **independent variable**(s), referred to as inputs, features, and explanatory or predictive variables (*X1, X2, X3*, etc.). When multiple independent variables are examined at the same time, they are called **covariates**. Sometimes when OLS regression uses only one independent variable, it is referred to as **bivariate regression**.

OLS regression is one of the many regression techniques. You use it when you are interested in exploring how one or multiple variables explain variation in a ratio- or interval-level variable. We will review the steps in conducting OLS regression below. After reviewing model assumptions, you will see how you can use regression analysis when you have one predictor. While you can use several predictors at once, that goes beyond the scope of the present chapter.

While this chapter is not a comprehensive overview of OLS regression, we are going to review important aspects of the technique, particularly those that pertain to techniques you must carry out in R.

Here are some *key assumptions* of OLS regression:

- *Linearity*. There must be a linear relationship between your predictor and outcome variable. If the relationship is nonlinear (e.g., it is curvilinear), predicted values will be wrong in a biased manner, meaning that predicted values will systematically miss the true pattern of the mean of Y (as related to the x-variables). We will discuss problems with nonlinearities below, including ways to diagnose and solve this problem.

- *Independence of errors*. Regression assumes that the errors from the prediction or **regression line** (or hyperplane) are independent. If there is dependency between the observations, you may have to use models that are more appropriate (e.g., multilevel models, spatial regression, Poisson regression). The term **heteroscedasticity**, meaning unequal scatter, is used to describe the correlation of model error, which violates the independence of error assumption.

- *Equal variances of errors*. When the variance of the residuals is unequal, you may need different estimation methods. This is, nonetheless, considered a minor issue. There is a small effect on the validity of *t*-test and *F*-test results, but generally, regression inferences are *robust* (meaning they don't change much) with regard to the variance issue.

- *Normality of errors*. The residuals should be normally distributed. Gelman and Hill (2007) discuss this as the least important of the assumptions because regression inferences tend to be *robust* with respect to non-normality of the errors. We will show you how to inspect normality of the residuals, not because this is a problem in and of itself, but because it may give you further evidence that there is some other problem with the model you are applying to your data, though it is important to note that your results can be sensitive to very large outliers. If this is a potential concern, refer to the steps presented in Chap. 4 for identifying and dropping outliers from your dataset.

- *Multicollinearity*. Variables that are highly correlated indicate that they are tapping into the same construct. When you include more than one independent variable as a predictor, they cannot be too highly correlated. If this problem does occur, it is referred to as **multicollinearity**. While there is no hard-and-fast rule, a Pearson's correlation of 0.6 or 0.7 is when you should start investigating further. Recall from Chap. 14 that you can examine this with several variables at once via a correlation matrix using the `ggcorr()` function from the `GGally` package. Below, we will also show you how to obtain the *variance inflation factor* (VIF) values for your model. You can also look for indicators of multicollinearity like model instability. When you add or remove a potentially collinear variable, some squirrelly things may begin to appear. To name a few, beta coefficients could change considerably or switch signs; you may find you have a very high R^2, which is just artificially inflated; you could have high standard errors for your coefficients; or you may have a significant overall model but no significant predictors.

We will go through how to test that some of the key assumptions are met and review some options that you can consider if you find that your model violates them in the sections below. While finding that some of the assumptions are violated does not necessarily mean that you have to scrap your model, it is important to use these diagnostics to illustrate that you have considered what the possible issues with your model are and if you find any serious issues that you address them.

Testing for Linearity

We will be exploring the research question: *Does age (age) predict perceived level of antisocial behavior in one's neighborhood (*antisocx *variable)?* For the antisocx variable, higher scores represent that the respondents perceive a good deal of antisocial behavior.

Now, let's write out our hypotheses:

> **Hypotheses**
>
> H_0: Age does not predict perceived level of antisocial behavior in one's neighborhood.
>
> H_A: Age predicts perceived level of antisocial behavior in one's neighborhood.

Before assessing whether there is a linear relationship between the two variables, let's look at their distribution. First, we can use the **summary()** function to obtain the measures of central tendency and dispersion.

```
summary(df$age)

##    Min. 1st Qu.  Median    Mean 3rd Qu.    Max.    NA's
##   16.00   34.00   48.00   49.17   63.00   99.00      22

summary(df$antisocx)

##    Min. 1st Qu.  Median    Mean 3rd Qu.    Max.    NA's
##  -4.015  -0.742  -0.005  -0.102   0.737   1.215    3926
```

You will see that this summary tells us that both variables have missing data. While you can just ignore these NAs, we are going to remove these cases and rerun our descriptives. The reason we are making this decision is because with regression, you are going to run into the issue of *listwise deletion*, which is when cases will be dropped from your analysis that are missing data on your dependent variable OR your independent variable(s). So when we obtain descriptives now, we are really only interested in those cases that won't be dropped from our analysis later on. We can use the `complete.cases()` function to drop these where we tell R to only retain cases in our dataset if they have valid responses for both key variables of interest. We can use the `nrow()` function to see how this impacts our sample size. And we do lose several cases :-/.

```
nrow(df) # Start with 5,193 cases

## [1] 5193

df <- df[(complete.cases(df$age) & complete.cases
      (df$antisocx)), ]
nrow(df) # Left with 1,259 cases after dropping NAs

## [1] 1259

# Summaries of just the 1,259 cases
summary(df$age)

##    Min. 1st Qu.  Median    Mean 3rd Qu.    Max.
##   16.00   33.50   48.00   48.74   63.00   98.00

summary(df$antisocx)

##       Min.  1st Qu.    Median      Mean   3rd Qu.      Max
## -4.014557 -0.741532  0.005403 -0.098637  0.736874  1.21526
```

Remember that we are just dealing with a subsample of the CSEW dataset. Imagine that we randomly select one of the respondents from the master dataset that is not in our current sample. What would you say if you were asked to provide your best guess as to the respondent's perceived antisocial behavior in the neighborhood (<u>antisocx</u>)? You would most likely say a value near the mean ($M = -0.099$) of the present sample.

Next, we can visually examine their distributions using the `qplot()` function.

```
qplot(x = age, data = df)
```

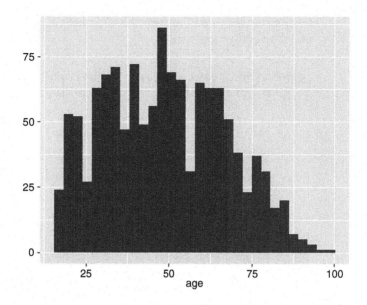

```
qplot(x = antisocx, data = df)
```

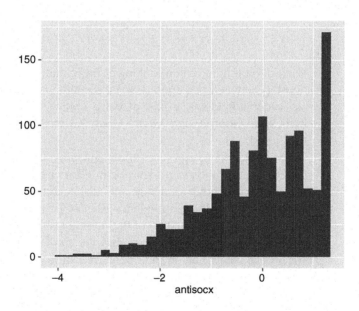

And we can see that the antisocx variable is a little negatively skewed.

Now, let's conduct a scatterplot to visualize their relationship by using the **ggplot()** function in the **ggplot2** package. Note here that we are examining how they covary together. This is different from regression because with regression, you are looking for some sort of causal relationship between the variables (X causes Y, rather than simply stating that they covary together).

```
ggplot(df, aes(x = age, y = antisocx)) +
  geom_point(alpha=.2, position="jitter")
```

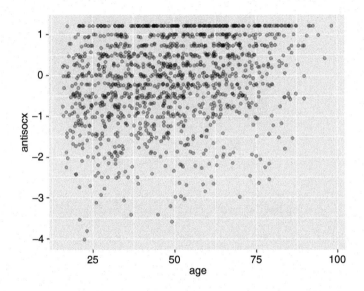

What do you think when looking at this scatterplot? Is there a linear relationship between perceptions of antisocial behavior and age? Does it look as if older individuals (x-axis) perceive a higher level of antisocial behavior in their neighborhood (y-axis)? I would say that there definitely appears to be a trend.

So, back to our question about guessing the new respondent's perceived level of antisocial behavior in the neighborhood. After reviewing measures of central tendency and dispersion before, you would most likely guess that the respondent's level of confidence would be a value near the mean ($M = -0.099$) of the present sample. But based on the scatterplot, what if you were told that the new respondent's age was 30? Would that change the level of perceived antisocial behavior you guess for that respondent? I certainly would not go with the overall mean or median as my prediction anymore. If somebody said to me the age of the respondent is 30, I would be more inclined to guess the mean value for the individuals *of that age* (referred to as the conditional mean), rather than the overall mean across all the individuals. Wouldn't you?

If we plot the conditional means, we can see that the mean of perceived antisocial behavior for those respondents around the age of 30 is around −0.3. So you may be better off guessing that. Notice how we are specifying that our trend line represents the mean of the variable on the y-axis (antisocx) and we want the means to be computed for each age (age).

```
ggplot() +
  geom_point(data=df, aes(x = age, y = antisocx), alpha=.2) +
  geom_line(data=df, aes(x = age, y = antisocx),
            stat='summary',
            fun.y=mean,
            color="blue",
            size=1)
```

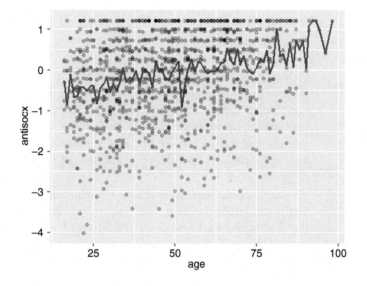

Or we can make the trend a little smoother by calculating average perceived antisocial behavior for age in increments of 5 years.

```
ggplot() +
  geom_point(data=df, aes(x = age, y = antisocx), alpha=.2) +
  geom_line(data=df, aes(x = round(age/5)*5, y = antisocx),
            stat='summary',
            fun.y=mean,
            color="blue",
            size=1)
```

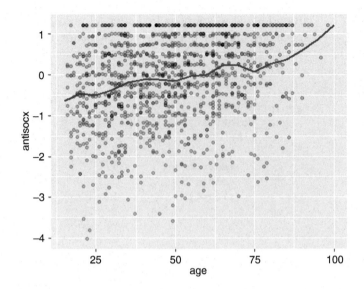

OLS regression (also referred to as simple linear regression) tackles this problem using a slightly different approach. Rather than focusing on the conditional mean (smoothed or not), it draws a straight line that tries to capture the trend in the data. If we focus in the region of the scatterplot that are less sparse, we see that this is an upward trend, suggesting that as age increases so do the perceptions of antisocial behavior in the neighborhood.

Simple linear regression draws a single straight line of predicted values as the model for the data. This line would be a model, a *simplification* of the real world like any other model (e.g., a toy pistol, an architectural drawing, a subway map), that assumes that there is approximately a linear relationship between X and Y.

Let's draw the regression line.

```
# method=lm asks for the linear regression line
# se=FALSE asks not to print confidence interval
# Other arguments specify the color, thickness of the line

ggplot(data = df, aes(x = age, y = antisocx)) +
  geom_point(alpha = .2, position = "jitter") +
  geom_smooth(method = "lm", se = FALSE, color = "red",
              size = 1)
```

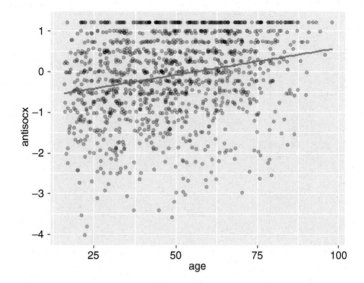

What that line is doing is giving you estimates (predictions) for the values of perceived level of antisocial behavior in the information that we have about age. It gives you one possible guess for the value of perceived antisocial behavior for every possible value of age and links them all together in a straight line.

Another way of thinking about this line is as the best possible summary of the cloud of points that are represented in the scatterplot (if we can assume that a straight line would do a good job doing this, and with a linear relationship, we can). If I were to tell you to draw a straight line that best represents this pattern of points, the regression line would be the one that best does it (if certain assumptions are met).

The linear model then is a model that takes the form of the equation of a straight line through the data. The line does not go through all the points. In fact, you can see it is a slightly less accurate representation than the (smoothed) conditional means:

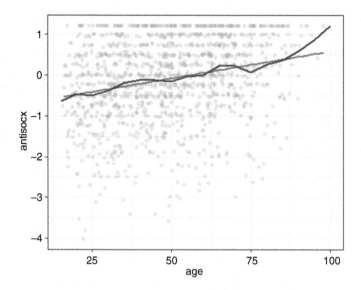

As Bock et al. (2012) highlight, "like all models of the real world, the line will be wrong–wrong in the sense that it can't match reality *exactly*. But it can help us understand how the variables are associated" (p. 179). A map is never a perfect representation of the world; the same happens with statistical models. Yet, as with maps, models can be helpful.

OLS Regression Model

As a reminder of the assumptions of OLS regression above, once you are at the point of running your model, you should have already established that a *linear relationship* exists between the independent variable and the dependent variable. You have checked for any large *outliers* and if they will potentially affect your results, transform your data (e.g., taking the log), or drop the outliers. And you have also made sure that if you plan to have more than 1 covariate, you already assessed potential multicollinearity concerns by conducting a correlation matrix of all independent variables. If you aren't positive that covariates pose a collinearity threat, we will discuss the calculation of VIF below. But you will also want to look for any problems with your model that are noted in the *OLS Regression Model Assumptions* section at the beginning of this chapter.

Additionally, while we do not delve into this topic (because we want you to buy our next book, hehe), we believe it is imperative to briefly touch upon covariate selection. We have explained that you can include more than one independent variable as a covariate (i.e., ~one covariate for every ten cases) and that you should look for signs of multicollinearity by reviewing a correlation matrix of your potential covariates. In creating your correlation matrix, you *do not* want to include your dependent variable in your correlation matrix. You will learn that some people select which variables to include as predictors in their model by selecting those that have statistically significant Pearson's r with their dependent variable (admittedly, we did this too when we didn't know any better). Instead, you will want to select variables by whether they are theoretically relevant. Otherwise, selecting based upon statistical significance will increase your chances of a type I error (finding a relationship that was significant just by chance alone). Okay, now that we got that off our chest, we can proceed.

To draw a regression line, we need to know two things:

1. We need to know where the line begins, what is the value of Y (our dependent variable) when X (our independent variable) is 0, so that we have a point from which to start drawing the line. The technical name for this point is the **intercept**.

2. And we need to know what the slope of that line is, that is, how inclined the line is, the angle of the line.

If you recall from elementary algebra (and you may not if you skipped this class like we did), the equation for any straight line is:

$$y = mx + b \hspace{3cm} \text{Equation 15.1}$$

In statistics, we use a slightly different notation, although the equation remains the same:

$$y = b0 + b1x \hspace{3cm} \text{Equation 15.2}$$

We need the origin of the line (**b0** or the y-intercept) and the slope of the line (**b1**). In linear regression models, like the one we cover here, when drawing the line, **R** tries to minimize the distance from every point in the scatterplot to the regression line using a method called *least squares estimation*. The reason for this is that your analysis draws a trend line, and then it calculates the distance from every point in the scatterplot to the trend line. The farther these points fall from the trend line, the more error your regression model will have. So with respect to this error, there are going to be some points that fall above the trend line (a positive error value), while other points will fall below the line (a negative error value). If we were to sum up these error values as is, the positives would cancel out the negatives and underreport our error, suggesting that our trend line was perfect. To get around this issue, the error values are squared before they are summed (since a negative * a negative equals a positive, they aren't canceled out anymore). Therefore, our regression model is trying to find a trend line fit that has the least (squared) error.

To fit the model, we use the `lm()` function using the formula specification (Y ~ X). Typically, you want to store your regression model in an object, which we will call fit_1:

```
fit_1 <- lm(antisocx ~ age, data = df)
```

You will see in your **RStudio** global environment space that there is a new object called **fit_1** with 12 elements in it. We can get a sense for what this object is and includes using the functions **class()** and **attributes()**:

```
class(fit_1)
## [1] "lm"

attributes(fit_1)

## $names
##  [1] "coefficients"  "residuals"  "effects"   "rank"
##  [5] "fitted.values" "assign"     "qr"        "df.residual"
##  [9] "xlevels"       "call"       "terms"     "model"
##
## $class
## [1] "lm"
```

R is telling us that this is an object of class **lm** and that it includes a number of attributes. One of the beauties of **R** is that you are producing all the results from running the model, and then putting them in an object, giving you the opportunity for using them later. A lot of the diagnostics that we will cover shortly work with various elements that we stored in this object. If you want to simply see the basic results from running the model, you can use the **summary()** function.

```
summary(fit_1)

##
## Call:
## lm(formula = antisocx ~ age, data = df)
##
## Residuals:
##     Min      1Q  Median      3Q     Max
## -3.5606 -0.6073  0.1196  0.8083  1.7357
##
## Coefficients:
##               Estimate Std. Error t value Pr(>|t|)
## (Intercept) -0.746338   0.081004  -9.214   <2e-16 ***
## age          0.013289   0.001557   8.534   <2e-16 ***
## ---
## Signif. codes: 0 '***' 0.001 '**' 0.01 '*' 0.05 '.'
## 0.1 ' ' 1
##
## Residual standard error: 1.004 on 1257 degrees of freedom
## Multiple R-squared:  0.05476, Adjusted R-squared: 0.05401
## F-statistic: 72.82 on 1 and 1257 DF, p-value: < 2.2e-16
```

Or if you prefer more parsimonious presentation, you could use the **display()** function from the **arm** package:

```
display(fit_1)

## lm(formula = antisocx ~ age, data = df)
##             coef.est coef.se
## (Intercept) -0.75     0.08
## age          0.01     0.00
## ---
## n = 1259, k = 2
## residual sd = 1.00, R-Squared = 0.05
```

Interpreting Model Output

Beta Coefficients

A **regression coefficient** (or beta coefficient) is a value that assesses the impact of the independent variable on the dependent variable. We then need the *b1* regression coefficient for our independent variable, the value that will shape the *slope* in this scenario. This value is 0.013289. This estimated regression coefficient for our independent variable has a convenient interpretation. When the value is positive, it tells us that *for every*

1 unit increase in X, there is a b1 increase on Y. If the coefficient is negative, then it represents a decrease on Y. Here, we can read it as "for every 1 year older, there is a 0.01 unit increase in level of perceived antisocial behavior in the neighborhood."

And since it took us way too long to realize this distinction when we learned regression, there is a difference between *b* (sometimes indicated by a capital *B*) and the fancy pants β. The *b* most often reported in OLS regression is in *unstandardized units*. If you are wondering whether your beta coefficients, *b*, are large or small, remember that they depend on the units being examined. For instance, if I were examining the effect of height in inches (*X*) on weight in pounds (*Y*), the interpretation of the beta coefficient, *b*, that is 0.30 would be "for every 1 *inch* increase in height, there is an increase in weight by 0.30 *pounds*." The fancy pants β indicates *standardized units*, which will range from −1 to 1. So using the same example but the β is 0.30, it would be interpreted as follows: "for every 1 *inch* increase in height, there is a 30% increase in how many *pounds* they weigh." That can be a big difference!

Statistical Significance

The *p*-value for each term (beta coefficient) tests the null hypothesis that the coefficient is equal to zero (no effect). A low *p*-value ($p < 0.05$) indicates that you can reject the null hypothesis. In other words, a predictor that has a low *p*-value is likely to be a meaningful addition to your model because changes in the predictor's value are statistically significantly related to changes in the response variable. Conversely, a larger (insignificant) *p*-value suggests that changes in the predictor are not associated with changes in the response. For statistically insignificant coefficients, while you can make statements about their general trend (positive or negative), we would not recommend that you interpret statistically insignificant beta coefficients.

In the output above, we can see that our *p*-value is very, very small—definitely under our cutoff alpha of 0.05. So, we can conclude that age significantly predicts level of perceived antisocial behavior and that we can reject the null hypothesis.

Hypotheses Conclusion

H_0: ~~Age does not predict perceived level of antisocial behavior in one's neighborhood.~~

H_A: Age predicts perceived level of antisocial behavior in one's neighborhood. [REJECT NULL]

However, we need to consider the coefficient as a measure of the effect size of this relationship. It is important to mention that with very large sample sizes, you should place less of an emphasis on p-values and more emphasis on the size of the beta coefficients because the p-values are very sensitive to sample size. With a very large sample size, you may have all statistically significant covariates (because of low error) even though the variables do not have much of an effect on your dependent variable.

You might see another p-value at the bottom of your regression output (last line of the output from the `summary()` function). Here, it says, "F-statistic: 72.82 on 1 and 1257 DF, p-value: $< 2.2e-16$." This shows you the results of an F-test printed at the bottom of the summary output and the associated p-value, which in this case is way below the conventional 0.05 cutoff that we use to declare statistical significance. This evaluates whether our model as a whole can predict our outcome of interest with high confidence. Especially if we had multiple predictors, we could conclude this as an indicator that at least one of our inputs must be related to our response variable (i.e., assuming there was no multicollinearity problem).

Y-Intercept

The first value you see in the *Estimate* column of the output from your `summary()` function of the regression is something called the *intercept*. In this case, the value of -0.7463377 estimated for the intercept is the *predicted* value for Y when X equals zero. This is the predicted value of perceived antisocial behavior *at 0 years old*.

Regression Line

With these two parameters, the coefficient and the intercept, we can draw that **regression line**—the line of best fit—through our data. Remember this:

```
ggplot(data = df, aes(x = age,
                      y = antisocx)) +
  geom_point(alpha = .2, position = "jitter") +
  geom_smooth(method = "lm", se = FALSE, color = "red",
              size = 1)
```

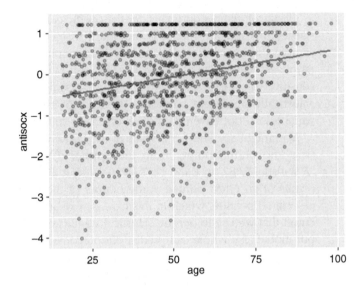

This line is drawn by knowing the intercept and the slope.

Regression as Prediction

Knowing the two parameters of the slope of the line (coefficient) and the y-intercept not only allows us to draw the line; we can also solve for any given value of X to make predictions. Now you get a better understanding for why the relationship between the independent and dependent variable needs to be linear. Let's go back to our guess-the-perceived-antisocial-behavior game. Imagine that I tell you that the age of the new respondent is 17. What would be your best bet now? We can simply go back to our regression line equation and insert the estimated parameters:

Or if you don't want to do the calculation yourself, you can use the **predict()** function:

```
y = b0 + b1x
y = -0.7463377 + 0.013289 (17)
y = -0.5204242
```

This suggests that −0.5204242 is the expected value of Y, perceived level of antisocial, when X age is 17. Of course, this is *according to our model* (a simplification of the real world—our simplification of the whole cloud of points into just one straight line). Look back at the scatterplot we produced earlier with the red line. Does it look as if the red line when X is 17 corresponds to a value of Y of −0.5204242? I would say yes!

Error Term

In the same way that we can compute the standard error when estimating the mean, we can compute standard errors for the regression coefficients to quantify our uncertainty about these estimates (referred to as **regression error** and represented by the symbol *e*). These standard errors can in turn be used to produce confidence intervals. This would require us to assume that the residuals are normally distributed. For a simple regression model, you are assuming that the values of Y are approximately normally distributed for each level of X. In those circumstances, we can trust the confidence intervals that we can draw around the regression line. You can also then perform standard hypothesis tests on the coefficients. As we saw before when summarizing the model, R will compute the standard errors and a *t*-test for each of the coefficients.

```
# First, you name your stored model and then you identify
# The new data has to be in a data frame format with
## matching variable names
predict(fit_1, data.frame(age = c(17)))

##          1
## -0.5204242
```

In our example, we can see that the coefficient for our predictor here is statistically significant.

We can also obtain confidence intervals for the estimated coefficients using the **confint()** function.

```
summary(fit_1)$coefficients

##               Estimate   Std. Error   t value     Pr(>|t|)
## (Intercept) -0.74633771 0.081003719 -9.213623 1.284153e-19
## age          0.01328903 0.001557232  8.533751 4.023312e-17
```

Percent of Variance Explained (R^2)

In the output above, we saw there was something called the residuals. The residuals are the differences between the observed values of Y for each case minus the predicted or expected value of Y—in other words, the distances between each point in the dataset and the regression line.

You see that we have our line, which is our predicted values, and then we have the black dots that are our actually observed values. The distance between them is essentially the amount by which we were wrong, and all these distances between observed and predicted values are our residuals. As we noted above, the least squares estimation essentially aims to reduce the squared average of all these distances; that's how it draws the line.

Why do we have residuals? Well, think about it. The fact that the line is not a perfect representation of the cloud of points makes sense, doesn't it? You cannot predict perfectly what the value of Y is for every individual just by looking ONLY at their perceptions of antisocial behavior! This line only uses information regarding perceptions of antisocial behavior. This means that there's bound to be some difference between our *predicted* perceived antisocial behavior given our knowledge of age (the regression line) and the *actual* perceived antisocial behavior (the actual location of the points in the scatterplot). There are other things that matter not being taken into account by our model to predict the values of Y. There are other things that surely matter in terms of understanding perceived level of antisocial behavior. And then, of course, we have measurement error and other forms of noise.

We can rewrite our equation like this if we want to represent each value of Y (rather than the predicted value of Y):

$$y = b0 + b1x + \text{residuals}$$

Equation 15.3

The residuals capture how much variation is unexplained (how much we still have to learn if we want to understand variation in Y). A good model tries to maximize explained variation and reduce the magnitude of the residuals. We can use information from the residuals to produce a measure of effect size, of how good our model is in predicting variation in our dependent variable. Remember our game where we try to guess perceived antisocial behavior (Y)? If we did not have any information about X (age), our best bet for Y would be the mean of Y. The regression line aims to improve that prediction. By knowing the values of X, we can build a regression line that aims to get us closer to the actual values of Y (see this with the variables *Age* and *Number of Arrests* in Fig. 15.1 below). For more detail, see Weisburd et al. (2021 on page 547).

Figure 15.1

The explained, unexplained, and total deviations from the mean for subject 13 (age = 20; arrests = 9)

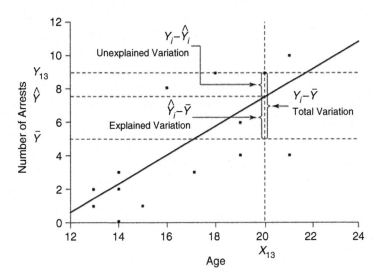

The distance between the mean (our best guess without any other piece of information) and the observed value of Y is what we call the *total variation*. The residual is the difference between our predicted value of Y and the observed value of Y. This is what we cannot explain (i.e., variation in Y that is *unexplained*). The difference between the mean value of Y and the expected value of Y (the value given by our regression line) is how much better we are doing with our prediction by using information about X (i.e., in our previous example, it would be variation in Y that can be *explained* by knowing age). How much closer the regression line gets us to the observed values. We can then contrast these two different sources of variation (explained and unexplained) to produce a single measure of how good our model is using R^2 (which is the percent of the variation that is explained). The formula is as follows:

$$R^2 = \frac{SSR}{SST} = \frac{\Sigma(\hat{y}_i - \bar{y})^2}{\Sigma(y_i - \bar{y})^2}$$

Equation 15.4

All this formula is doing is taking a ratio of the explained variation (the squared differences between the regression line and the mean of Y for each observation) by the total variation (the squared differences of the observed values of Y for each observation from the mean of Y). This gives us a measure of the *percentage of variation in Y that is explained by X.* If this sounds familiar, it is because it's a measure similar to *eta* squared in ANOVA that we cover in the earlier chapter.

We can take this value as a measure of the strength of our model (as long as you don't have a multicollinearity problem, of course!). If you look at the **R** output, you will see that the R^2 for our model was about .05 (look at the multiple r-squared value in the output). We can say that our model explains 5% of the variance in the level of perceived antisocial behavior.

To continue emphasizing your appreciation of the object-oriented nature of **R**, when we run the `summary()` function, we are simply generating a list object of the class `summary.lm`.

```
confint(fit_1)

##                  2.5 %        97.5 %
## (Intercept)  -0.90525510  -0.58742032
## age           0.01023397   0.01634409
```

This means that we can access its elements if we wish. So, for example, to obtain just the r-squared, we could ask for:

```
attributes(summary(fit_1))

## $names
## [1] "call"           "terms"        "residuals"    "coefficients"
## [5] "aliased"        "sigma"        "df"           "r.squared"
## [9] "adj.r.squared"  "fstatistic"   "cov.unscaled"
##
## $class
## [1] "summary.lm"
```

Knowing how to interpret this is important. R^2 ranges from 0 to 1. The greater it is, the more powerful our model is, the more explaining we are doing, and the better we are able to account for variation in our outcome Y with our input—in other words, the stronger the relationship is between Y and X. As with all the other measures of effect size, interpretation is a matter of judgment. You are advised to see what other researchers report in relation to the particular outcome that you may be exploring.

There is not established cutoff for precisely what R^2 value is acceptable. But to give an idea of what we tend to find in our field, Weisburd and Piquero (2008) analyzed R^2 values in published articles testing criminological theories ($n = 169$) and found that they reported a mean r-squared of 0.389 (SD = 0.220). And of course, when it comes to us being peer reviewers who love to complain, think about whether there are truly worthwhile implications from a regression model where only 2% of the variation in the dependent variable can be explained from the observed data. Also, Weisburd et al. (2021) suggest that in criminal justice, you rarely see values for R^2 greater than 0.40. Thus, if your R^2 is larger than 0.40, you can assume you have a powerful model or that something may be wrong with your model :-/. When, on the other hand, R^2 is lower than 0.15 or 0.10, the model is likely to be viewed as relatively weak. Our observed R^2 here is rather poor. There is considerable room for improvement if we want to develop a better model to explain perceived level of antisocial behavior. In any case, many people would argue that R^2 is a bit overrated. You need to be aware of what it measures and the context in which you are using it.

Variance Inflation Factor

When you are conducting a linear regression model, there is a function available that will provide you the variance inflation factor (VIF). As noted above, VIF is used to test whether you have multicollinearity. There is debate about how high VIF must get before there is a multicollinearity concern—some say 5, while others say 10, is the appropriate cutoff.

In R, you can get VIF values by using the `vif()` function from the `car` package. And to demonstrate this, we are going to include a second covariate in our model.

```
summary(fit_1)$r.squared

## [1] 0.05476277
```

The low VIF values indicate that including both variables, age (age) and confidence in the police (confx), in the same model does not pose any multicollinearity concerns.

Application Activities

Problem 1:

Research shows that confidence in the police is important for promoting social order but levels of confidence differ between communities and between people of different demographic characteristics (Tyler and Fagan 2008). Age is one of the things associated with increased confidence. Conduct OLS regression using the `lm()` and `summary()` functions to determine whether age (age) significantly predicts confidence in the police (confx) using the CSEW 2013/2014 dataset (`df`). You will first want to reload your dataset into the object `df` since we dropped cases during the walkthrough. Then examine the distribution of the two variables separately using the `summary()` function and then depict how the two covary by using `ggplot()` to create a scatterplot with a trend line. Based on your model, use the `predict()` function to predict confidence level in the police (confx) at age 45 (age).

Problem 2:

Cao, Frank, and Cullen (1996) show using data from the United States that confidence in the police is most determined by community context rather than individual characteristics. In particular, fear of crime has shown to impact levels of confidence even when other sociodemographic characteristics are held constant. Using data from the CSEW 2013/14 dataset (`df`) and the `lm()` and `summary()` functions, determine whether fear of crime (worryx) significantly predicts confidence in the police (confx). Using `summary()$r.squared`, how much variation in your dependent variable can be explained by your independent variable?

Key Terms

Bivariate regression A technique for predicting change in a dependent variable using one independent variable.

Dependent variable (*Y*) The variable assumed by the researcher to be influenced by one or more independent variables.

Heteroscedasticity A situation in which the variances of scores on two or more variables are not equal. Heteroscedasticity violates one of the assumptions of the parametric test of statistical significance for the correlation coefficient.

Independent variable (*X*) A variable assumed by the researcher to have an

impact on the value of the dependent variable, *Y*.

Multicollinearity Condition in a multivariate regression model in which independent variables examined are very strongly intercorrelated. Multicollinearity leads to unstable regression coefficients.

OLS regression See *ordinary least squares regression analysis.*

Ordinary least squares regression analysis A type of regression analysis in which the sum of squared errors from the regression line is minimized.

Percent of variance explained (*R²*) A measure for evaluating how well the regression model predicts values of Y. It represents the improvement in predicting Y that the regression line provides over the mean of Y.

Regression coefficient (b) A statistic used to assess the influence of an independent variable, X, on a dependent variable, Y. The regression coefficient b is interpreted as the estimated change in Y that is associated with a one-unit change in X.

Regression error (e) The difference between the predicted value of Y and the actual value of Y.

Regression line The line predicting values of Y. The line is plotted from knowledge of the Y-intercept and the regression coefficient.

Regression model The hypothesized statement by the researcher of the factor or factors that define the value of the dependent variable, Y. The model is normally expressed in equation form.

Y-intercept (b_0) The expected value of Y when $X = 0$. The Y-intercept is used in predicting values of Y.

Functions Introduced in this Chapter

FUNCTION	DESCRIPTION (PACKAGE)
complete.cases()	Returns only complete cases that do not have NAs (base **R**)
confint()	Computes confidence intervals for parameters in a fitted model (base **R**)
display()	Gives a clean printout of lm, glm, and other such objects (**arm**)
ggtitle()	Adds a title or subtitle to a graph made using **gglot()** (**ggplot2**)
lm()	Fit linear models (base **R**)
predict()	Makes predictions from the results of model fitting functions (base **R**)
qplot()	Creates a variety of plots/graphs (base **R**)
summary()$coefficients	Extract coefficients only from summary (base **R**)
summary()$r.squared	Extract **R** squared only from summary (base **R**)
vif()	Calculate the variance inflation for OLS or other linear models (**car**)

References

Bock, D. E., Velleman, P. F., & De Veaux, R. D. (2012). *Stats: modeling the world*. Boston: Addison-Wesley.

Cullen, F. T., Cao, L., Frank, J., Langworthy, R. H., Browning, S. L., Kopache, R., & Stevenson, T. J. (1996). Stop or I'll shoot: Racial differences in support for police use of deadly force. *American Behavioral Scientist, 39*(4), 449–460.

Gelman, A., & Hill, J. (2007). *Data analysis using regression and multilevel/hierarchical models*. New York, NY, USA: Cambridge University Press.

Tyler, T. R., & Fagan, J. (2008). Legitimacy and cooperation: Why do people help the police fight crime in their communities? *Ohio State Journal of Criminal Law, 6*, 231.

Weisburd, D., Britt, C., Wilson, D., & Wooditch, A. (2021). *Basics in statistics in criminology and criminal justice*, Edition 5. Springer Science & Business Media.

Weisburd, D., & Piquero, A. R. (2008). How well do criminologists explain crime? Statistical modeling in published studies. *Crime and Justice, 37*(1), 453–502.

Appendix

Appendix 1: Navigating R

1.1. Installing and Loading Packages

You will find that installing packages can be a pain. This section will try to make it as painless as possible. You can check what packages are loaded, as well as load packages, using the *Packages* tab. We suggest that you load packages using code so when you run the code in the future, the package loads automatically.

The first thing you want to do is install the desired package using the `install.packages()` function, and it can then be loaded with the `library()` function, which we suggest to use over the `require()` function. This can be done as follows:

```
install.packages("PackageName")   # Install package

library(PackageName)   # Load package
```

Was the package successfully loaded? If yes, GREAT! And you can stop reading this section. If it failed :-(keep reading and try a few trouble shooting steps.

Package not found:

Make sure that you typed the code correctly. Perhaps you forgot the period between install and packages or the S at the end of the word packages. Also, check to make sure that there are quotation marks around the package name when you install the package, but no quotation marks when you load the package. Remember as well that R is case sensitive.

Package XXX not available:

1. Sometimes R can be buggy and not allow you to set repositories. If step 1 fails, We have found the most success with the code below. Make sure to use the `library()` function afterward if the installation was successful.

```
install.packages("PackageName",
                 repos='https://cloud.r-project.org')
```

© The Editor(s) (if applicable) and The Author(s), under exclusive license to
Springer Nature Switzerland AG 2021
A. Wooditch et al., *A Beginner's Guide to Statistics for Criminology and Criminal Justice Using R*, https://doi.org/10.1007/978-3-030-50625-4

2. If the prior step fails, make sure that the device you are using is connected to the Internet and rerun the function.

3. R may not be checking in the right place to find the package. You can try to fix this by typing `setRepositories()`. You then want to enter the values 1 (for CRAN). Run `setRepositories()` again, and then enter 5 (for CRAN extras).

4. Still no work? Throw the laptop against the wall. No, just kidding. First, recheck that you have completed all prior steps correctly. Second, if that does not work, I would search the specific error that you are receiving online. There are many online forums that are very helpful in solving this issue.

1.2. Specifying Packages

In some circumstances, different functions will have the same name in different packages, or a package will contain a function with the same name as a function available in base R. Just because functions have the same name, it does not mean that they do the same thing or behave in the same way. For example, base R has a function called `range()` which simply calculates the range of values in a vector. However, the package called `mosaic` used in Chapter 6 also includes a function called `range()`, which behaves a little differently, containing additional options. You might have noticed that when you load packages, R will give you warnings about the function names which are conflicting. By default, R will use the function from the package which you loaded last. To avoid any confusion, you can actually specify which package you want to use by using `::` before the function name, either with the package name or simply `base` for base R.

```
base::range(numeric_vector) # Uses the range() function
                            ## from base R

mosaic::range(numeric_vector) # Uses the range() function
                              ## from mosaic
```

1.3. Projects and Working Directories

Working with `here()` As noted in Chapter 2, we recommend that you use R projects. Wherever your R project is saved will be the default working directory. This is very helpful when it comes to loading or saving data, because you don't have to specify the whole working directory each time. However, doing this yourself might bring up problems, largely because working directories can differ between operating systems (e.g., Windows and Mac). Your code might work for you, but not for other people (or somebody else's code won't work for you!). A useful way to address this is to use the `here()` function from the `here` package, in tandem with an R project. Instead of specifying the working directory manually, you can input each section of the directory within `here()` and stick them altogether for you in a way that works consistently.

```
# Not recommended: specify whole working directory outside
## of a project
df <- read_csv(file = "C:/Users/your_name/Documents/my_
                       project_folder/Datasets/my_file.csv")

# Improvement: work from your project
# But, this might not work for other people!
df <- read_csv(file = "Datasets/my_file.csv")

# Ideal situation: work from your R project and use here()
df <- read_csv(here("Datasets", "my_file.csv"))
```

1.4. Setting Working Directory

Although we recommend that you use R projects, and use working directories via the **here()** function, it is possible to set the working directory manually from within R using the function **setwd()**. How you do this varies between Windows and Mac, as demonstrated below.

Windows

Note that in Windows, you cannot simply copy and paste your desired working directory. You need to set the directory using two backward slashes or, alternatively, one forward slash.

```
# Either use two backward slashes
setwd("C:\\Users\\your_name\\Documents\\my_project_folder")

# Or change backward slashes to forward slashes
setwd("C:/Users/your_name/Documents/my_project_folder")
```

Mac

To set your working directory on a Mac:

```
setwd("/Users/your_name/Documents/my_project")
```

1.5. Get Working Directory

You can check to see if your working directory was successfully defined, or simply check what it is, by using **getwd()** on its own.

```
getwd()
```

1.6.   Opening Data Files and Exporting Data

R is capable of reading and exporting data in numerous different formats, many of which are used in other software. Here, we make use of functions from the packages **haven**, **readr**, and **readxl**, contained within the **tidyverse**, as well as functions from the **openxlsx** and **foreign** packages.

1.6.1.   R Data Files

R data files have the file extension .R (or .RDA if the file was created in an older version of R). Note that if you don't assign the dataset to an object, R specifies a dataset name for you.

- Read: **load(file)** loads your .rda file into the R environment.

- Write: **save(x, path)** saves your data frame **x** into an R data file (.rda) specified in path.

```
# .rda Example
load("Dataset Name.rda") # Imports your .rda file

# Exports your data as an .rda file
write(ncvs, file = "New Dataset Name.rda")
```

1.6.2.   General Delimited

- Read: **read_delim(file, delim, ...)** from the **readr** package reads in delimited files, where users can specify the delimiter in the **delim** argument. If you are importing a comma- or tab-delimited file, see below.

- Write: **write_delim(x, path, delim = " ", na = "NA", append = FALSE, col_names = TRUE,...)** from the **readr** package writes R data objects **x** to a delimited file specified in **path**. The delimiter being used should be entered into the **delim** argument. The default arguments for this function include that the string that should be used for missing values is **NA**; the new file should replace the old and not be appended to the bottom (set **append = TRUE** for the opposite) and that the column names will be included at the top of the file.

```
# General Delimited Example
ncvs <- read_delim("Dataset Name.txt",
       delim = "\t", col_names = TRUE) # Importing a
                                       ## tab-delimited
                                       ## text file

write_delim(ncvs, "New Dataset Name.txt", delim = "\t",
na = "NA", append = FALSE, col_names = TRUE) # Exporting the
                                       ## tab-delimited
                                       ## text file
```

1.6.3. Comma Separated

- Read: `read_csv(file, ...)` from the **readr** package imports comma-separated files. You can specify whether or not you want the first row of your data to be considered the variable names. `read_csv2(file, ...)` can also be used for the ; separator.

- Write: `write_csv(x, path, na = "NA", append = FALSE, col_names = TRUE,...)` writes your data frame **x** to a comma-separated file specified in `path`. The default arguments for this function include that the string that should be used for missing values is **NA**; the new file should replace the old and not be appended to the bottom (set **append = TRUE** for the opposite); and the column names will be included at the top of the file. `write_csv2()` may be used for the ; separator.

```
# .csv Example
# Importing CSV file with the header
ncvs <- read_csv("Dataset Name.csv", col_names = TRUE)

# Importing CSV file without header
ncvs <- read_csv("Dataset Name.csv", col_names = FALSE)


# Exporting as a new CSV file with headers
write_csv(ncvs, file = "NewName.csv", na = "NA",
append = FALSE, col_names = TRUE)

# Exporting as a new CSV file without headers
write_csv(ncvs, file = " NewName.csv", na = "NA",
append = FALSE, col_names = FALSE)
```

1.6.4. Tab Separated

- Read: `read_tsv(file, ...)` from the **readr** package imports a tab-delimited file.

- Write: `write_tsv(x, path, na = "NA", append = FALSE, col_names = TRUE, ...)` from the **readr** package can be used to write a data frame or matrix **x** to a tab-delimited file. `col_names` must be either **True or False** and specifies whether the column names should be written to the top of the file.

```
# .tsv Example

# Import the tab-delimited text file
ncvs <- read_tsv("Dataset Name.tsv", col_names = TRUE)

# Export as a tab-delimited text file
write_tsv(ncvs, file = "NewName.tsv", na = "NA",
          append = FALSE, col_names = TRUE)
```

1.6.5. Excel

- Read: `read_excel(file, ...)` imports both .xls and .xlsx files into R through the `readxl` package. `read_excel(file, sheet = "name")` and `read_excel(file, sheet = 2)` both import a specific sheet from the Excel file that you want to use, either by name or index.

- Write: `write.xlsx(x, path, ...)` from the `openxlsx` package enables you to write your data frame `x` as an Excel file specified in `path`.

```
# Excel Example

# Import excel file as the object ncvs
ncvs <- read_excel("Dataset Name.xlsx")

# Export as dataset "New Dataset Name.xlsx"
write.xlsx(ncvs, file = "New Dataset Name.xlsx")
```

1.6.6. dBASE

- Read: `read.dbf(file, ...)` from the package `foreign` may be used to read DBF files.

- Write: `write.dbf(x, path, ...)` can write the R data frame `x` in DBF format.

```
# dBASE Example

# Import dbf dataset as the object ncvs
ncvs <- read.dbf("Dataset Name.dbf")

# Export as dataset named New Dataset Name.dbf
write.dbf(ncvs, file = "New Dataset Name.dbf")
```

1.6.7. Stata

- Read: `read_dta(file, ...)` reads *.dta* files using the package `haven`.

- Write: `write_dta(x, path, version = 14, ...)` writes your data to a Stata *.dta* file. This currently works with Stata versions 8–15.

```
# Stata Example

# Import Stata dataset as the object ncvs
ncvs <- read_dta("Dataset Name.dta")

# Export as Stata dataset named New Dataset Name.dta
write_dta(ncvs, file = "New Dataset Name.dta")
```

1.6.8. SPSS

- Read: `read_sav(file, ...)` from the package **haven** reads *.sav* files, and `read_por()` can be used for older SPSS files.

- Write: `write_sav(x, path, ...)`.

```
# SPSS Example

# Import SPSS dataset as the object named ncvs
ncvs <- read_sav("Dataset Name.sav")

# Export as SPSS dataset named New Dataset Name.sav
write_sav(ncvs, file = "New Dataset Name.sav")
```

1.6.9. SAS

- Read: `read_sas(file, ...)` from the **haven** package reads *.sas7bdat* files, and `read_xpt()` can be used to open SAS transport files (versions 5 and 8)

- Write: `write_sas(x, path, ...)` writes your data to a SAS format file specified in **path**, though this functionality is currently experimental. Make sure to keep apprised of package updates to get the most out of these functions.

```
# SAS Example

# Import SAS dataset
ncvs <- read_sas("Dataset Name.sas7bdat")

# Write to a SAS data file named New Dataset Name.sasb7dat
write_sas(ncvs, file = "New Dataset Name.sasb7dat")
```

1.6.10. From Web URL

You can load data directly from the web as long as you have the URL. To do so, you will want to create an object with the permanent **url** address. Then, we use a function to read the data into **R**. The data that can be saved using an **api** is in tab-separated format; therefore, we use the `read.table()` function from base **R**. We pass two arguments to the function. The `sep= '\t'` is telling **R** this file is tab separated. The `header = T` function is telling **R** that is **TRUE** (T) that this file has a first row that acts as a header (this row has the name of the variables). See example below where we load the data into an object named *sharkey*:

```
# URL Example
data_url <- "https://dataverse.harvard.edu/api/access/
            datafile/:persistentId?persistentId=doi:
            10.7910/DVN/46WIH0/ARS2VS"

sharkey <- read.table(url(data_url), sep = '\t',header = T)
```

1.6.11. Systat

- Read: read.systat(file, ...) reads *.sys* or *.syd* files using the foreign package.

- Write: The foreign package does not currently support writing data in R as a Systat file. Make sure to keep apprised of package updates to get the most out of these functions.

```
# Systat Example
ncvs <- read.systat("Dataset Name.syd") # Import Systat file
```

1.6.12. Minitab

- Read: read.mtp(file, ...) reads *.mtp* files using the foreign package.

- Write: The foreign package does not currently support writing data in R as an *.mtp* file. Make sure to keep apprised of package updates to get the most out of these functions.

```
# Minitab Example
ncvs <- read.mtp("Dataset Name.mtp") # Import .mtp dataset
```

1.6.13. Matlab

- Read: read.mat(file, ...) reads *.mat* files using the rmatio package.

- Write: write.mat(x, path,...) to save R objects as a MAT file.

```
# Matlab Example
ncvs <- read.mat("Dataset Name.mat") # Import MAT file

# Write object ncvs to a MAT file
write.mat(ncvs, file = "New Dataset Name.mat")
```

1.6.14. JSON

- Read: `read_json(file, ...)` reads JSON files using the `jsonlite` package.

- Write: `write_json(x, path,...)` to save R objects in JSON format.

```
# JSON Example
ncvs <- read_json("Dataset Name.json") # Import JSON file

# Write object ncvs to a JSON file
write_json(ncvs, file = "New Dataset Name.json")
```

1.7. Viewing Data Frame

It is good practice to do this to ensure R has read the data correctly and there's nothing terribly wrong with your dataset. It can also give you a first impression for what the data look like. If you are used to spreadsheet-like views of data, you can use the `View()` function, which should open this view in R Studio. This can also be used to view R objects.

```
# Example with a dataset named burglary_df
View(burglary_df)
```

1.8. Using `attach()` and `detach()`

The `attach` function attaches the dataset name to the R file path so you can access variables of a dataset without calling the dataset name. You can turn off the attach function using `detach()`.

```
# Without *Attach*:
df_name$my_variable

# With *Attach*:
attach(df_name)
my_variable

# Turn off *Attach*
detach("df_name")
```

1.9. Interrupting R

Sometimes R can take a long time to execute a task if you have asked it to perform a particularly complex or computationally demanding operation. In cases such as these, a small red stop sign will appear in the top right corner of your console in **RStudio**. Click on this stop sign to interrupt the process. You can also use the *Esc* key in Windows or Mac. If for some reason this still does not halt the process, you may need to wait out the operation or navigate to your operating system's task manager and quit **RStudio** altogether. Take caution, however, that exiting the program will cause any unsaved work to be lost. It is best practice to save your work, and save it often!

1.10. Keyboard Shortcuts

Though it is possible to use your cursor to navigate and execute tasks within the **RStudio** IDE, **RStudio** has a large number of keyboard shortcuts you can leverage without having to use your mouse. To check on the available shortcuts for **RStudio**, simply navigate to the *Tools* menu in the task bar, and select *Keyboard shortcuts help* from the dropdown. Users even have the option of customizing their keyboard shortcuts. Table A1 lists just a few common shortcuts that may come in handy for most users (adapted from this article: https://support.rstudio.com/hc/en-us/articles/200711853-Keyboard-Shortcuts).

Table A1   R Keyboard Shortcuts

TASK	SHORTCUT (WINDOWS/LINUX)	SHORTCUT (MAC)
Clear console	Ctrl + L	Ctrl + L
Navigate function history	Up/Down	Up/Down
Interrupt executing function	Esc	Esc
New document (except Chrome/Windows)	Ctrl+ Shift + N	Cmd + Shift + N
New document (Chrome only)	Ctrl + Alt + Shift + N	Cmd + Shift + Alt + N
Open document	Ctrl + O	Cmd + O
Save document	Ctrl + S	Cmd + S
Run current line/section	Ctrl + Enter	Cmd + Return
Run current document	Ctrl + Alt + R	Cmd + Option + R
Insert assignment operator	Alt + -	Option + -
Insert pipe operator	Ctrl + Shift + M	Cmd + Shift + M
Search R Help	Ctrl + Alt + F1	Ctrl + Option + F1
Quit session	Ctrl + Q	Cmd + Q

Again, be sure to check the *Keyboard shortcuts help* menu in your version of **RStudio** to see the available shortcuts.

Appendix 2: Data Transformation

Data transformation is often a necessary task in the data analysis process. Of course, R has multiple ways of accomplishing the various transformations you may need to do. For most of the tasks in this section, we focus on base R and **tidyverse** methods.

2.1. Recoding or Creating a New Variable

There are many different ways one can achieve generating or recoding a variable. For instance, we can use the **mutate()** and **case_when()** functions from **dplyr** to create transformed variables based on some criteria.

We can also create new variables, based on some computation or combination of other variables. In our data frame, df, we want to recode a variable called <u>shot</u>, which is a character variable of whether someone was injured via gunshot or another method.

```
# Recode the variable injury_type into variable called "shot"
df <- df %>%
mutate(shot = case_when
       (injury_type %in% "gun" ~ "Gun shot",
        injury_type %in% "stab" ~ "Not Gun Shot"))
```

You can also create new variables based on some calculation. For instance, if you wanted to create a variable that was a ratio of two variables, you could simply divide one variable by the other within the mutate() function.

```
# Create a new variable that is a calculation
# In this case, a ratio of var1 to var2
df <- df %>%
   group_by(sex) %>%
   mutate(ratio = var1/var2)
```

Or you could create a new variable that was equal to the sum of four variables divided by four.

```
# Create a new variable that is equal to the sum of four
## vars divided by four
df <- df %>%
   group_by(sex) %>%
   mutate(someindexscore = (var1 + var2 + var3 + var4)/4)
```

You also may want to add a totally new column to your data frame. You can use the add_column() function for this. The following example uses this function to create an ID variable for our data frame, df:

```
# Create a new column that is a row ID
add_column(df, newid = 1:nrow(df))
```

These are just several key ways to recode variables using dplyr. There are many functions that can perform various tasks that might be useful to you as you are cleaning your data. Which functions you choose simply depends on what you need to do with your data.

2.2. Binning Variables

Binning variables is useful, for example, when you need to create categories of a continuous variable, or when you simply want to collapse a certain number of categories into a fewer number of categories. Using functions from **dplyr** and **forcats**, like **mutate()** and **case_when()**, or **fct_collapse()**, you can define how you want your variable to be binned. For instance, below, we create the variable injury location that collapses six different places people could have been injured into three categories: home, school, and other.

```r
# Create a new collapsed character variable injury_location
## from numeric values
df <- df %>%
  mutate(injury_location = case_when(location %in% 0 ~ "Home",
                                     location %in% 1 ~ "School",
                                     location %in% 2:5 ~ "Other"))

# Create collapsed version of variable if it's a factor using
## fct_collapse()
# Manually decide your factor levels
df$injury_location <- fct_collapse(df$location,
  other = c("Work", "Park", "Mall", "Other"),
  school = "School",
  home = "Home")
```

If you have a continuous variable like age or number of arrests, you may want to be able to bin them into broader categories under certain circumstances. In the example below, we are converting a continuous variable of the number of full-time sworn officers in each law enforcement agency (Q_8) into an ordinal measure of agency size (agcysize).

```r
# Create bins of agency size from the variable Q_8
bwcs <- bwcs %>%
  mutate(agcysize=case_when(
    Q_8 %in% 0:10 ~ "0-10 FTS",
    Q_8 %in% 11:50 ~ "11-50 FTS",
    Q_8 %in% 51:100 ~ "51-100 FTS",
    Q_8 %in% 101:500 ~ "101-500 FTS",
    Q_8 %in% 501:1000 ~ "501-1000 FTS",
    Q_8 >= 1001 ~ ">1000 FTS"))
```

2.3. Dealing with Missing Data

Missing data are a common occurrence in criminological research. It might arise due to a variety of reasons. In police-recorded crime data, it might be due to recording issues, or perhaps the information was simply not available or unknown (e.g., an offender's home address). In survey data, respondents might have refused to answer a question, or the respondent might have simply dropped out of participating. How to deal with missing values is a field of research in itself and should be considered carefully. One important reason for this is because missing data might be missing for an underlying systematic reason which impacts on your research. For instance, many people don't like answering questions about their income, but perhaps certain demographic groups (or people on certain incomes) are especially unlikely to answer this question. It would be unwise to simply remove all these people from your data, because you would end up with a biased sample only containing people who were willing to discuss their income. So, consider these issues carefully when dealing with your missing data! With that in mind, the following functions might be of use.

First, let's create an example data frame containing information about the number of prior offenses committed by a sample of ten offenders. The column crime_count contains missing values, because some of our offenders did not want to discuss their offending history. Note that **R** actually treats missings as missings using **NA**. This might seem obvious, but many software assign a specific value like **9999** to define a missing value. Note that **NA** is *not* the same as stating **NA**, which would be treated as a character, and therefore not missing!

```
df <- data.frame(
  id = 1:10,
  crime_count = c(1,4,0,NA,6,0,23,NA,54,NA))
```

To remove observations with missing values (which as stated above, is not always appropriate), we can use **drop_na()** from the **tidyr** package. Make sure you have this package installed and loaded before trying the following code. Because the data frame is so small, we will just print the output to the *Console* without assigning it to anything.

```
drop_na(data = df, crime_count)
```

Note that if you do not specify a variable, **drop_na()** will just remove any observations with missings in any column.

We can also replace missing values with another value using **replace_na()**, which is also from **tidyr**. Let's say we wanted to just replace missings with zeros. Again, in reality this might not be a good idea! We can do this for any particular column, but in this example, we only have one, so we only need to specify crime_count.

```
replace_na(data = df, list(crime_count = 0))
```

The replacement does not have to be a number. Here, we just assign *refused to answer* to these values.

```
replace_na(data = df, list(crime_count = "refused to answer"))
```

If we were to do things the other way round, we can also replace observed (non-missing) values with missings using **na_if()** in the **dplyr** package. This function is designed to be used within **mutate()** (see Chapter 2) to create a new variable. Here, we just replace crime count values of zero with missings.

```
df %>%
  mutate(na_example = na_if(x = crime_count, y = 0))
```

2.4.   Selecting Specific Rows, Columns, or Cells

Oftentimes in criminological research and data analysis in general, we only need to work with a subset of a dataset. The **dplyr** package offers ways of selecting various subsets of your data. For instance, one can make selections based on rows, certain columns, or even cells. Making a selection based on rows is equivalent to keeping certain *observations* in your dataset, while making a selection based on columns is equivalent to keeping certain *variables* in your dataset. The following code provides some examples of how to use the **slice()**, **filter()**, and **select()** functions from **dplyr** to keep what we need of our data and nothing more. We demonstrate how to use these functions on our data frame, **df**.

2.4.1.   Selecting Rows (or Cases/Observations)

```
# Subset the first 100 rows of data using the
## slice() function
first100 <- df %>%
  slice(1:100)

# Alternatively...
first100 <- df[c(1:100),]
```

2.4.2. Selecting Columns (or Variables)

```
# Subset the first 30 variables (or columns) in your data
## frame using the select() function
first30 <- df %>%
  select(1:30)

# Alternatively...
first30  <- df[,c(1:30)]

# Same as above, but using the variable names
first30 <- df %>%
  select(Var1:Var30)
```

You can also use `select()` in conjunction with special functions like `starts_with()`, `ends_with()`, `contains()`, `matches()`, `num_range()`, `one_of()`, and `everything()` to more easily filter out the variables you want to select.

```
# Select only variables beginning with "crime"
crime <- df %>%
  select(starts_with("crime"))

# Select only variables ending with "year2"
crime2 <- df %>%
  select(ends_with("year2"))
```

2.4.3. Selecting Cells

Selecting certain cells in R is easy. Note that you can also use this way of specifying cells for recoding.

Here, we are selecting/recoding a cell that falls on the 109th row and in the 4th column.

```
df[109, 4]     # Row 109, column 4

df[109, 4]<-NA # Code cell as missing

df[109, 4]<-99 # Change cell value to 99
```

2.5. Selecting Cases Based on Criteria

We have covered how to go about selecting your subset by rows and columns, but you may also want to subset your data by some other criteria. For instance, you want to examine only males, or only youth, but your samples contain females and senior citizens. If you need to select cases from your data frame that meet certain conditions, you can use the `filter()` function from `dplyr`. Assume in the following example that we want to perform an analysis on a sample of recidivists. We can filter on the dummy variable <u>recidivist</u> such that only cases where recidivist is equal to 1 are kept. We also want only adults in our sample, so we can filter on age as well.

```
# Subset rows based on some condition(s) using filter()
adult_recidivist_sample <- df %>%
    filter(recidivist == 1 & age > 17)
```

2.6. Add Columns to a Data Frame

Unless you are lucky, you will sometimes need to merge multiple data sources together for your analyses. The `dplyr` package allows users to merge multiple data frames together through different *join* functions. Each type of join merges your data a slightly different way.

2.6.1. Inner Join

The `inner_join()` function keeps only cases that exist in *both* datasets you are merging. This means that if you have an ID for someone in your first dataset, but not in your second, that case will be dropped in the merged version.

```
# Inner join
df3 <- inner_join(df1, df2, by = "ID")
```

2.6.2. Left Join

The `left_join()` function does not drop ALL unmatched cases, but keeps unmatched cases from the first data frame, and simply assigning it an `NA` for columns from the second data frame. If the second data frame also had an unmatched case, this would be dropped.

```
# Left join
df3 <- left_join(df1, df2, by = "ID")
```

2.6.3. Right Join

The `right_join()` function is the same as the `left_join()` function, except that any unmatched cases from the second dataset are kept this time, and the unmatched cases from the first dataset are dropped.

```
# Right join
df3 <- right_join(df1, df2, by = "ID")
```

2.6.4. Full Join

The `full_join()` function returns all of the columns from both datasets and returns a **NA** when there are no matching values.

```
# Full join
df3 <- full_join(df1, df2, by = "ID")
```

2.7. Add Rows to a Data Frame

You may want to add more cases to your data frame rather than adding columns. This can be done by using the `rbind()` function from base **R** where you specify the names of the objects you want to add together (can be vector, matrix, or data frame). To use this function with a data frame, make sure that the variable names in data frames being combined match.

```
# Add rows with rbind()
New_df<-rbind(df1, df2)
```

2.8. Applying Functions to Every Column

If you want to apply a function to all columns in your data frame, you can use one of the `apply()` family of functions from base **R**. Some key functions from this family include `apply()`, `lapply()`, `sapply()`, and `tapply()`.

2.8.1. Using apply()

The `apply()` function does exactly what it sounds like—it applies a function to an array or matrix. You can choose whether to apply the function to rows, columns, or both. Note that to pass the function to rows, you will use the number 1, and to pass the function to columns, the number 2. This function then returns either a vector, or an array, or list of values.

```
# apply()

# Applies the function mean to all COLUMNS in df
apply(df, 2, mean)

# Applies the function mean to all ROWS in df
apply(df, 1, mean)
```

2.8.2. Using lapply()

Using the `lapply()` function applies a function to all elements of a list and returns a list of results.

```
# lapply()

# Applies the function mean to the list "mylist"
lapply(mylist, mean)
```

2.8.3. Using sapply()

The `sapply()` function is similar to `lapply()`, except that instead of returning a list, it returns a vector or matrix.

```
# sapply()

# Applies the function mean to the List "mylist"
sapply(mylist, mean)
```

2.8.4. Using tapply()

The `tapply()` function is useful in that it allows users to apply a function to parts of a vector rather than the whole thing. For instance, if you wanted to apply a function to groups within a vector, you can simply specify the vector that you want to apply the function to, the grouping vector, and finally, the function itself. For instance, if you want to calculate the mean number of officers by law enforcement agency type, you could do the following:

```
# tapply()

# Calculates the mean number of officers per agency type
tapply(df$num_officers, df$agencytype, mean)
```

2.9. Calculating Variable Transformations

Sometimes we need to transform our variables before we include them in a statistical model. You can use the mathematical operations discussed in Chapter 1 on most variables in R (if your variable is numeric!). The following are merely a few examples of key transformations you may want to make.

2.9.1. Logarithmic Transformation

Use the `log10()` function from base R to calculate the base 10 logarithm of a vector.

```
# Create a vector a
a <- c(50, 100, 40, 62, 922, 4000)
a

# transform a using Log
b <- log(a)
b
```

2.9.2. Natural Log

To perform a natural log transformation on a vector, you can use the `log()` function, also available through base R.

```
# Create a vector named "a"
a <- c(50, 100, 40, 62, 922, 4000)
a

# Transform "a" using log()
b <- log(a)
b
```

2.9.3. Exponentiation

Exponentiating a value or set of values in R is very straightforward. You can perform calculations of values directly in R like a calculator.

```
# 10 squared
10^2

# 5 cubed
5^3
```

You can also perform calculations on vectors of values.

```
# create a vector named "c"
c <- c(10, 33, 52, 900, 2246)

# Square "c"
c^2

# Raise "c" to the 4th power
c^4
```

These are just several data transformations you may want to make. Luckily, with the use of R objects and vectorized operations, it is relatively easy to transform your data to fit your specific needs.

2.10. Summarize a Data Frame by Groups

With the `dplyr` package, you can summarize variable(s) within groups. For instance, in this example, imagine we want to calculate the mean and standard deviation of inmates' age (AGE) by their gender (GENDER), and the variables are stored in a data frame named `df`.

```
df %>%
group_by(GENDER) %>%
  summarize(mean_age = mean(AGE, na.rm = TRUE),
  sd_age = sd(AGE, na.rm = TRUE))
```

You can choose to store this as a data frame (named new_df).

```
new_df <- (df %>%
            group_by(GENDER) %>%
            summarize(mean_age = mean(AGE, na.rm = TRUE),
            sd_age = sd(AGE, na.rm = TRUE)))
```

2.11.   Reshaping Data Frames

Reshaping data is a task many analysts must perform at one time or another. How else are you supposed to format your time series data to examine changes in delinquency over time? Though the task itself seems like it may be long and arduous, R, and more specifically tidyr, can make this process much smoother than what you might first expect.

2.11.1.   Into Wide Format

Load the library for tidyr, and use the spread() function to convert your data into wide format. You just need to specify the data frame you want to reshape (df, in this case), as well as the variable that you will convert to multiple variables or column names (intervention period).

```
# Convert data frame into wide format
wide_df <- df %>% spread(key = intervention_period,
                         value = num_crimes)
```

You can also use the newer approach to reshaping data in tidyr, pivot_wider(). This function works in a similar fashion, though it is still being updated, unlike the spread() function. Rather than specify the *key* and *value* column names, the pivot_wider() function allows you to specify the columns that uniquely identify each observation (though the default is that all columns in your data frame will be selected), as well as the columns from which to get the new column names (names from) and values from (values from). The following example will create a new data frame with multiple columns beginning with intervention period and will include the number of crimes in each cell in the appropriate intervention period column.

```
# Convert data frame into Wide format
wide_df <- pivot_wider(id_cols = id,
                       names_from  = intervention_period,
                       values_from = num_crimes)
```

2.11.2. Into Long Format

If on the flip side we want to take our 20 different variables indicating each intervention period and collapse it into a single column, use the **gather()** function to reshape wide format to long. Remember to specify both the *key* and the *value* columns, or what variables you want to gather *on*, and their values.

```
# Convert data frame into long format using "gather"
long_df <- df %>% gather(key = intervention_period,
                         value = num_crimes)
```

Again, you can also use the newer approach offered by **tidyr**: the **pivot_longer()** function. In the following example, we first need to specify the columns we want to pivot on or make longer (in this case, variables marking the intervention period), then the new column name for the pivoted column names, and then finally the new column name for the values associated with these columns.

```
# Convert data frame into long format using "pivot_longer()"
long_df <- df %>% pivot_longer(cols = starts_with("period"),
names_to = "intervention_period", values_to = "num_crimes")
```

Appendix 3: Formatting

3.1. Changing Classes

3.1.1. To Numeric Class

After importing data into R, you will often need to change the class of some of your variables. In the example below, the variable <u>age</u> was stored as a character class, i.e., the numbers are stored as strings rather than numbers. To change the class of the <u>age</u> variable, you can use the base R **as.numeric()** function.

```
# Change the "age" variable in the ncvs data frame
## to numeric class
ncvs$age <- as.numeric(ncvs$age)

# Dplyr method to change multiple variables to numeric
# Changes variables x, y, and z to numeric class
ncvs <- ncvs %>%
    mutate_at(vars(x, y, z), list(as.numeric))
```

3.1.2. To Character Class

Sometimes, you may want to change a variable to a character class or string. For example, if you import a dataset (<u>df</u>) that contains a column of zip codes (<u>zip</u>), R may treat this column as a numeric class initially. However, you may want zip code to be treated as a string variable. To change the class of <u>zip</u>, you can use the base R `as.character()` function.

```
# Change the "zip" variable in the data frame to a character
## class variable
df$zip <- as.character(df$zip)

# Dplyr method to change multiple variables to character
# Changes variables x, y, and z to character class
df <- df %>%
    mutate_at(vars(x, y, z), list(as.character))
```

3.1.3. To Factor Class

You may also need to convert variables to a factor class. This can be accomplished with the base R `as.factor()`, or the `as_factor()` function from the **forcats** package. There is a difference between the two functions in how levels are defined. Be sure to review the documentation for whichever function you choose. Let's convert the variable <u>sex</u>, a character variable, to a factor.

```
# Change the "sex" variable in the data frame to a factor
## class variable
df$sex2 <- as.factor(df$sex)

# Forcats method to change variable to a factor
df$sex2 <- df %>% as_factor(sex)
```

3.2. Formatting Dates

As noted in Chapter 3, research in criminology and criminal justice is increasingly making use of longitudinal and time-stamped data. For that reason, it is useful to know how to work with dates in R. There is a specific package in R used for working with dates called **lubridate**. Ensure that you have this package installed and load it using `library()` as you learned in the earlier chapters of this book.

First, let's create a simple example dataset to work with. You will find that a great deal of data, such as police-recorded crime records, come with dates in this kind of format. Here, we will use the popular format of DD-MM-YYYY to denote some specific days of the year in the variable <u>day_fac</u>, with a separate variable <u>count</u> denoting the number of events (e.g., crime counts) on that day.

Remember, we are using *DD-MM-YYYY* format, so the first date is 15 February 2012, and so on.

```
df <- data.frame(
  day_fac = c("15-02-2012","21-01-2012","01-03-2012",
              "01-04-2012","15-04-2012 ","01-12-2012"),
  count = c(54,102,32,57,301,1612)
  )
```

Notice that when we check the class of day_fac, it is a factor. Sometimes when you load in data like this (e.g., using `read_csv()`) it will be treated as a character. Either way, the fact is that R does not know that this variable is a date.

```
class(df$day_fac)
```

One implication of this is that when want to do things like arrange rows by date, R does it inappropriately. For example, it thinks that *01-12-2012* (1 December 2012) comes before *15-02-2012* (15 February 2012).

```
# This will just print the arranged df to your Console
arrange(df, day_fac)
```

Using the **lubridate** package, we can ensure that R treats dates correctly, either by reclassifying an existing variable or creating a new one. Here, the appropriate function from **lubridate** is `dmy()` because we know that the date format is *DD-MM-YYYY*. To retain the original for comparison, we will just create a new variable called day_dmy.

```
df <- df %>%
  mutate(day_dmy = dmy(day_fac))
```

Now when we check the class, it confirms that the new day_dmy variable is a date.

```
class(df$day_dmy)
```

This time, when we arrange by the new date, it gets it right.

```
# This will just print the arranged df to your Console
arrange(df, day_dmy)
```

3.3. Extract Parts of Dates from a String

Perhaps you have a date variable stored as a string, but you really need a column with just one part of the date, such as the year. See the example below for how you can extract a part of a date using a `substr()` function from base R, the `separate()` function from `tidyr`, or by using functions from the `lubridate` package.

```
# Extract parts of the date you need when the date
## is stored as a string
df <- data.frame(
  date = c("01-01-2015", "01-02-2015" , "01-01-2016",
           "01-02-2016"), count = c(100, 200, 300, 400))

# The first value is position in the string you want
## to start your subset
df$year <- substr(df$date, 7, 10)


# The second value is what position in the string you want
## to end your subset
df$month <- substr(df$date, 4, 5)
df$day <- substr(df$date, 1, 2)

# You can also use the tidyr function separate()
df <- df %>% separate(date, c("Month", "Day", "Year"),
                      sep = "-")

# Alternatively, you can transform the string variable to
## date format
# Use the year() function from lubridate

# Transforms string to the month, day, year date format
df <- df %>%
  mutate(date2 = mdy(date))

# Extracts the year from the MDY formatted variable
df <- df %>%
  mutate(year2 = year(date2))
```

The `lubridate` package has many other options depending on the format of your dates. It also has advanced functionality with timings such as hours, seconds (even milliseconds, nanoseconds, and so on), as well as time zones. However, hopefully the above demonstration showcases how important it is to treat dates appropriately in R and how useful the `lubridate` package is!

Appendix 4: Pimp My ggplot

4.1. Shape Options

In Chapter 3, we covered data visualization using **ggplot2**. This included the use of geometries such as **geom_line()** and **geom_point()**. We also mapped variables to different aesthetics including **shape** and **linetype**. In doing so, we saw some of the common shapes (e.g., circles and squares) and line types (e.g., dotted and dashed) used to display data. By adapting some code from the **ggplot2** documentation, we can visualize the 25 different shapes available. Note that the position of each shape on the y-axis corresponds to its unique number. So, if you wanted all your data points to be shaped with the + symbol, you would specify **shape = 3**.

```
points_df <- data.frame(x = 1:5 , y = 1:25, option = 1:25)

ggplot(data = points_df) +
  geom_point(mapping = aes(x = x, y = y, shape = option),
             size = 5) +
  scale_shape_identity()
```

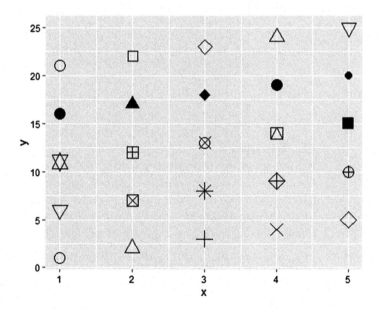

It is worth being aware that shapes might respond differently to additional aesthetics such as fill and color. This demonstrates important distinctions between shapes that might otherwise appear identical (e.g., 1 and 21).

```
ggplot(data = points_df) +
  geom_point(mapping = aes(x = x, y = y, shape = option),
             size = 5, fill = "salmon",
             color = "dodgerblue") +
  scale_shape_identity()
```

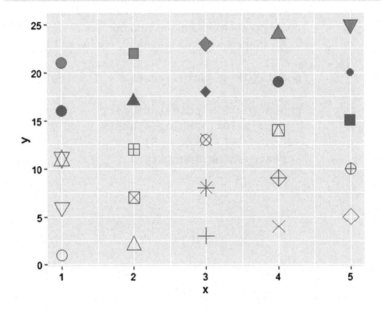

4.2. Line Types

For line types, we can view the names of the options available in the help documentation ?linetype. There are six options by default (excluding a blank one). Like the shapes, these options can be referred to by number (0–6). To take a look at some of these options, we can create a basic data frame containing the line type names and visualize it.

```
lines_df <- data.frame(options = c("blank", "solid",
                                   "dashed", "dotted",
                                   "dotdash", "longdash"))

ggplot(data = lines_df) +
  geom_segment(mapping = aes(x = 0, xend = 1, y = options,
                             yend = options,
                             linetype = options)) +
  scale_linetype_identity()
```

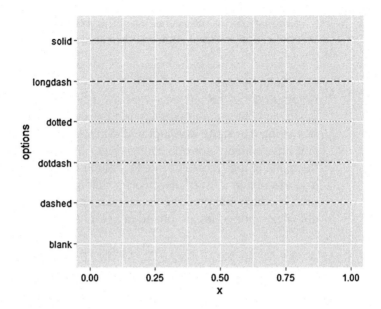

4.3. Font Types

The function `element_blank()` assigns nothing, and as such is often used to remove something (e.g., axis ticks). For instance, to remove the x-axis title, we would add the following to the `theme()` function:

```
theme(axis.title.x = element_blank())
```

The function `element_text()` is used to specify options to text (e.g., font style or size). For instance, to change the y-axis text to size **10**, at a **90** degree angle, in font style **mono**, and in bold type, we would add the following to `theme()`:

```
theme(axis.text.y = element_text(size = 10,
                                 angle = 90,
                                 family = "mono",
                                 face = "bold"))
```

The function `element_rect()` is used to specify options relating to panel borders or backgrounds. To make the plot background pink, for example, we would use the following within `theme()`:

```
theme(plot.background = element_rect(fill = "pink"))
```

The function `element_line()` is for lines, such as the grid lines (e.g., panel grid) of your graphic. So, to change the panel grid line color, we would add:

```
theme(panel.grid = element_line(color = "black"))
```

You may also want to check out the **extrafont** package if you would like more options to change the appearance of the text in R.

4.4.   Color Options

Colors in R can be referenced just as they are in HTML/CSS, where red, green, and blue are represented using hexadecimal (*hex*) values (**00** to **FF**) in a string that starts with a pound symbol, e.g., **#000099**. R also has several pre-defined color options that you can use instead by just specifying the name of the color, e.g., **"red"**, **"darkred"**, **"tomato"**, and **"salmon"**. You can obtain a list of these colors simply by running the function **colors()**, which will print the list of color names to your console. The available hex color codes are provided in Fig. A4.1.

Figure A4.1   *Hex Code Color Options*

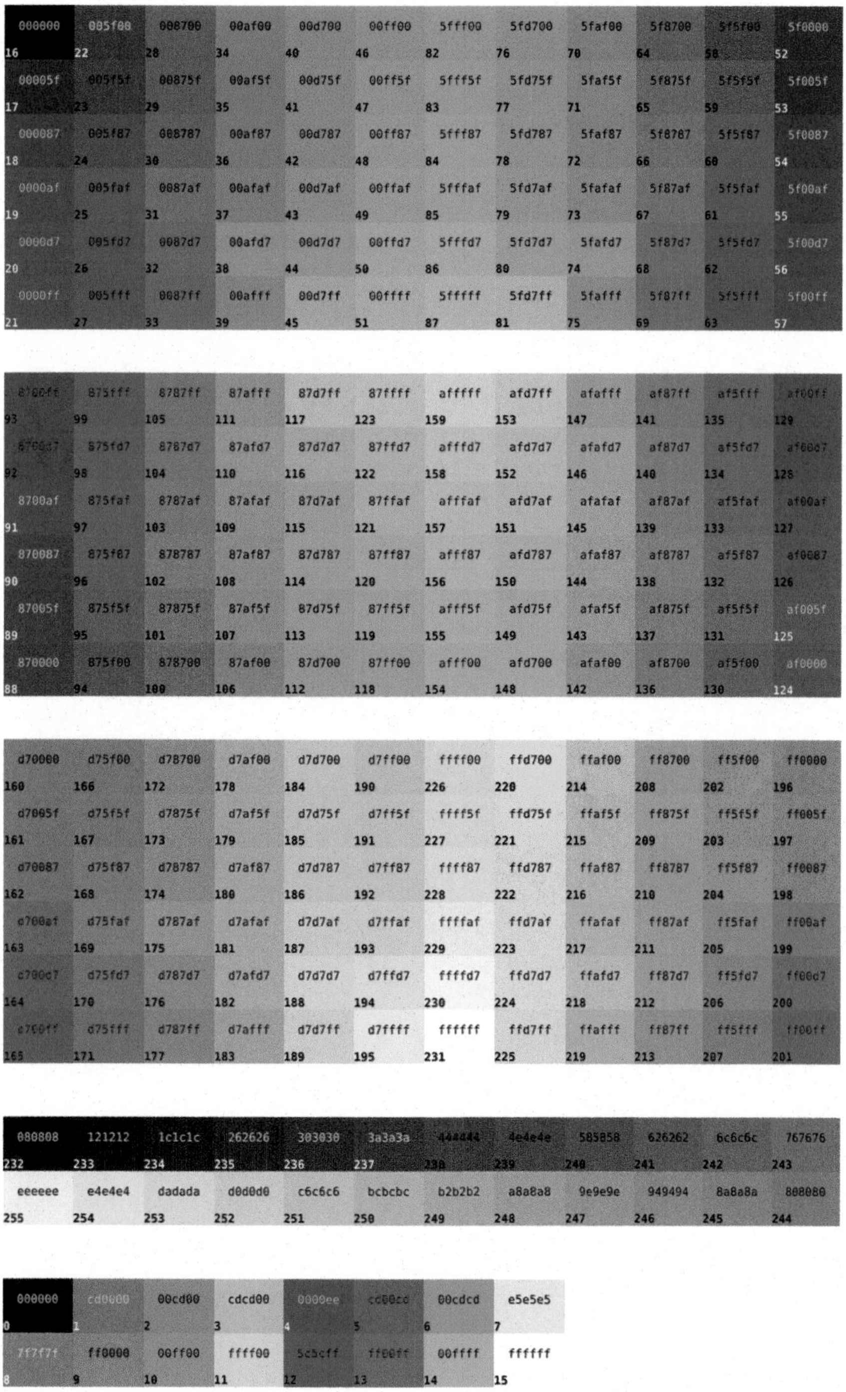

4.4.1. *ggplot2 Color Options*

You can also visualize the colors themselves using some of the skills picked up in Chapter 3, with some additional tweaks. Here, we just show a sample of colors, because there are far too many (over six hundred!) in total. Remember to ensure that the relevant libraries are loaded before you try this code, such as by using `library(ggplot2)`. For this example, we use `ggplot2`, `stringr`, and `dplyr`.

```r
# Pull all colors containing the words pink, violet or purple
colors_df <- data.frame(col_names = colors()) %>%
              filter(str_detect(col_names,
                    "pink|violet|purple"))

# Visualize these colors in a tile plot
ggplot(data = colors_df) +
  theme_minimal() +
  geom_tile(aes(x = col_names, fill =
            as.factor(1:nrow(colors_df)), y = 1)) +
  scale_fill_manual(values = colors_df$col_names) +
  coord_flip() +
  theme(legend.position = "none",
        axis.title = element_blank(),
        axis.text.x = element_blank())
```

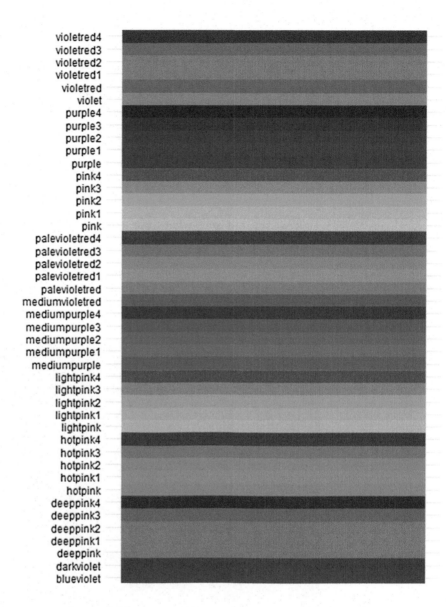

4.4.2. Color Palettes

Rather than refer to colors manually by name, we can use functions available within the **scales** package to extract the hex value names for the default **ggplot2** palette, or any other palette available.

```
# Print hex value names (in this example, for six colors)
hue_pal()(6) # default for ggplot2

## [1] "#F8766D" "#B79F00" "#00BA38" "#00BFC4" "#619CFF"
      "#F564E3"

# Specific palette name, e.g., spectral
brewer_pal(palette = "Spectral")(6)
## [1] "#D53E4F" "#FC8D59" "#FEE08B" "#E6F598" "#99D594"
      "#3288BD"
```

If we are not sure what these colors look like, we can also visualize them, along with the respective hex values.

```
# Visualize hex values with names
show_col(hue_pal()(6)) # default for ggplot2
```

```
# Specific palette name e.g. spectral
show_col(brewer_pal(palette = "Spectral")(6))
```

#D53E4F	#FC8D59	#FEE08B
#E6F598	#99D594	#3288BD

Or simply visualize all the palettes available, along with their respective palette names, using the **RColorBrewer** package.

```
display.brewer.all()
```

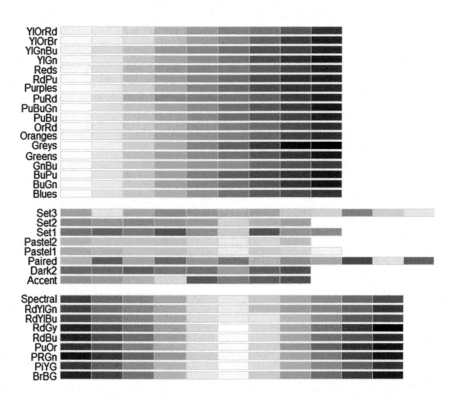

Appendix 5: Saving Output

5.1. Exporting Plots

In Chapter 3, we covered how to explore your data using the visualization tools available in ggplot2. Once you've created a visual with the R environment, you will likely want to save it for use in a paper or presentation. The simplest way to do this is to use the *Export* tab from the *Plots* window in the RStudio environment. One of the downsides of this method is that it is not reproducible. Someone running your code (including your future self) might get the same graphic within R but then export it using different settings (e.g., format, dimensions). For that reason, we recommend using the function ggsave() within ggplot2. It allows you to export your graphics in a way that is reproducible. It is also flexible, with numerous different options around dimensions, formats, and resolution, which saves you a bunch of time when producing lots of different visuals.

To start with, you will want to generate your graphic and assign it to an object. If you want to run through this code, take a look at the first example using police-recorded crime data in Chapter 3.

```
my_plot <- ggplot(data = burglary_df, mapping = aes
                  (x = incscore,
                   y = burglary_count))+ geom_point()
```

You can then input this object into the ggsave() function, using the arguments available within the function to specify our preferences. A brief explanation of each is given using comments in the below code chunk, but you can view the help documentation using ?ggsave to get the full details. Note that we don't specify where to save the file, so by default it will be saved to whatever the current working directory is. Remember that you can check this using getwd(). If you want to specify a working directory, you can either include it before the file name or use the path option within the function.

```
ggsave(plot = my_plot,                     # name of ggplot object
       filename = "my_plot_file.png",      # file name
       device = "png",                     # device i.e. file format
       units = "cm",                       # units of dimensions
       width = 10,                         # width dimension
       height = 8,                         # height dimension
       dpi = 300)                          # pixel density,
                                           ## i.e., resolution
```

It's worth noting that **ggsave()** will guess the device (i.e., file format) based on the extension used within the **filename** argument. However, in the above example, we have been explicit and stated this using **device = "png"**. There are a number of other formats available (e.g., pdf, tiff, jpeg).

Appendix 6: List of Data Sources and Dataset Names

CHAPTER	DATA SOURCE	FILE NAME(S)
1	NA	NA
2	National Crime Victimization Survey (NCVS)	NCVS lone offender assaults 1992 to 2013.sav
3	2017 crime data from Greater Manchester, England	gmp_2017.csv; gmp_monthly_2017.csv
4	2016 LEMAS-Body Worn Camera Supplement	37302-0001-Data.rda
5	2004 Survey of Inmates in State and Federal Correctional Facilities (SISFCF)	04572-0001-Data.Rda
6	Simulated data	NA
7	Simulated data	NA
8	Simulated data	NA
9	British Crime Survey	*bcs_2007_8_teaching_data_unrestricted.dta*
10	Synthetic data containing information about IQ scores of prisoners	NA
11	National Youth Survey	*nys_1_ID.dta, nys_2_ID.dta*
12	Stop and searches carried out in London by police	*stop_search_london.csv*
13	Seattle Neighborhoods and Crime Survey	Seattle_Neighborhoods_Crime_RandomSample.dta
14	Prof. Sharkey et al.'s dataset to study the effect of nonprofit organizations in the levels of crime	sharkey.csv
15	Crime Survey for England and Wales	csew1314_teaching.csv

Appendix 7: Citations to Packages/Software

PACKAGE/ SOFTWARE	CITATION
arm	Gelman, A., & Hill, J. (2007). Data analysis using regression and multi-level hierarchical models (Vol. 1). New York, NY, USA: Cambridge University Press
car	Fox, J., & Weisberg, S. (2019). An R Companion to Applied Regression, Third edition. Sage, Thousand Oaks CA. https://socialsciences.mcmaster.ca/jfox/Books/Companion/
DescTools	Signorell, A., et al. (2020). DescTools: Tools for Descriptive Statistics. R package version 0.99.34, https://cran.r-project.org/package=DescTools
dplyr	Wickham, H., François, R., Henry, L. & Müller, K. (2019). dplyr: A Grammar of Data Manipulation. R package version 0.8.3. https://CRAN.R-project.org/package=dplyr
forcats	Wickham, H. (2019). forcats: Tools for Working with Categorical Variables (Factors). R package version 0.4.0. https://CRAN.R-project.org/package=forcats
Ggally	Schloerke, B., et al. (2020). GGally: Extension to 'ggplot2'. R package version 1.5.0. https://CRAN.R-project.org/package=GGally
ggplot2	Wickham, H. (2016). ggplot2: Elegant Graphics for Data Analysis. Springer-Verlag New York
gmodels	Warnes, G.C., Bolker, B., Lumley, T. & Johnson, R.C. (2018). gmodels: Various R Programming Tools for Model Fitting. R package version 2.18.1. https://CRAN.R-project.org/package=gmodels
GoodmanKruskal	Pearson, R. (2016) Goodman Kruskal: association analysis for categorical variables. R package version 0.0.2. https://CRAN.R-project.org/package=GoodmanKruskal
haven	Wickham, H. & Miller, E. (2019). haven: Import and Export 'SPSS', 'Stata' and 'SAS' Files. R package version 2.2.0. https://CRAN.R-project.org/package=haven
here	Müller, K. (2017). here: A Simpler Way to Find Your Files. R package version 0.1. https://CRAN.R-project.org/package=here
labelled	Larmarange, J. (2019). labelled: Manipulating Labelled Data. R package version 2.2.1. https://CRAN.R-project.org/package=labelled
modeest	Poncet, P. (2019). modeest: Mode Estimation. R package version 2.4.0. https://CRAN.R-project.org/package=modeest
moments	Komsta, L. & Novomestky, F. (2015). moments: Moments, cumulants, skewness, kurtosis and related tests. R package version 0.14. https://CRAN.R-project.org/package=moments
mosaic	Pruim, R., Kaplan, D.T., & Horton, N.J. (2017). The mosaic Package: Helping Students to 'Think with Data' Using R. The R Journal, 9(1):77-102
qualvar	Gombin, J. (2018). qualvar: Implements Indices of Qualitative Variation Proposed by Wilcox (1973). R package version 0.2.0. https://CRAN.R-project.org/package=qualvar
R	R Core Team (2020). R: A language and environment for statistical computing. R Foundation for Statistical Computing, Vienna, Austria. URL https://www.R-project.org/
readr	Wickham, H., Hester, J. & Francois, R. (2018). readr: Read Rectangular Text Data. R package version 1.3.1. https://CRAN.R-project.org/package=readr

PACKAGE/ SOFTWARE	CITATION
`Rstudio`	RStudio Team (2016). RStudio: Integrated Development for R. RStudio, Inc., Boston, MA URL http://www.rstudio.com/
`sjlabelled`	Lüdecke, D. (2020). sjlabelled: Labelled Data Utility Functions. R package version 1.1.3. doi: 10.5281/zenodo.1249215 (URL: https://doi.org/10.5281/zenodo.1249215), URL: https://CRAN.R-project.org/package=sjlabelled
`skimr`	Waring, E., Quinn, M., McNamara, A., Arino de la Rubia, E., Zhu, H. & Ellis, S. (2020). skimr: Compact and Flexible Summaries of Data. R package version 2.1. https://CRAN.R-project.org/package=skimr
`tibble`	Müller, K. & Wickham, H. (2019). tibble: Simple Data Frames. R package version 2.1.3. https://CRAN.R-project.org/package=tibble
`tidyverse`	Wickham et al., (2019). Welcome to the tidyverse. Journal of Open Source Software, 4(43), 1686, https://doi.org/10.21105/joss.01686
`tigerstats`	Robinson, R. & White, H. (2016). tigerstats: R Functions for Elementary Statistics. R package version 0.3. https://CRAN.R-project.org/package=tigerstats

Appendix 8: Index of R Functions

FUNCTION	DESCRIPTION (PACKAGE)	PAGE #S
`abs()`	Calculates the absolute value (base **R**)	9, 20, 162
`add_column()`	Adds columns to a data frame (`tibble`)	31, 38, 279
`add_labels()`	Add value labels to a variable (`sjlabelled`)	29, 37, 38
`add_row()`	Add rows to a data frame (`tibble`)	234, 244
`add_value_labels()`	Add value labels to a variable (`labelled`)	172, 182
`aes()`	Mapping aesthetics to variables (`ggplot2`)	43, 44, 46-55, 57, 60, 71–73, 92, 96, 107, 101, 103, 130, 186–188, 195, 198, 199, 230, 234, 235, 252–254, 261, 293, 294, 298, 302
`aov()`	Fit an analysis of variance model (base **R**)	191, 193, 194, 196, 204–206, 208
`apply()`	Applies a function to elements of an array or matrix (base **R**)	285
`arrange()`	Sorts rows by a given variable(s) (`dplyr`)	34, 37, 38
`array()`	Stores data in 1 dimension (vector) or 1+ dimension (matrix) (base **R**)	16, 20
`as_factor()`	Changes the class of an object to factor class (`forcats`)	139–141, 143, 145, 147, 151, 290
`as.character()`	Changes the class of an object to character (base **R**)	290
`as.data.frame()`	Checks if data frame and tries to coerce if not (base **R**)	17, 20, 142
`as.factor()`	Coerce vector to factor, including specifying levels (base **R**)	53–58, 60, 290, 298
`as.numeric()`	Changes the class of an object to numeric (base **R**)	29, 220, 289

FUNCTION	DESCRIPTION (PACKAGE)	PAGE #S
`as.vector()`	Coerce an object into a vector (base **R**)	82, 88
`attach()`	Commonly used to attach a data frame object for easier access (base **R**)	79, 81, 88
`attributes()`	Access object attributes, such as value labels (base **R**)	88, 137, 138, 182, 218, 223, 258, 265
`bind_rows()`	Combine data frame(s) together row-wise (`dplyr`)	97, 106
`BinomCI()`	Compute confidence intervals for binomial proportions (`DescTools`)	128–130, 132, 133
`boxplot()`	Produce a box and whisker plot (base **R**)	186–188
`c()`	Concatenates elements to create vectors (base **R**)	14, 16–18, 29, 71, 124–126, 170, 177, 213, 215, 216, 219, 221, 238, 263, 281, 283, 286, 287, 291, 292
`case_when()`	Allows users to vectorize multiple if or if else statements (`dplyr`)	33, 34, 37, 38, 72, 177, 278–280
`cat()`	Combines/concatinates character values and prints them (base **R**)	162, 165, 168
`ceiling()`	Always round up (base **R**)	9, 20
`chisq.test()`	Produces the chi-square test (base **R**)	148–150, 153, 212, 213, 215
`class()`	Check the class of an object (base **R**)	148–150, 153, 212, 213, 215
`complete.cases()`	Returns only complete cases that do not have NAs (base **R**)	250, 268
`confint()`	Computes confidence intervals for parameters in a fitted model (base **R**)	263, 265, 268
`contains()`	Used in conjunction with `select()`, selects only variables that contains a certain string (`dplyr`)	283
`cor.test(…method = "kendall")`	Conducts a Kendall's correlation test (`stats`)	225, 238
`cor.test()`	Obtains correlation coefficient (base **R**)	220, 221, 232, 233, 235, 236, 238, 244
`cor()`	Produces the correlation of two variables (base **R**)	232, 233, 235–237, 243, 244
`count()`	Counts the number of occurrences (`dplyr`)	31, 33, 38
`CrossTable()`	Produces contingency tables (`gmodels`)	142–145, 147, 148, 151–153
`cut()`	Divides by the specified interval (base **R**)	207, 208
`data.frame()`	Create a new data frame object (base **R**)	17–20, 93, 142, 157, 158, 263, 281, 291–294, 298
`dbinom()`	Find probability of events occurring X number of times (`stats`)	116–118
`detach()`	Turns off the `attach()` function (base **R**)	79, 88, 277
`diff()`	Computes differences between values in a numeric vector (base **R**)	84, 85, 87, 88
`dim()`	Check the dimensions of an **R** object (base **R**)	16, 20, 63, 137

FUNCTION	DESCRIPTION (PACKAGE)	PAGE #S
`display()`	Gives a clean printout of `lm`, `glm`, and other such objects (`arm`)	259, 268
`DM()`	Computes deviation from the mode (`qualvar`)	82, 87, 88
`dmy()`	Creates a date variable in the format of DD-MM-YYYY (`lubridate`)	291
`do()`	Loop for resampling (`mosaic`)	95, 97
`drop_na()`	Removes observations with missing values (`tidyr`)	281
`element_blank()`	Assigns nothing to the component of the graphic it is called in (`ggplot2`)	295, 298
`element_line()`	Used to specify options relating to lines (`ggplot2`)	295
`element_rect()`	Used to specify options relating to panel borders or backgrounds (`ggplot2`)	295
`element_text()`	Refer to a text element in thematic options—see Index (`ggplot2`)	70–73, 76, 187, 295
`ends_with()`	Used in conjunction with `select()`, selects only variables that end with some suffix (`dplyr`)	283
`everything()`	Used in conjunction with `select()`, selects all variables (`dplyr`)	283
`facet_wrap()`	Facet graphics by one or more variables (`ggplot2`)	55, 58, 60, 71
`factor()`	Creates a factor (base **R**)	30, 31, 38, 53–55, 57, 58, 60, 139–141, 143, 145, 147, 151, 187, 213, 215, 216, 219, 221, 290, 298
`factorial()`	Compute the factorial of a numeric vector (base **R**)	114, 115, 118
`fct_explicit_na()`	Provides missing values an explicit factor level (`forcats`)	140, 141, 153
`filter()`	Subsets a data frame to rows when a condition is true (`dplyr`)	36–38, 69, 82, 153, 229, 237, 282, 283, 284, 298
`fisher.test()`	Produces Fisher's exact test (base **R**)	149, 153
`fitted()`	Extract fitted values from objects when modeling functions (base **R**)	193, 194, 208
`floor()`	Always round down (base **R**)	9, 20
`for()`	Initiates a for loop (base **R**)	111, 112
`full_join()`	Joins two data frames together, keeping all columns from both data frames and returning an **NA** when there are no matching values (`dplyr`)	285
`function()`	Creates a user-specified function (base **R**)	162, 164, 165, 168
`gather()`	Reshapes a data frame to long format (`tidyr`)	289
`geom_bar()`	Geometry layer for bar plot (`ggplot2`)	54, 60
`geom_boxplot()`	Geometry layer for box plot (`ggplot2`)	57, 60, 70–72, 187, 188
`geom_density()`	Geometry layer for density plots (`ggplot2`)	97, 101, 106, 195, 198, 199

FUNCTION	DESCRIPTION (PACKAGE)	PAGE #S
geom_errorbar()	Draw error bars by specifying maximum and minimum value (**ggplot2**)	106, 130, 132
geom_histogram()	Geometry layer for histograms (**ggplot2**)	52, 53, 58, 60, 73, 92, 96
geom_line()	Geometry layer for line charts (**ggplot2**)	56, 60, 234, 253, 293
geom_point()	Geometry layer for scatterplots (**ggplot2**)	43–47, 50, 51, 55, 57, 59, 60, 103, 130, 234, 235, 252–254, 261, 293, 294, 302
geom_smooth()	Geometry layer for smoothed lines (**ggplot2**)	59, 60, 235, 254, 261
geom_vline()	Geometry layer for adding vertical lines (**ggplot2**)	92, 96, 101, 103, 106
get_labels()	Returns value labels of labelled data (**sjlabelled**)	27, 30, 38
getwd()	Returns the current working directory (base **R**)	271, 302, 23
ggcorr()	Visualize a correlation matrix (**GGally**)	239–241, 244, 248
ggpairs()	Makes a matrix of plots, e.g., correlations, scatterplots (**GGally**)	241–244
ggplot()	Initialize a ggplot graphic, i.e., specify data, aesthetics (**ggplot2**)	43–48, 50-55, 57, 59, 60, 70, 71, 73–75, 92, 96, 101, 103, 104 129, 130, 186, 187, 188, 196, 198, 199, 208, 230, 234, 235, 251-253, 261, 267, 293, 294, 298, 299, 302
ggsave()	Saves plot as a file (**ggplot2**)	302, 303
ggtitle()	Adds a title or subtitle to a graph made using **gglot()** (**ggplot2**)	71–73, 268
GKtau()	Conducts the Goodman-Kruskal measure of association (**GoodmanKruskal**)	216, 223, 225
GoodmanKruskalGamma()	Conducts Goodman-Kruskal measure of association (**DescTools**)	218, 219, 223, 225
group_by()	Group observations by variable(s) for performing operations (**dplyr**)	64, 66, 67, 75, 76, 88, 95, 97, 140, 141, 172, 173, 177, 190, 243, 279, 288
guides()	Used to customize plot legend when using **ggplot()** (**ggplot2**)	187, 188, 208
head()	Returns the first parts of a vector, matrix, table, or data frame (base **R**)	34, 38, 94, 186
here()	Find a project's files based on the current working directory (**here**)	41, 79, 137, 171, 185, 211, 229, 235, 247
if_else()	Tests conditions for true or false, taking on values for each (**dplyr**)	102, 106
inner_join()	Joins two data frames together, keeping only data that exists in both datasets (**dplyr**)	284

FUNCTION	DESCRIPTION (PACKAGE)	PAGE #S
install.packages()	Installs non-base R packages (base R)	23, 24, 38, 41, 63, 79, 90, 120, 136, 156, 171, 185, 211, 229, 247, 269
IQR()	Compute interquartile range (base R)	69, 76
is.na()	Returns TRUE when values are missing, FALSE if not (base R)	80–82, 88, 139
KendallTauB()	Conducts the Kendall measure of association (DescTools)	220, 221, 223, 225
kruskal.test()	Performs a Kruskal-Wallis rank sum test (base R)	202, 208
labs()	Specify labels for ggplot object, e.g., title, caption (ggplot2)	49–51, 53, 54, 57, 60, 70–73
Lambda()	Conducts the measure of association (DescTools)	216, 223, 225
lapply()	Applies a function to all elements of a list, returning a list (base R)	285, 286
left_join()	Joins two data frames together, keeping unmatched cases from the first data frame (dplyr)	284
leveneTest()	Computes Levene's test for homogeneity of variance across groups (car)	192, 193, 206, 208
library()	loads the installed non-base R package (base R)	23, 24, 38, 41, 59, 63, 79, 90, 120, 136, 156, 171, 185, 211, 229, 247, 269, 290
list()	Create a list (base R)	16, 20, 282, 289, 290
lm()	Fit linear models (base R)	258, 259, 267, 268
load()	Loads an R datafile (.R or .Rda) (base R)	63, 79, 272
log()	Computes the natural logarithm (base R)	235, 286, 287
log10()	Computes common (i.e., base 10) logarithms (base R)	187, 188, 199, 200, 208, 286
matches()	Used in conjunction with select(), selects only variables that match a regular expression (dplyr)	283
matrix()	Creates a vector with two dimensions (base R)	15, 19, 20
max()	Returns the maximum value (base R)	64, 75, 76
mdy()	Creates a date variable in the format of MM-DD-YYYY (lubridate)	292
mean()	Compute arithmetic mean (base R)	64–67, 75, 76, 87, 88, 92–98, 100, 101, 141, 159, 177, 190, 288
median()	Compute the median (base R)	66, 67, 75, 76
merge()	Merge datasets by common row or columns names (base R)	180, 182
min()	Returns the minimum value (base R)	64, 65, 75, 76
mlv()	Compute the mode (modeest)	64, 67, 76, 80, 81

FUNCTION	DESCRIPTION (PACKAGE)	PAGE #S
mutate()	Creates new vectors or transforms existing ones (dplyr)	32–34, 37, 38, 59, 72, 102, 153, 177, 182, 278, 279, 280, 282, 291, 292
n()	Count observations, within summarize(), mutate(), or filter() (dplyr)	32
na_if()	Replace non-missing values with missing values (dplyr)	282
names()	Provides the element names (base R)	16, 20
nrow()	Counts the number of rows (base R)	31, 38, 154, 158, 250, 279, 298
num_range()	Used in conjunction with select(), selects only variables that match a numerical range (dplyr)	283
oneway.test()	Tests if 2+ samples from normal distributions have same means (base R)	195, 208
pairwise.t.test()	Pairwise comparisons between group levels (base R)	203, 208
par()	Set graphics parameters such as margins (base R)	71, 76
paste()	Combines a series of string text (base R)	112, 114, 118
pbinom()	Find cumulative probability of a binomial probability distribution (stats)	117, 118
Phi()	Conducts the measure of association (DescTools)	212–214, 223, 225
pivot_longer()	Reshapes a data frame to long format (tidyr)	289
pivot_wider()	Reshapes a data frame to wide format (tidyr)	288
pnorm()	Probability of random variable following normaldistribution (base R)	162, 168
pnormGC()	Compute probabilities for normal random variables (tigerstats)	159, 160, 168
predict()	Makes predictions from the results of model fitting functions (base R)	262, 267, 268
print()	Prints arguments and returns it invisibly (base R)	15, 20, 111–113
prop_z_test()	Function created in Chapter 10 for a single-sample z-test for proportions	164, 166, 168
prop.test()	Test null hypothesis that proportions in groups are the same (base R)	124–126, 131, 133, 176, 177, 181
qplot()	Creates a variety of plots/graphs (base R)	250, 251, 268
qqline()	Adds a reference line to Q-Q plot produced by qqnorm() (base R)	196, 208
qqnorm()	Produces a normal Q-Q plot of the variable (base R)	196, 208
qqPlot()	Draws theoretical quantile-comparison plots for variables (car)	197, 200, 208
quantile()	Compute quantiles as per specified probabilities (base R)	69, 76
range()	Compute the minimum and maximum values (base R)	84, 85, 270, 283

FUNCTION	DESCRIPTION (PACKAGE)	PAGE #S
rbind()	Appends rows to a data frame (base R)	285
read_csv()	Read in comma separated values file (readr)	41, 60, 185, 229, 247, 271, 273, 291
read_delim()	Reads in a delimited file (readr)	272
read_dta()	Imports a .dta Stata file (haven)	137, 153, 171, 211, 274
read_excel()	Reads in an .xls or .xlsx file (readxl)	274
read_json()	Reads in a JSON file (jsonlite)	277
read_sas()	Reads in a SAS format file (haven)	275
read_sav()	Reads in an SPSS .sav file (haven)	275
read_spss()	Imports SPSS .sav files (haven)	24, 38
read_tsv()	Reads in a tab-separated file (readr)	273
read.dbf()	Reads in a .dbf file (foreign)	274
read.mat()	Reads in a Matlab file (rmatio)	276
read.mtp()	Reads in a Minitab file (foreign)	276
read.systat()	Reads in a Systat file (foreign)	276
read.table()	Reads in data in tabular format (base R)	275
recode()	Replaces values of a integer/factor variable	172, 182
remove_labels()	Removes value labels from a variable (sjlabelled)	28, 29, 38
remove_var_label()	Removes a variable's label (labelled)	28, 38
replace_na()	Replaces missing values with another value (tidyr)	281, 282
require()	Attempts to load a package in R, returning a logical value of whether the attempt was successful or not (base R)	269
resid()	Extract residuals from objects returned by modeling functions (base R)	193, 194, 196, 208
return()	Used in functions to tell R what to return/ print for the user (base R)	162, 168
right_join()	Joins two data frames together, keeping unmatched cases from the second data frame (dplyr)	284
rm()	Remove object from R environment (base R)	229, 244
rnorm()	Create synthetic normally distributed data (base R)	92, 93, 106, 157, 158
round()	Rounds to nearest whole number or specified number of decimals (base R)	23, 94, 157, 158, 234, 253
sample()	Randomly sample from a vector or data frame (mosaic)	32, 94, 95, 97, 99, 100, 106
sapply()	Applies a function over a vector or list (base R)	285, 286
save()	Saves an R data file (base R)	272
scale_color_brewer()	Default color scheme options (ggplot2)	46, 48, 50, 51, 60
scale_color_ viridis_d()	Colorblind-friendly palettes from viridis package (ggplot2)	48
scale_fill_discrete()	Specify fill of discrete aesthetics, e.g., color palette (ggplot2)	97, 106
scale_y_log10()	Log scales the y-axis on your chart (ggplot2)	187, 188, 208

FUNCTION	DESCRIPTION (PACKAGE)	PAGE #S
scale()	Mean centers or re-scales a numeric variable (base **R**)	158, 168
ScheffeTest()	Scheffé's test for pairwise and otherwise comparisons (**DescTools**)	204, 208
sd()	Computes standard deviation of a numeric vector (base **R**)	86, 88, 99–102, 159, 288
select()	Select columns to retain or drop (**dplyr**)	32, 35, 36, 38, 229, 234, 282, 283
separate()	Separates a string by the given separator (**tidyr**)	292
set.seed()	Random number generator start point (base **R**)	93, 106
setRepositories()	Sets the repository from which R should search for a package (base **R**)	270
setwd()	Sets the working directory (base **R**)	24, 271
single_t_test()	Function created in Chapter 10 for single-sample *t*-tests for means	165, 166, 168
skewness()	Calculate degree of skewness in a numeric vector (**modeest**)	74–76
skim()	Provide summary statistics specific to object class (**skimr**)	67, 76, 80, 84, 173
slice()	Select rows based on their position in the data frame (**dplyr**)	36, 38, 282
SomersDelta()	Conducts Somers' measure of association (**DescTools**)	222, 223, 225
spread()	Reshapes a data frame to wide format (**tidyr**)	288
sqrt()	Finds the square root (base **R**)	9, 20, 100, 162, 164–167
starts_with()	Used in conjunction with select(), selects only variables that start with some prefix (**dplyr**)	283, 289
str()	Returns internal structure of an R object (base **R**)	88, 142
StuartTauC()	Conducts the Kendall measure of association (**DescTools**)	221, 225
substr()	Selects part of a string (base **R**)	291, 292
sum()	Sum values in a vector (base **R**)	67, 139, 177
summarize()	Create new summary variable(s), e.g., counts, mean (**dplyr**)	82, 88, 95, 97, 99, 100, 104, 140, 141, 153, 172, 177, 190, 243, 288
summary.lm()	Summary method for class **lm** (base **R**)	205, 208, 265
summary()	Produce summary of model results (base **R**)	69, 76, 84, 86, 191, 249, 258, 259, 261, 263, 265–267
summary()$coefficients	Extract coefficients only from summary (base **R**)	268
summary()$r.squared	Extract R squared only from summary (base **R**)	267, 268

FUNCTION	DESCRIPTION (PACKAGE)	PAGE #S
symbox()	Transforms x to a series of selected powers and displays box plots (car)	199, 208
t.test()	Performs one and two sample *t*-tests on vectors of data (base R)	175, 181, 182, 203
table()	Generates a frequency table (base R)	27, 30, 53, 82, 83, 102, 102, 139, 140, 142, 150, 189, 213, 215, 216, 219, 221, 276
tapply()	Applies a function to parts of a vector (base R)	285, 286
theme_bw()	The traditional dark-on-white ggplot theme (ggplot2)	187, 188, 195, 199, 208
theme_minimal()	Default minimalist theme for ggplot graphics (ggplot2)	50, 51, 60, 130, 298
theme()	Customize ggplot graphics (ggplot2)	50, 60, 70–73, 187, 188, 295, 298
TukeyHSD()	Implements Tukey's honest significant difference method (base R)	204, 208
var_label()	Returns or sets a variable label (labelled)	27–29, 37, 38
var.test()	Performs an *F*-test to compare the variances of two samples from normal populations (base R)	174, 181, 182
var()	Computes variance (base R)	85, 86, 88
View()	View data in new window (base R)	17, 20, 25, 34, 35, 37, 42, 63, 94, 137, 171, 180, 211, 277
vif()	Calculate the variance inflation for OLS or other linear models (car)	266, 268
which()	Provides the position of the elements such as in a row (base R)	158
while()	Initiates a while loop (base R)	114, 118
with()	Evaluates an expression, often used to specify the data you want to use (base R)	142, 143, 145, 147, 151, 153
write_csv()	Writes a comma-separated file (readr)	273
write_delim()	Writes a delimited file (readr)	272
write_dta()	Writes a Stata .dta file (haven)	274
write_json()	Writes a JSON file (jsonlite)	277
write_sas()	Writes a SAS format file (haven)	275
write_sav()	Writes an SPSS .sav file (haven)	275
write_tsv()	Writes a tab-separated file (readr)	273
write.dbf()	Writes a .dbf file (foreign)	274
write.mat()	Writes a Matlab (MAT) file (rmatio)	276
write.xlsx()	Writes an Excel file (.xlsx) (openxlsx)	274
year()	Extracts the year from a date (lubridate)	292
z_test()	Function created in Chapter 10 for a single-sample *z*-test	161, 162, 164–166, 168

Glossary

68-95-99.7 rule Empirical rule that states that 68% of the cases in a normal distribution should fall within 1 standard deviation of the mean (so within a z-score of -1 and +1); 95% of the cases in the distribution should fall within 2 standard deviations of the mean (so within a z-score of -2 and +2); and 99.7% of the cases in the distribution should fall within 3 standard deviations of the mean (so within a z-score of -3 and +3). In the real world, you will likely not find a distribution where this rule is exact.

Aesthetics Describe visual characteristics that represent the data.

Arrangements The different ways events can be ordered and result in a single outcome. For example, there is only one arrangement for gaining the outcome of ten heads in ten tosses of a coin. There are, however, ten different arrangements for gaining the outcome of nine heads in ten tosses of a coin.

Array A three-dimensional data structure that can contain homogenous elements (of the same class).

Assignment operators Symbols used to make assignations to objects.

Atomic vector A one-dimensional data structure that can contain homogeneous elements (of the same class).

Bell Curve See Gaussian distribution.

Binomial distribution The probability or sampling distribution for an event that has only two possible outcomes.

Binomial formula The means of determining the probability that a given set of binomial events will occur in all its possible arrangements.

Bivariate regression A technique for predicting change in a dependent variable using one independent variable.

Bonferroni correction A post-hoc pairwise comparison of means that controls the type I error rate by dividing the selected α-level by the number of pairwise comparisons made.

Central limit theorem A theorem that states: "If repeated independent random samples of size N are drawn from a population, as N grows large, the sampling distribution of sample means will be approximately normal." The central limit theorem enables the researcher to make inferences about an unknown population using a normal sampling distribution.

© The Editor(s) (if applicable) and The Author(s), under exclusive license to
Springer Nature Switzerland AG 2021
A. Wooditch et al., *A Beginner's Guide to Statistics for Criminology and Criminal Justice Using* R, https://doi.org/10.1007/978-3-030-50625-4

Chi-square statistic The test statistic resulting from applying the chi-square formula to the observed and expected frequencies for each cell. This statistic tells us how much the observed distribution differs from that expected under the null hypothesis.

Coefficient of variation (CV) A measure of dispersion calculated by dividing the standard deviation by the mean.

Comments Code annotations that are not interpreted by R.

Concordant pairs of observations Pairs of observations that have consistent rankings on two ordinal variables.

Confidence interval An interval of values around a statistic (usually a point estimate). If we were to draw repeated samples and calculate a 95% confidence interval for each, then in only 5 in 100 of these samples would the interval fail to include the true population parameter. In the case of a 99% confidence interval, only 1 in 100 samples would fail to include the true population parameter.

Contingency table A tabular way of viewing the relationship between categorical variables (also referred to as cross tabs).

Covariation A measure of the extent to which two variables vary together relative to their respective means. The covariation between the two variables serves as the numerator for the equation to calculate Pearson's *r*.

Cramer's V A measure of association for two nominal variables that adjusts the chi-square statistic by the sample size. V is appropriate when at least one of the nominal variables has more than two categories.

Data Information used to answer a research question; typically will be stored in a data frame. Data (plural) are made up of numerous datum (singular).

Data frame A data structure that is defined by the number of rows and columns.

Data transformation An adjustment of data to a different unit or scale (normally to deal with normality issues).

Dependent sample *t*-test A test of statistical significance that is used when two samples are not independent.

Dependent variable (Y) The variable assumed by the researcher to be influenced by one or more independent variables.

Directional hypothesis A research hypothesis that indicates a specific type of outcome by specifying the nature of the relationship that is expected.

Discordant pairs of observations Pairs of observations that have inconsistent rankings on two ordinal variables.

Environment Where objects are stored.

Eta squared The proportion of the total sum of squares that is accounted for by the between sum of squares. Eta squared is sometimes referred to as the percent of variance explained.

Expected frequency The number of observations one would predict for a cell if the null hypothesis were true.

External validity The extent to which a study sample is reflective of the population from which it is drawn. A study is said to have high external validity when the sample used is representative of the population to which inferences are made.

_F_-distribution A continuous probability distribution used as the null distribution in ANOVA.

Gamma (γ) PRE measure of association for two ordinal variables that uses information about concordant and discordant pairs of observations within a table. Gamma has a standardized scale ranging from −1.0 to 1.0.

Gaussian distribution Normal distribution or bell curve.

Geom Abbreviation for geometries from the `ggplot2` package.

Geometries Describe the objects that represent the data.

Goodman and Kruskal's lambda (λ) PRE measure of association for two nominal variables that uses information about the modal category of the dependent variable for each category of the independent variable. Lambda has a standardized scale ranging from 0 to 1.0.

Goodman and Kruskal's tau (τ) PRE measure of association for two nominal variables that uses information about the proportional distribution of cases within a table. Tau has a standardized scale ranging from 0 to 1.0. For this measure, the researcher must define the independent and dependent variables.

Heteroscedasticity A situation in which the variances of scores on two or more variables are not equal. Heteroscedasticity violates one of the assumptions of the parametric test of statistical significance for the correlation coefficient.

Independent Describing two events when the occurrence of one does not affect the occurrence of the other.

Independent sample _t_-test A test of statistical significance that examines the difference observed between the means of two unrelated samples.

Independent variable (X) A variable assumed by the researcher to have an impact on the value of the dependent variable, Y.

Index of qualitative variation (IQV) A measure of dispersion calculated by dividing the sum of the possible pairs of observed scores by the sum of the possible pairs of expected scores (when cases are equally distributed across categories).

Inferential statistics A broad area of statistics that provides the researcher with tools for making statements about populations on the basis of knowledge about samples. Inferential statistics allow the researcher to make inferences regarding populations from information gained in samples.

Interval/ratio variables Numeric variables with equal intervals between values; functionally the same, yet ratio-level variables have a true zero.

Kendall's tau Measures the strength and direction of two rank-ordered variables on a standardized scale between 0 and 1.0, whereby higher values indicate a stronger relationship.

Kendall's τ_b PRE measure of association for two ordinal variables that uses information about concordant pairs, discordant pairs, and pairs of observations tied on both variables examined. τ_b has a standardized scale ranging from −1.0 to 1.0 and is appropriate only when the number of rows equals the number of columns in a table.

Kendall's τ_c A measure of association for two ordinal variables that uses information about concordant pairs, discordant pairs, and pairs of observations tied on both variables examined. τ_c has a standardized scale ranging from −1.0 to 1.0 and is appropriate when the number of rows is not equal to the number of columns in a table.

Kruskal-Wallis test A nonparametric test of statistical significance for multiple groups, requiring at least an ordinal scale of measurement.

Levene's test A test of the equality of variances.

Linear relationship An association between two variables whose joint distribution may be represented in linear form when plotted on a scatter diagram.

List A one-dimensional data structure that can contain heterogenous elements (of different classes).

Logical operators Boolean operators that return TRUE or FALSE.

Marginal The value in the margin of a table that totals the scores in the appropriate column or row.

Matrix A specific type of array that has at least two columns and two rows and can contain homogeneous elements (of the same class).

Mean A measure of central tendency calculated by dividing the sum of the scores by the number of cases.

Measures of central tendency Descriptive statistics that allow us to identify the typical case in a sample or population. Measures of central tendency are measures of typicality.

Median A measure of central tendency calculated by identifying the value or category of the score that occupies the middle position in the distribution of scores.

Mode A measure of central tendency calculated by identifying the score or category that occurs most frequently.

Multicollinearity Condition in a multivariate regression model in which independent variables examined are very strongly intercorrelated. Multicollinearity leads to unstable regression coefficients

Multiple comparisons problem The problem associated with the chance of obtaining a false-positive (type I error) increase as the number of comparisons increase.

Multiplication rule The means for determining the probability that a series of events will jointly occur.

Nominal variables Categorical, unordered variables.

Non-directional hypothesis A research hypothesis that does not indicate a specific type of outcome, stating only that there is a relationship or a difference.

Nonparametric tests Tests that do not make an assumption about the distribution of the population; also called distribution-free tests.

Normal distribution A bell-shaped frequency distribution, symmetrical in form. Its mean, mode, and median are always the same. The percentage of cases between the mean and points at a measured distance from the mean is fixed.

Null hypothesis A statement that reduces the research question to a simple assertion to be tested by the researcher. The null hypothesis normally suggests that there is no relationship or no difference.

Object A specialized data structure; everything in R is an object.

Observed frequency The observed result of the study, recorded in a cell.

OLS regression See ordinary least squares regression analysis.

One-way analysis of variance (ANOVA) A parametric test of statistical significance that assesses whether differences in the means of several samples (groups) can lead the researcher to reject the null hypothesis that the means of the populations from which the samples are drawn are the same.

Ordinal variables Categorical, ordered variables.

Ordinary least squares regression analysis A type of regression analysis in which the sum of squared errors from the regression line is minimized.

Outliers A single or small number of exceptional cases that substantially deviate from the general pattern of scores.

Packages Modules that expand what R can do.

Parametric tests Tests that make an assumption about the shape of the population distribution.

Pearson's correlation coefficient See Pearson 's *r*.

Pearson's *r* A commonly used measure of association between two variables. Pearson's r measures the strength and direction of linear relationships on a standardized scale from –1.0 to 1.0.

Percent of variance explained (R^2) A measure for evaluating how well the regression model predicts values of Y. It represents the improvement in predicting Y that the regression line provides over the mean of Y.

Phi (φ) A measure of association for two nominal variables that adjusts the chi-square statistic by the sample size. Phi is appropriate only for nominal variables that each has two categories.

Population The universe of cases that the researcher seeks to study. The population of cases is fixed at a particular time (e.g., the population of the United States). However, populations usually change across time.

Population distribution The frequency distribution of a particular variable within a population.

Project A self-contained working directory.

Proportional reduction in error (PRE) The proportional reduction in errors made when the value of one measure is predicted using information about the second measure.

QQ-plot Used to check for normality of data, plots the correlation between the sample and a normal distribution.

R A language and free software environment used for statistical computing.

R Script Where R programming code is written and stored.

Range A measure of dispersion calculated by subtracting the smallest score from the largest score. The range may also be calculated from specific points in a distribution, such as the 5th and 95th percentile scores.

Regression coefficient (*b*) A statistic used to assess the influence of an independent variable, X, on a dependent variable, Y. The regression coefficient b is interpreted as the estimated change in Y that is associated with a one-unit change in X.

Regression error (*e*) The difference between the predicted value of Y and the actual value of Y.

Regression line The line predicting values of Y. The line is plotted from knowledge of the Y-intercept and the regression coefficient.

Regression model The hypothesized statement by the researcher of the factor or factors that define the value of the dependent variable, Y. The model is normally expressed in equation form.

Reproducibility When there is a record of one's research such that these steps can be repeated by others and the findings reproduced.

Residual An index of the relative deviation of the observed frequency from the expected frequency for a cell of a contingency table. It is useful for guiding the interpretation of an association between two nominal variables.

RStudio An integrated development environment (IDE) designed specifically for R.

Sample A set of actual observations or cases drawn from a population.

Sampling distribution A distribution of all the results of a very large number of samples, each one of the same size and drawn from the same population under the same conditions. Ordinarily, sampling distributions are derived using probability theory and are based on probability distributions.

Sample statistic A characteristic of a sample—for example, the mean number of previous convictions in a random sample of 1,000 prisoners.

Scatterplot A graph whose two axes are defined by two variables and upon which a point is plotted for each subject in a sample according to its score on the two variables.

Scheffé's test A multiple comparison test that accounts for family-wise error rate by weighting the test statistic by the mean squared error, between-samples degrees of freedom, and group sizes.

Single-sample *t*-test A test of statistical significance that is used to examine whether a sample is drawn from a specific population with a known or hypothesized mean. In a *t*-test, the standard deviation of the population to which the sample is being compared is unknown.

Single-sample *z*-test A test of statistical significance that is used to examine whether a sample is drawn from a specific population with a known or hypothesized mean. In a *z*-test, the standard deviation of the population to which the sample is being compared either is known or—as in the case of a proportion—is defined by the null hypothesis.

Somers' D PRE measure of association for two ordinal variables that uses information about concordant pairs, discordant pairs, and pairs of observations tied on the independent variable. Somers' D has a standardized scale ranging from −1.0 to 1.0.

Spearman's correlation coefficient See Spearman 's rho.

Spearman's rho (r_s) A measure of association between two rank-ordered variables. Spearman's r measures the strength and direction of linear relationships on a standardized scale between −1.0 and 1.0.

Standard deviation A measure of dispersion calculated by taking the square root of the variance.

Standard deviation unit A unit of measurement used to describe the deviation of a specific score or value from the mean in a *z* distribution.

Standard error The standard deviation of a sampling distribution.

Synthetic data Computer-generated data.

Test for equality of variance An *F*-test used to assess the null hypothesis that the two population variances are equal.

Themes Customizations that can alter the general appearance of a plot.

Tibble Modern version of base R's data frame (simpler and more user-friendly) that is from the *tidyverse* package.

Tied pairs of observations (ties) Pairs of observation that have the same ranking on two ordinal variables.

Tukey's honestly significant difference (HSD) A parametric test of statistical significance, adjusted for making pairwise comparisons. The HSD test defines the difference between the pairwise comparisons required to reject the null hypothesis.

Type I error Also known as alpha error and false positive. The mistake made when a researcher rejects the null hypothesis on the basis of a sample statistic (i.e., claiming that there is a relationship) when in fact the null hypothesis is true (i.e., there is actually no such relationship in the population).

Variance (s^2) A measure of dispersion calculated by adding together the squared deviation of each score from the mean and then dividing the sum by the number of cases.

Variation ratio A measure of dispersion calculated by subtracting the proportion of cases in the modal category from 1.

Welch's ANOVA ANOVA test for when the equality of variances assumption (homoscedasticity) is not met.

Y-intercept (b_0) The expected value of Y when X = 0. The Y-intercept is used in predicting values of Y.

z-score Score that represents an observation in standard deviation units from the mean.

Index

Printed by Printforce, United Kingdom